HELLENISTIC CULTURE AND SOCIETY

General Editors: Anthony W. Bulloch, Erich S. Gruen,
A. A. Long, and Andrew F. Stewart

I. Alexander to Actium: The Historical Evolution of the Hellenistic Age, by *Peter Green*
II. Hellenism in the East: The Interaction of Greek and Non-Greek Civilizations from Syria to Central Asia after Alexander, edited by *Amélie Kuhrt* and *Susan Sherwin-White*
III. The Question of "Eclecticism": Studies in Later Greek Philosophy, edited by *J. M. Dillon* and *A. A. Long*
IV. Antigonus the One-Eyed and the Creation of the Hellenistic State, by *Richard A. Billows*
V. A History of Macedonia, by *R. Malcolm Errington*, translated by *Catherine Errington*
VI. Attic Letter-Cutters of 229 to 86 B.C., by *Stephen V. Tracy*
VII. The Vanished Library: A Wonder of the Ancient World, by *Luciano Canfora*
VIII. Hellenistic Philosophy of Mind, by *Julia Annas*
IX. Hellenistic Culture and History, by *Peter Green* et al.
X. The Best of the Argonauts: The Redefinition of the Epic Hero in Book 1 of Apollonius's *Argonautica*, by *James J. Clauss*
XI. Faces of Power: Alexander's Image and Hellenistic Politics, by *Andrew Stewart*
XII. Images and Ideologies: Self-Definition in the Hellenistic World, by *A. W. Bulloch* et al.
XIII. From Samarkand to Sardis: A New Approach to the Seleucid Empire, by *Susan Sherwin-White* and *Amélie Kuhrt*

The Best of the Argonauts

The Best of the Argonauts

The Redefinition of the Epic Hero in Book 1 of Apollonius's *Argonautica*

James J. Clauss

University of California Press

Berkeley • Los Angeles • Oxford

University of California Press
Berkeley and Los Angeles, California

University of California Press, Ltd.
Oxford, England

©1993 by
The Regents of the University of California

Library of Congress Cataloguing-in-Publication Data

Clauss, James Joseph.
  The Best of the Argonauts : the redefinition of the epic hero in
book 1 of Apollonius's *Argonautica* / James J. Clauss.
    p.   cm. – (Hellenistic culture and society; 10)
  Includes bibliographical references and index.
  ISBN 0-520-07925-6 (alk. paper)
  1. Apollonius, Rhodius. Argonautica. 2. Argonauts (Greek
mythology) in literature. 3. Epic poetry, Greek—History and
criticism. 4. Jason (Greek mythology) in literature. 5. Heroes-
-Greece-Mythology. 6. Heroes in literature. I. Title
II. Series.
PA3872.Z4C57 1993
883'.01–dc20   92-4983
                                                                                           CIP

9 8 7 6 5 4 3 2 1

Familiæ Carissimæ

O bright Apollo,
τίν' ἄνδρα, τίν' ἥρωα, τίνα θεόν
What god, man, or hero
Shall I place a tin wreath upon!

EZRA POUND, HUGH SELWYN MAUBERLEY III.57–60

CONTENTS

	Preface	xi
	Abbreviations and References	xv
	Introduction: Themes and Methodology	1
1	The Argonautic Program	
	The Proemium (*Argo.* 1.1–22)	14
2	The Argonautic Hero in Question	
	The Catalogue (*Argo.* 1.23–233)	26
3	Unheroic Contrasts	
	The Departure from Iolcus (*Argo.* 1.234–316)	37
4	The Best of the Argonauts Defined	
	Preparations at Pagasae (*Argo.* 1.317–518)	57
5	The Wrath of Thetis	
	Journey from Pagasae to Lemnos (*Argo.* 1.519–608)	88
6	ἢ νῆσος ἢ νόστος	
	Sojourn on Lemnos (*Argo.* 1.609–909)	106
7	Initiation and Lustration	
	Sojourn on Oros Arkton (*Argo.* 1.910–1152)	148
8	The Best of the Argonauts	
	Heracles Abandoned (*Argo.* 1.1153–1362)	176
	Select Bibliography	215
	General Index	227
	Index Locorum	233

PREFACE

THE BEST OF THE ARGONAUTS is a thoroughly reconceived and rewritten version of my doctoral dissertation, "Allusion and the Narrative Style of Apollonius Rhodius: A Detailed Study of Book 1 of the Argonautica" (diss. Berkeley 1983). In my dissertation, I analyzed the narrative of Book 1 strictly from the point of view of the poet's allusive and structural techniques. The study succeeded in providing me with a methodology for exposing and interpreting allusions in the text to earlier and contemporary writers. I set aside the completed dissertation for several years in order to study allusion in other writers with the hope of returning to Apollonius with a more mature and sophisticated understanding of intertextuality, and indeed, work on Horace (*TAPhA* 115 [1985] 197–206), Callimachus (*ClAnt* 5 [1986] 155–70), Ovid (*HSCPh* 92 [1988] 297–314), Vergil (*AJP* 109 [1988] 309–20), and Theocritus (*QUCC*, n.s., 36 [1990] 129–40) has greatly enhanced my ability to identify and discuss the influence that one or more texts exert on another.

In addition to refining my ability to understand and articulate my understanding of Hellenistic narrative technique, I expanded my earlier investigation of the *Argonautica* by considering Book 1 within the larger context of ancient discourse on the hero. In the process, I discovered a recurring theme that sets Jason's status among the Argonauts against the backdrop of archaic, classical, and Hellenistic conceptions of the heroic figure. Although the issue of Jason as antihero or nonhero is far from new, in Book 1 Apollonius appeals to a central question in the Homeric epics: Who is the best among the heroes? My new work thus combines an analysis of

Apollonius's allusive technique, structural patterns, and concept of the hero. In merging these topics, I happily discovered that many of the allusions I discussed in my dissertation concerned, directly or indirectly, the nature of the Argonautic hero. So, while *The Best of the Argonauts* is a revised dissertation, its focus is quite different from the earlier version. The style of the present version is better, but I fear that I have not been able to rid my work completely of that most infelicitous of academic dialects, dissertationese, for which I ask the reader's indulgence.

I would like to mention those groups and individuals from whose assistance I benefited. First of all, the College of Arts and Sciences and the Graduate School of the University of Washington granted me release time from teaching to work on the *Argonautica*. I continued to receive encouragement and advice on a variety of issues from my professors at the University of California, Berkeley: William S. Anderson, Mark Griffith, Erich S. Gruen, and especially Anthony W. Bulloch, whose belief that my dissertation had some merit gave me the confidence I needed to proceed with revision. My colleagues, past and present, in the Department of Classics (Lawrence J. Bliquez, Sheila M. Colwell, Catherine C. Connors, William R. Dunn, Alain M. Gowing, William C. Grummel, Stephen E. Hinds, Merle K. Langdon, Pierre A. MacKay, John B. McDiarmid, and Paul Pascal) have enhanced my research through their personal warmth and stimulating conversations on this and other related topics. In particular, I would like to thank Mary Whitlock Blundell and Michael R. Halleran for their useful comments on the entire manuscript and Daniel P. Harmon for his painstaking reading of and detailed comments on the final version. I would also like to acknowledge the assiduous reference checking of David Hart, my research assistant, and the technical advice of Pierre and Theo MacKay, who have done such a splendid job of typesetting my manuscript. I am also very grateful to Mary Lamprech and Paul Psoinos of the University of California Press for their thoughtful work and advice, and would like to acknowledge the useful criticisms of the referees, Edward Phinney and Michael Haslam, both of whom allowed themselves to be identified.

Above all, I am deeply indebted to my family, immediate and extended, for their support and affection, and it is to them all that I dedicate this book: to my parents, Jim, Sr., and Marion, for not insisting that I become a doctor, lawyer, or insurance man; to my sisters, Katie, Mari, and Becki, for continuing to worship their only brother as they should, and their husbands John and David; to my in-laws, Norbert, Rita, Tony, his wife Lillian, Chuck, Michael, and Rosaire Betti, for accepting me as part of the family, even though I am not Italian or from Jessup; to my children, Gerard, Michael, and Elizabeth, for their loving abuse as vengeance for their dad's constant teasing; and to my wife, Louise, for ... κλῦτέ νυν· οὐ μὲν πάντα πέλει θέμις ὔμμι δαῆναι / ἀτρεκές!

ABBREVIATIONS AND REFERENCES

Abbreviations of Greek and Roman authors and their works, journals, lexica, and encyclopedias are those found in Liddell and Scott's *Greek-English Lexicon*; P. G. W. Glare, ed., *Oxford Latin Dictionary*; *L'Année Philologique*; and those in standard use (e.g., LSJ, *RE*, Roscher, etc.). In addition to these I make special note of the following abbreviations:

TEXTS, COMMENTARIES, AND INDICES OF THE *ARGONAUTICA*

Ardizzoni	A. Ardizzoni, *Le Argonautiche libro I* (Rome 1967)
Campbell	M. Campbell, *Echoes and Imitations of Early Epic in Apollonius Rhodius,* Mnemosyne Supplement 72 (Leiden 1981)
Campbell (Index)	M. Campbell, *Index Verborum in Apollonium Rhodium* (Hildesheim 1983)
Fränkel (OCT)	H. Fränkel, *Apollonii Rhodii Argonautica* (Oxford 1961)
Fränkel	H. Fränkel, *Noten zu den Argonautika des Apollonios* (Munich 1968)
Hunter	R. L. Hunter, *Apollonius of Rhodes Argonautica Book III* (Cambridge 1989)
Livrea	E. Livrea, *Apollonii Rhodii Argonauticon Liber IV* (Florence 1973)
Mooney	G. W. Mooney, *The Argonautica of Apollonius Rhodius* (reprint: Amsterdam 1987)
Vian	F. Vian, *Apollonios de Rhodes Argonautiques chants I-II* (Paris 1974)

Vian (2)	F. Vian, *Apollonios de Rhodes Argonautiques chant III* (Paris 1980)
Vian (3)	F. Vian, *Apollonios de Rhodes Argonautiques chant IV* (Paris 1981)
Wendel	C. Wendel, *Scholia in Apollonium Rhodium Vetera* (Berlin 1935)

OTHER TEXTS, COMMENTARIES, INDICES, AND LEXICA

Bond	G. W. Bond, *Euripides: Hypsipyle* (Oxford 1963)
Davies	M. Davies, *Epicorum Græcorum Fragmenta* (Göttingen 1988)
Dunbar	H. Dunbar, *A Complete Concordance to the Odyssey of Homer*, rev. B. Marzullo (reprint: Hildesheim 1971)
FGrHist	F. Jacoby, *Die Fragmente der griechischen Historiker* (Berlin 1923–)
FHG	C. Müller and T. Müller, *Fragmenta Historicorum Græcorum* (Paris 1841–70)
GGM	C. Müller, *Geographici Græci Minores* (Paris, 1855–61)
LIMC	*Lexicon Iconographicum Mythologiæ Classicæ* (Zurich 1981–)
Linnenkugel	A. Linnenkugel, *De Lucillo Tarrhæo Epigrammatum Poeta, Grammatico, Rhetore* (Paderborn 1926)
M&W	R. Merkelbach and M. L. West, *Fragmenta Hesiodea* (Oxford 1967)
Pf.	R. Pfeiffer, *Callimachus*, vols. 1 and 2 (Oxford 1949–53)
PMG	D. L. Page, *Poetæ Melici Græci* (Oxford 1962)
Powell	J. U. Powell, *Collectanea Alexandrina* (Oxford 1925)
Prendergast	G. L. Prendergast, *A Complete Concordance of the Iliad of Homer*, rev. B. Marzullo (reprint: Hildesheim 1962)
Radt	S. Radt, *Tragicorum Græcorum Fragmenta* (*TrGF*), vols. 3 (Æschylus) and 4 (Sophocles) (Göttingen 1985, 1977, respectively)

SH	H. Lloyd-Jones and P. Parsons, *Supplementum Hellenisticum,* Texte und Kommentare Band 11 (Berlin 1983)
Snell	B. Snell and H. Mæhler, *Pindari Carmina cum Fragmentis,* 2 vols. (Leipzig: vol. 1 1984⁷, vol. 2 1975⁴)
TGL	*Thesaurus Græcæ Linguæ,* ed. B. Hase, G. Dindorf, and L. Dindorf (Paris 1831–65)
TLG	*Thesaurus Linguæ Græcæ* (University of California, Irvine, 1987), read on the Packard Ibycus System
Wyss	B. Wyss, *Antimachi Colophonii Reliquiæ* (Berlin 1936)

SPECIAL STUDIES

I refer to the following studies in abbreviated form; all others will be cited in full in the notes:

Beye	C. R. Beye, *Epic and Romance in the Argonautica of Apollonius* (Carbondale 1982)
Blumberg	K. W. Blumberg, "Untersuchungen zur epischen Technik des Apollonios von Rhodos" (diss. Leipzig 1931)
Collins	J. F. Collins, "Studies in Book 1 of the Argonautica of Apollonius Rhodius" (diss. Columbia 1967)
Delage	E. Delage, *La géographie dans les Argonautiques d'Apollonios de Rhodes* (Paris 1930)
Giangrande	G. Giangrande, *Zu Sprachgebrauch Technik und Text des Apollonios Rhodios* (Amsterdam 1973)
Händel	P. Händel, *Beobachtungen zur epischen Technik des Apollonios Rhodios* (Munich 1954)
Hunter (2)	R. L. Hunter, "'Short on Heroics': Jason in the Argonautica," *CQ* 38 (1988) 436–53
Hurst	A. Hurst, *Apollonius de Rhodes: Manière et cohérence* (Bern 1967)
Knorr	E. Knorr, *De Apollonii Rhodii Argonauticorum Fontibus Quæstiones Selectæ* (Leipzig 1902)
Lawall	G. Lawall, "Apollonius' *Argonautica*: Jason as Anti-hero," *YClS* 19 (1966) 121–69

Levin   D. N. Levin, *Apollonius' Argonautica Re-examined,
I: The Neglected First and Second Books*,
Mnemosyne Supplement 13 (Leiden 1971)

SIGLA

An equivalence symbol (≈) signifies that the word or phrase referred to on the left is similar or identical to that on the right. A word or phrase underlined <u>once</u> signifies an imitation of a word or phrase that occurs in a passage discussed immediately afterwards, where, if quoted, it is also underlined <u>once</u>. A word or phrase underlined <u>twice</u> signifies an imitation of a word or phrase that occurs in a second passage discussed immediately afterwards, where, if quoted, it is also underlined <u>twice</u>. A word or phrase underlined with a <u>dotted line</u> signifies a freer adaptation of a word or phrase that occurs in the passage discussed immediately afterwards, where it is also underlined with a <u>dotted line</u>.

INTRODUCTION

Themes and Methodology

ANYONE WHO approaches the *Argonautica* for the first time, whether in the original or in translation, will find this epic unusual and challenging for a variety of reasons. First, the reader must have a detailed knowledge of the earlier versions of the Argonautic tale; he or she must also be reasonably conversant with archaic, classical, and contemporary Hellenistic literature, with scholarly debates on problematic texts, and even with the literary theories of the day. Second, the poet himself enters the narrative on several occasions to comment on or even apologize for what is taking place and interrupts the time frame of the story on many occasions with numerous etiological explanations that effectively carry the reader from the heroic age of the story into the author's present. Moreover, the narrative proceeds in a noticeably staccato movement, constantly punctuated by seemingly independent, self-contained episodes that have a structure and theme of their own. Most disconcerting of all, however, the central figure, Jason, while ultimately managing to complete his heroic quest in the course of the epic, clearly lacks the heroic stature of an Achilles or an Odysseus.

This is a curious and demanding poem. Yet in writing it, Apollonius took a great step forward in the writing of epic verse by bringing this archaic genre up to date at a time when some literary theorists, like Callimachus and Theocritus, believed—as most do today—that the epic genre was passé.[1] In response to this

---

1. I shall not here enter into the issue of the supposed argument between Callimachus and Apollonius. This, I believe, has been sufficiently discredited

small but influential movement, Apollonius writes what is in effect a Callimachean epic.² In the *Argonautica*, the poet takes us on an intellectual journey through Greek and non-Greek lands, culture, history, and literature. By engaging his readers' knowledge of the Hellenic culture of the past, Apollonius brings them by way of his many striking contrasts into an exciting, albeit uncertain, present in which, like the Argonauts, they must leave behind their belief in and reliance upon heroes such as Heracles and face a world run by Jasons. And yet such a *Weltanschauung* need not grow out of a pessimistic attitude in which the poet luxuriates in the self-pitying recognition that there are no more heroes;³ nor does Apollonius necessarily betray or subvert with his authorial and etiological interruptions the medium through which these lost heroes had been and continued to be celebrated up to his own day.⁴ Rather, at a time when greater-than-life heroes like Heracles no longer existed in the collective mind, Apollonius created for his *Argonautica* a real-life hero, vulnerable, dependent on the help of others, even morally questionable, but ultimately successful in his ἄεθλος as were the heroes of the *Iliad* and *Odyssey*, each of whom within these poems achieved the distinction of being called ἄριστος Ἀχαιῶν, "the best of the Achæans." The honorific term

---

by M. R. Lefkowitz, "The Quarrel between Callimachus and Apollonius," *ZPE* 40 (1980) 1–19 (= *The Lives of the Greek Poets* [Baltimore 1981] 117–35).

2. On the literary affinity between these poets, see W. Steffan, "De Veteribus et Novis Poeticis in Apollonii Rhodii Argonauticis Obviis," *Meander* 19 (1964) 77–87 (summary in Latin p. 121); M. G. Ciani, "Apollonio Rodio: Gli studi e le prospettive attuali," *A&R* 15 (1970) 80–88; T. M. Klein, "Callimachus, Apollonius Rhodius, and the Concept of the Big Book," *Eranos* 73 (1975) 16–25, and "Callimachus' Two *Ætia* Prologues," *ZAnt* 26 (1976) 357–61; and, more recently, G. O. Hutchinson, *Hellenistic Poetry* (Oxford 1988) 85–97; this issue is vigorously addressed by M. Margolies DeForest in her forthcoming book *Heroes in a Toy Boat*, a copy of which she has kindly sent me prior to publication. For a recent attempt to make sense of Apollonius's Rhodian exile and the esthetic discourse between Callimachus and Apollonius, see E.-R. Schwinge, *Künstlichkeit von Kunst* (Munich 1986) 153–54.

3. As argued by, for example, Lawall 167, and G. Karl Galinsky, *The Herakles Theme* (Oxford 1972) 114.

4. As M. Fusillo, *Il tempo delle Argonautiche* (Rome 1985) 136–42, and T. M. Klein, "The Role of Callimachus in the Development of the Concept of Counter-Genre," *Latomus* 33 (1974) 217–31, suggest; cf. most recently, S. Goldhill, *The Poet's Voice: Essays on Poetics and Greek Literature* (Cambridge 1991) 284–333.

ἄριστος, according to Nagy, "serves as a formal measure of a given hero's supremacy in his own epic tradition."[5] Thus, in focusing on what sets Jason apart from the other men on the expedition, what makes him "the best of the Argonauts," Apollonius can be seen as entering into a discourse on the hero that is a traditional feature of epic poetry.

From this point of view, Book 1 of the *Argonautica* serves as an introduction to the whole poem; for in this first book Apollonius forges a new kind of hero within the context of a recurrent thematic contrast between the man of skill and the man of strength. By the end of the book, this hero will establish himself as the best of the Argonauts, the proper leader for a group whose goal is, as Jason states, shared and not private (Ἀλλά, φίλοι, ξυνὸς γὰρ ἐς Ἑλλάδα νόστος ὀπίσσω, / ξυναὶ δ' ἄμμι πέλονται ἐς Αἰήταο κέλευθοι, 1.336–37 ["But, my friends, our return back to Greece is a matter of common concern, and our journey to the palace of Æëtes is also of common concern"]).[6] And for the rest of the poem, this new, Hellenistic hero will encounter a series of increasingly difficult, even bizarre, obstacles to the ultimate completion of his quest. He will succeed in overcoming these obstacles both through—and despite—his clearly circumscribed personal skills and with the assistance of his crew and of many others along the way, the most important of whom is Medea.[7] Nevertheless, when

---

5. G. Nagy, *Greek Mythology and Poetics* (Ithaca 1990) 13. In the first four chapters of his earlier book *The Best of the Achæans* (Baltimore 1979), a work that has suggested to me the title and focus of the present book (our methods, however, will be seen to be quite different), Nagy demonstrates at greater length how Achilles in the *Iliad* and Odysseus in the *Odyssey* vie for and attain the title "Best of the Achæans." Other characters in the poems may claim, with some right, to be "the best" within a given category (e.g., Teucer is the best archer among the Achæans; cf. *Il.* 13.313–14) or even for a brief moment are in fact the best among the whole group (e.g., Diomedes during his *aristeia* in *Il.* 5 [103, 414] or Ajax when he fights Hector in *Il.* 7 [289]). Nonetheless, completion of the central contest or ἆεθλος of the poem (the killing of Hector in the *Iliad* and the winning of Penelope in the *Odyssey*) is what sets the "Best of the Achæans" apart from all others.

6. I shall provide my own translations for all the citations set off as extracts and for some important passages or phrases, like this one, embedded in my text for the convenience of the reader.

7. Because of the limited focus of this study, I shall not have the opportunity to examine the role that Medea plays in the poem or to take up the issue of viewing her achievements as "heroic" in bringing about the success of the

Jason emerges from the crisis surrounding the loss of Heracles at the end of Book 1, a crisis that threatens to scuttle the expedition, he establishes his *modus operandi* for the expedition and the kind of hero he will be.

In the chapters that follow, I shall examine Book 1 section by section in order of occurrence. In the Proemium (Chapter 1), Apollonius identifies not only the topic of his epic (the Argonautic expedition, which Pelias ordered Jason to lead as a means of getting rid of the one fated to kill him), but also, as I shall argue, his poetic approach. In the Catalogue (Chapter 2), Apollonius introduces the thematic contrast mentioned above by organizing the Argonauts in two groups, one headed by a man of skill (Orpheus) and the other by a man of strength (Heracles). Allusion is also made to the question that lies at the heart of the present book: Who is the best of the Argonauts? The narrative proper begins at the home of Æson (Chapter 3), where we get our first extended picture of the protagonist and his family. On the beach at Pagasae (Chapter 4), Jason begins the expedition with a call for the election of the best of the Argonauts as captain, whom he envisages as a man of diplomatic skill. Events prior to their departure suggest that Jason might well be that man. In describing their departure (Chapter 5), Apollonius again contrasts strength and skill, while at the same time alluding to the failed marriage of Peleus and Thetis, which possesses striking similarities to Jason's future marriage with Medea. In the following three episodes, Apollonius explicitly compares Jason's and Heracles' approaches to action. On Lemnos (Chapter 6), the Argonauts face the first threat to their mission and ultimate return to Greece (νόστος) as the Lemnian women tempt them with a life of sensuality on their island (νῆσος). There Jason gives evidence of his ability to attract women and his tendency toward a passive approach; Heracles espouses the old heroic code of individual action. On Oros Arkton, later known as Cyzicus (Chapter 7), Heracles' battle with the Gegeneis is set alongside Jason's armed encounter with his former hosts, the Doliones, in which he kills their king, Cyzicus. The divine anger that the dynamic Heracles provokes subsides after a

---

expedition. On this, see, e.g., M. DeForest (supra n. 2); Beye 120–32; and B. Pavlock, *Eros, Imitation and the Epic Tradition* (Ithaca 1990) 19–68.

sign is sent to the sleeping Jason, who performs the appropriate expiatory rites. Finally, in Mysia (Chapter 8), the timely appearance and message of Glaucus settles the divisive argument caused by the abandonment of Heracles, who shortly before revealed the extent of his enormous strength by driving the *Argo* by himself; in his adept handling of the angry Telamon, Jason exorcises the group of any residual bad feelings. In this, he fulfills an intrinsic part of the definition of the best of the Argonauts that he gave on the beach at Pagasae. At the end of the book, the Argonauts can proceed to Colchis without Heracles; for they have in Jason the best leader for them, one who promotes harmony so that as a unified group they can accomplish what a Heracles can do on his own as a matter of course.

ALLUSION AND STRUCTURE

Two features of Apollonius's narrative style are particularly conspicuous both in Book 1 and throughout the rest of the poem: his ubiquitous allusion to other writers, especially Homer, and the carefully balanced structural organization of his episodes. In examining the evolution of Jason's heroic role,[8] I have found it essential to identify the various subtexts that inform our understanding of the narrative and to observe the structure of an episode that in many cases sets in relief the imitation of one or more significant passages.

Allusion

Even without the aid of the numerous studies available on Apollonian imitation, a reader familiar with the *Iliad* and *Odyssey* who comes to the *Argonautica* for the first time would immediately observe that the Alexandrian poet borrows heavily from the Homeric poems.[9] In composing his epic, Apollonius has successfully

---

8. Hunter (2) 436–37, and T. M. Klein, "Apollonius' Jason: Hero and Scoundrel," *QUCC*, n.s., 13 (1983) 115–23, both provide useful summaries of scholarly opinion on the character of Jason.

9. As Händel 7 succinctly states, "Vor allem und immer wieder ist da die Bedingung Homer." Campbell's monograph *Echoes and Imitations of Early Epic in Apollonius Rhodius*, cited in Abbreviations and References, vividly underscores Apollonius's debt to Homer; for a more discursive treatment, cf. J. F. Carspecken, "Apollonius Rhodius and the Homeric Epic," *YCIS* 13 (1952) 33–143.

created what Emile Cahen has styled the "presque homérique."[10] The poet not only employs Homer's vocabulary and syntax, either with slight variation (*imitatio cum variatione*) or in inverted form (*oppositio in imitando*),[11] he also reproduces *variæ lectiones*,[12] *hapax* and *dis legomena* in the *Iliad* and *Odyssey*[13] and semantic unica in the *Homerica*,[14] imitates Homeric ambiguities,[15] and extends the number of Homeric defective verbs.[16] Apollonius even appears to enter into debates with other scholars on issues of usage or interpretation of Homeric vocabulary by featuring a word in a context that requires his particular solution to the philological controversy.[17] In short, it is readily apparent that Apollonius had it in mind to produce a lexical analogue to the Homeric poems.[18]

---

10. E. Cahen, *Callimaque et son œuvre poétique* (Paris 1929) 519-25; cf. M. G. Ciani, "Poesia come enigma (Considerazioni sulla poesia di Apollonio Rodio)," *Scritti in onore di C. Diano* (Bologna 1975) 77-111; and M. Fantuzzi, "Omero 'autore' di Apollonio Rodio: Le formule introduttive al discorso diretto," *MD* 13 (1986) 67-82. As M. W. Haslam, "Apollonius Rhodius and the Papyri," *ICS* 3 (1978) 54-61 has shown, this feature of the narrative is so conspicuous that it has even made the text of the *Argonautica* susceptible to corruption (e.g., when a scribe inadvertently recalls and copies a Homeric expression that Apollonius was adapting).
11. See, for example, G. Giangrande, "'Arte Allusiva' and Alexandrian Epic Poetry," *CQ* 17 (1967), and "Aspects of Apollonius Rhodius' Language," *Papers of the Liverpool Latin Seminar 1976*, ed. F. Cairns (Liverpool 1977), 271-91, and E. Livrea, "L'épos philologique: Apollonius de Rhodes et quelques homérismes méconnus," *AC* 49 (1980) 146-60.
12. G. Giangrande, "The Utilization of Homeric Variants by Apollonius Rhodius: A Methodological Canon of Research," *QUCC* 15 (1973) 73-81; cf. Giangrande 8-9.
13. See G. Giangrande, "Hellenistic Poetry and Homer," *AC* 39 (1970) 46-77; cf. G. Caggia, "Due parole omeriche in Apollonio Rodio (ἐφιάομαι in 1.459 e ἀίδηλος in 3.1132)," *RFIC* 100 (1972) 23-31.
14. See, for example, A. Ardizzoni, "'Trappole' e infortuni apolloniani," *GIF* 30 (1978) 275-87.
15. See Caggia (supra n. 13) and "Un caso di bivalenza semantica in Apollonio Rodio," *GIF* 26 (1974) 33-40; cf. G. Giangrande, "Polisemia del linguaggio nella poesia alessandrina," *QUCC* 24 (1977) 97-106.
16. See G. Giangrande, "A Passage in Apollonius," *CQ* 21 (1971) 146-48; cf. P. M. Fraser, *Ptolemaic Alexandria* (Oxford 1972) 1.633-34.
17. As shown, for instance, by R. Merkel, *Apollonii Argonautica* (Leipzig 1854) lxxi-xcviii; cf. M. Campbell, "Three Notes on Alexandrine Poetry," *Hermes* 102 (1974) 42-46; and E. Livrea, "Una 'tecnica allusiva' apolloniana alla luce dell'esegesi omerica alessandrina," *SIFC* 44 (1972) 231-43.
18. R. F. Thomas, "Vergil's *Georgics* and the Art of Reference," *HSCPh* 90 (1986) 171-98, provides a very useful discussion on the various types

It is not reasonable to assume, however, that the successful creation of a convincing "presque homérique" as a kind of poetic instantiation of his philological research was Apollonius's main goal. As it stands, the manifestly Homeric texture of the narrative naturally brings with it a whole array of generic expectations: the invocation of the Muse, the catalogue, the duel, and the heroic choice, to mention but a few. These and other canonical or celebrated features of the Homeric poems, when they occur in transmogrified form in the *Argonautica*, invite comparison with their archaic models. As I shall argue, Apollonius turns his audience to specific Homeric texts in order to set up a contrast between the traditional action and outlook of the ancient heroes and those of his own. The Argonautic narrative is thus not a glossographical landscape whose primary function is to provide a mythic backdrop for a scholar's academic wars, although these are waged, but rather an evocative setting for the achievement of a truly heroic feat by a less than heroic figure who turns out to be a kind of Alexandrian Yankee in King Pelias's court. In what follows, I shall study the parallels and contrasts between the Hellenistic actors and their literary stage by focusing on the particular words, phrases, or lines whose wider settings entail situations that are similar to, identical to, or exactly the opposite of the new Argonautic context. For often when we see the heroes and heroines of the *Argonautica* in contexts reflecting specific Homeric incidents, the stark difference between the two worlds becomes all the more marked. Herein lies the special power and attraction of the allusive technique.

I shall call special attention to the more complex instances of allusion where Apollonius "contaminates"—to use the term suggested by Terence (cf. *An.* 16) and adopted by many modern scholars[19]—several passages that one might describe as *non ita*

---

of allusion; what he and J. Farrell, *Vergil's Georgics and the Traditions of Ancient Epic* (Oxford 1991), say about the *Georgics* applies to the *Argonautica* as well.

19. See, for example, I. M. Le M. Du Quesnay, "From Polyphemus to Corydon" [p. 212, n. 86], and F. Cairns, "Self-imitation within a Generic Framework: Ovid, *Amores* 2.9 and 3.11 and the *renuntiatio amoris*" [p. 121], both in *Creative Imitation and Latin Literature*, ed. D. West and T. Woodman (London 1979). Although *contaminare* in context is a negative term and refers to

dissimili argumento (ibid. 11). The episode in which Apollonius describes Jason leaving home offers a good example of such *contaminatio* (examined at length in Chapter 3). The poet casts the response to Jason's departure in such a way that he recalls various passsages in the *Iliad* where Homeric characters were responding to the death (actual and threatened) of Hector; in particular, Jason's mother, Alcimede, calls Andromache to mind. Moreover, when portraying Alcimede's desperate reaction to her son's imminent departure from home, Apollonius compares her to a young girl "falling upon and embracing" (ἀμφιπεσοῦσα) her old nurse. In point of fact, ἀμφιπεσοῦσα is a *hapax legomenon* found at *Od.* 8.523, where the tearful Odysseus is likened to a woman falling upon the body of her recently slain husband who was fighting on behalf of the city, a situation similar to that encountered by Andromache. Such *contaminationes* do not merely underscore the high level of originality in Apollonius's manipulation of the Homeric poems and other earlier and contemporary poetry; rather, the points where two or more literary models intersect below the surface of the narrative frequently add to the reader's understanding and appreciation of the narrative proper.

Apollonius by no means restricts his glance to the Homeric poems. The influence of practically all areas of previous and contemporary literature and scholarship can be observed, although understandably to a lesser degree than that of Homer. Of particular note are Pindar's fourth *Pythian*, Attic tragedy, and the poetry of Callimachus, especially the *Ætia* and *Hecale*.[20] The traditional heroic Jason to be found in Pindar's account of the Argonautic expedition told in the fourth *Pythian* stands in sharp contrast with Apollonius's Jason. In the opening of the poem, Apollonius appears to call this contrast to the reader's attention (Chapter 1).

---

the process of "spoiling plays for other dramatists ... [by] unfairly reducing the store of Greek plays available for adoption" (thus S. Goldberg, *Understanding Terence* [Princeton 1986] 95), it is a convenient term for describing the practice of conflating several models into a new and original piece. Goldberg's analysis of the effects of *contaminatio* in the *Adelphœ* and *Eunuchus* (ibid. 97–122) shows how effective such a conflation of models was in the Terentian plays.

20. With regard to the influence of the *Hecale* on the *Argonautica*, one should now consult A. S. Hollis, *Callimachus: Hecale* (Oxford 1990) 27, 388.

In the case of tragedy,[21] in addition to introducing tragic vocabulary into his epic,[22] Apollonius imported the tragic debate and monologue, especially in Book 3. Foremost among the Athenian plays that inform our reading of the *Argonautica* is Euripides' *Medea*. R. L. Hunter well summarizes the importance of this play in the reading of the Alexandrian epic:[23]

> A[pollonius] assumes in his readers an intimate knowledge of this famous play, and its action hangs over *Arg.* even when it is not specifically recalled. More significant than the actual foreshadowing of Jason's abandonment of Medea through the figure of Ariadne and of Medea's infanticide is the constant interplay between the arguments and gestures of the two texts; A[pollonius] models his Jason and his Medea with an eye to their "subsequent" history in Euripides' tragedy. The two texts become mutually explicative; *Arg.* shows us how the origins of the tragedy lay far back, and the tragedy lends deep resonance and "tragic" irony to the events of the epic.

The "'subsequent' history in Euripides' tragedy" will surface in Jason's departure from home (Chapter 3), the sailing of the *Argo* from Pagasae (Chapter 5), and Jason's encounter with Hypsipyle on Lemnos (Chapter 6).[24] There are a number of verbal points of contact between the *Argonautica* and the surviving poems and fragments of Callimachus. Two passages in Book 1 of the *Argonautica* that seem to reflect Callimachean models will

---

21. Cf. F. Stössl, *Apollonios Rhodios: Interpretationen zur Erzählungskunst und Quellenverwertung* (Bern 1941), who treats at length Apollonius's debt to Athenian drama—with a heavy hand, in my opinion.

22. Cf., for instance, A. Ardizzoni, "Note apolloniane," *Maia* 20 (1968) 14, and M. Fantuzzi, "Varianti d'autore nelle Argonautiche d'Apollonio Rodio," *A&A* 29 (1983) 146–61.

23. Hunter 18–19; cf. also Hunter's paper "Medea's Flight: The Fourth Book of the *Argonautica*," *CQ* 37 (1987) 129–39; and most recently A. R. Dyck, "On the Way from Colchis to Corinth: Medea in Book 4 of the 'Argonautica,'" *Hermes* 117 (1989) 455–70, and V. Knight, "Apollonius Rhodius, Argonautica 4.167–70 and Euripides' *Medea*," *CQ* 41 (1991) 248–50.

24. Surprisingly, I have not found correspondences, verbal or contextual, between the *Argonautica* and fragments of fifth-century tragedies dealing with the Argonautic myth (e.g., Euripides' *Hypsipyle*) particularly helpful in interpreting the Hellenistic epic or Jason's heroic status therein. I suspect that if more were available, this situation would change considerably. For a list of Athenian plays that deal with the Argonautic cycle, see Vian xxxvi–vii.

receive special attention: Jason's prayer to Apollo on the beach at Pagasae (Chapter 4) and the celebration of Rhea's mysteries on Mount Dindymon (Chapter 7). Finally, it would appear that the *Lyde* of Antimachus had considerable influence on Apollonius,[25] but because the fragmentary remains of the poem are so few we shall never know how the recollection of this elegiac narrative might have affected the interpretation of the Alexandrian epic.

The *Argonautica* is a poem rich in allusions to so many different writers composing different works in a variety of genres, including even so unexpected a writer as Herodotus (Chapter 5), that it would be impossible to take every reference into account in the present discussion.[26] Rather, as I mentioned above, I shall concentrate on those imitations that I believe invite the reader to recall the wider context of the word, phrase, line, or lines that the poet has worked into the fabric of his narrative. This allusive technique presupposes an audience that possesses, and actively engages in their reading of the poem, a comprehensive knowledge of past and contemporary literature in order to see the important suggestions being made between the lines. By relying as heavily as he does on the subtext to fill in the interstices of the narrative proper, Apollonius shares the burden of composition with the reader. Approaching the *Argonautica* without a considerable literary background, a reader would surely find Apollonius's poem a rather dull adventure story embedded in an antiquarian's travelogue, relieved only by a few interesting moments in Book 3 when Medea falls in love; the *doctus lector*, on the other hand, encounters not another mediocre epic about another hero on yet another legendary quest but a sophisticated poem whose double-tiered narrative informs and suggests, and whose meaning can be grasped only by a creative reading that sees both levels of the text.

---

25. See Wyss xlviii ff.; for examples of Antimachus's influence on Book 1, see, for example, lines 243 ($\approx$ fr. 72 Wyss), 1008 ($\approx$ fr. 71 Wyss), 1115–16 ($\approx$ fr. 53 Wyss), 1235 ($\approx$ fr. 44 Wyss).

26. Campbell has done a remarkable job of collecting many of these in his useful index, and the different commentators (Mooney, Ardizzoni, Fränkel, Vian) have recorded other archaic, classical, and Hellenistic reminiscences that have been observed to date.

Structure

As scholars have observed, Apollonius paid special attention to the arrangement of his episodes.[27] Although one might disagree on the configuration of a particular episode or on a section within, it should be clear to anyone who looks at the flow of the narrative that Apollonius organized his material in the symmetrically balanced ring-composition form; that is, one or more things mentioned at the beginning of a section or subsection are echoed at the end. He advertises this structural principle in the Proemium and continues it with great regularity throughout the poem. Naturally, if he applied the straightforward ring (A–B–A) in every case, the movement of the poem would become overly regular and eventually soporific. Instead, the poet varies the basic ring in a number of ways. The ring can be extended (e.g., A–B–C–D–C–B–A; cf. Chapter 3) or its main components can have balanced structures particular to themselves (e.g., A [a–b–a]–B–A [a–b–c–d–c–b–a]; cf. Chapter 6). The structural symmetry at times becomes so involved that even the subsections themselves have a ring format (e.g., A [a{α–β–α}–b{α–β–α}]–B–A [a–b–c–b–a]; cf. Chapter 8). Not every episode possesses a neat, thematically balanced structure; yet even in such episodes, subsections can be found with a symmetrical organization (e.g., A [a–b–a]–B [a–b–a]–C [a–b–c–d–e]; cf. Chapter 4). In short, Apollonius uses the

---

27. In addition to passing comments regarding Apollonius's symmetrical structure in or within specific episodes (e.g., Blumberg 17; Vian 255 ad 579; Levin 38; A. Köhnken, *Apollonios Rhodios und Theokrit* [Göttingen 1965] 17–25), there are three studies that have looked exclusively at this aspect of the Argonautic narrative: Hurst; P. Thierstein, *Bau der Szenen in den Argonautika des Apollonios Rhodios* (Bern 1971); and J. Preininger, *Der Aufbau der Argonautika des Apollonios Rhodios* (Vienna 1976). Hurst's analysis is by far the most exhaustive (he deals with the entire poem), sensitive, and informative of the three. Thierstein too makes many fine comments on the interrelationships between elements in the episodes that he discusses (4.1232–1619, 1.1153–1362, 2.720–898, 2.899–1029, 4.109–82). Both, however, have created and employed a complex system of terms that gives undue importance to a structural approach that is fundamentally simple. In the *Argonautica*, the medium is not the message. Preininger pushes his structural interpretation to the extreme, suggesting that the structure of the poem is a reflection of the poet's model, the temple of Apollo at Bassae, whose dimensions he calculated and imitated in such a way that 100 verses equals 100 centimeters; in their various combinations, he argues, the verses are to be read as musical notation.

ancient ring-composition technique throughout the book in a variety of configurations.[28] This asymmetrical symmetry, as it were, enlivens the flow of the narrative and provides clear evidence of the extraordinary control that Apollonius exerted over his narrative, which embraces so vast an amount of learning, both literary and antiquarian.[29]

Discussions of structure can be tedious, and I shall keep mine to a minimum. As I mentioned above, I do not aver that the structure of the episodes is significant *per se*; nor do I think that it necessarily reveals the soul of the writer or his time. Rather, I have found that when dealing with the *Argonautica*, recognition of the structure can be almost as crucial as the identification of an allusion; for the regularity of the structure in a poem as involved and erudite as this allows the reader to observe the important thematic and conceptual correspondences that the poet wants to highlight. Important images, dramatic moments, and/or allusions often lie in the central positions of the various rings. Very simply put, by locating the focal points of the rings the reader can isolate a significant element or elements of the narrative. Therefore, for each episode I shall briefly discuss the structure, using the system employed above: I employ capital letters to mark the main sections of the episode (A–B–C), minuscule for the subsections (a–b–c), Greek minuscule for the sub-subsections (α–β–γ), and italics in all three to mark corresponding sections (A–B–*A*, a–b–*a*, α–β–*α*). Although such a system may appear clumsy, the results will justify the attention given this technical feature of the poem.

Each chapter begins with a short introduction. After I analyze the structure of an episode and establish what its focal points are, I shall examine the sections and subsections in the order of occurrence, except in Chapter 3, where it proved to be more useful to start in the middle. The discussion of each episode will conclude with a summary statement in which I pull together the various

---

28. On ring composition in archaic literature, cf., for example, B. A. van Groningen, *La composition littéraire archaïque grecque* (Amsterdam 1958); and J. H. Gaisser, "A Structural Analysis of the Digressions in the *Iliad* and *Odyssey*," *HSCPh* 73 (1969) 1–43.

29. On the tension between these two features of the narrative, cf. Händel 7–8, Hurst 9–35.

strands of my argument and relate them to the larger and more important issue of Book 1: the nature and identity of the best of the Argonauts.[30]

IT may seem odd that the present study of the hero of the *Argonautica* is limited to Book 1 and that a sequential reading of the text has been preferred over a thematic analysis. The narrative of this book and of the poem in general, however, encourages the approach I have taken. First, it is at the conclusion of Book 1 that Apollonius identifies Jason as the hero of the epic and fully exposes the nature of his heroism in contradistinction to the quintessential archaic hero, Heracles. As such, the book has a unity and integrity that, not having been observed, merits our attention. Readers of the *Argonautica* must come to terms with who Jason is and what he represents within the epic tradition before leaving the familiar Hellenic topography and entering the strange world that lies beyond the crashing Symplegades. Second, the identification of the "best" among the Argonauts unfolds gradually and in a linear fashion, beginning from the Proemium and extending through to the final moment of the book; each episode provides another angle from which to view Jason, all heading to a disquieting but inevitable conclusion.

30. The text I use throughout is that of Vian unless I specify otherwise.

1

The Argonautic Program
The Proemium (*Argo.* 1.1–22)

THE HIGH DEGREE of self-consciousness that characterizes the work of Hellenistic poets and the Roman epigoni no longer requires introduction, explanation, or, for that matter, apology. Scholars over the past several decades have shown the remarkable extent to which these Greek and Roman artists in the composition of a poem simultaneously reflect upon its literary underpinnings with great ingenuity. A well-known example of this phenomenon is Callimachus's "negative priamel," in which he lists things he detests, professes to hate them all because they are common, and then suddenly addresses the specific issue at hand, the handsome Lysanias, whose love proves to be distressingly common (*Epigr.* 28 Pf.).[1] Among the items that the poet contemns is the cyclic poem. In expressing his frustration with Lysanias, Callimachus at the same time establishes his view that the traditional post-Homeric epic appeals only to vulgar tastes;[2] in doing so, he gives an unconventional twist to the priamel.[3]

Not surprisingly, nowhere does the articulation of a poetic program appear more frequently than at the beginning of a poem

---

1. A. Henrichs, "Callimachus Epigram 28: A Fastidious Priamel," *HSCPh* 83 (1979) 207–12 provides a very useful discussion of this poem.
2. See A. W. Bulloch, "Hellenistic Poetry," *The Cambridge History of Classical Literature*, 1 (1985) 560.
3. E.-R. Schwinge's monograph *Künstlichkeit von Kunst* (Munich 1986), despite my disagreement with his general thesis (see *AJP* 109 [1988] 447–49), offers an interesting and useful analysis of this epigram (pp. 5–9) and of the self-conscious nature of Alexandrian poetry (2–29). On the use of priamels in Hellenistic poetry in general, cf. W. H. Race, *The Classical Priamel from Homer to Boethius*, Mnemosyne Suppl. 74 (Leiden 1982) 99–109.

or of a collection of poems. Again Callimachus provides the best example in the response to his critics set at the beginning of the second edition of the Ætia (fr. 1 Pf.). In addition to rebuffing the vituperative criticisms of his detractors, Callimachus identifies the kind of poetry that will follow in his new edition: not a continuous poem about a hero or a king in thousands of lines (i.e., something akin to a cyclic epic), but a work that is characterized by its brevity (ὀλιγόστιχος) and subtlety (Μοῦσα λεπταλέη). The contrast between long, sustained poetry on a single subject and short segments on different topics[4] reverberates throughout the passage in a series of lively, contrasting images: Callimachus's short verse and his many years, the long flight of the cranes after killing the short Pygmies, and the long flight of the Massagetae's arrows in contrast to the sweet and small nightingales, the fat sacrificial victim and the slender Muse, the common highways versus unused paths, the braying of the ass against the sweet echo of the cicada, and finally the fate of Enceladus under Ætna as opposed to that of the dew-eating Tithonus.[5] These colorful antitheses establish not only the kind of poetry that Callimachus writes and that the reader can expect to encounter in the new edition of the Ætia (attenuated accounts of topics handled in an unorthodox manner) but even the general organizing principle of contrasting ætia: the serene sacrifice to the Graces (Ætia fr. 3–7 Pf.) is set alongside the boisterous and blasphemous sacrifices to Apollo and Heracles (Ætia fr. 7–21 Pf. + SH 250–51); Heracles' victory over the Nemean lion makes a striking contrast with Molorchus's triumph over the Nemean mice (SH 254–69); Book 3 begins with Berenice's Nemean victory (ibid.), while Book 4 concludes with the catasterism of Berenice's lock of hair (Ætia fr. 110 Pf.). In the Proemium to the *Argonautica*, Apollonius too alerts the reader to the approach he will take in his epic; he does so not through an overt statement of purpose, but, like Callimachus, by subtle implication.

The *Argonautica* begins in an arresting fashion: Ἀρχόμενος σέο, Φοῖβε, παλαιγενέων κλέα φωτῶν / μνήσομαι ... (1–2). The

---

4. The only reasonable interpretation of ὀλιγόστιχος (Ætia fr. 1.9 Pf.), pace N. Hopkinson, *A Hellenistic Anthology* (Cambridge 1988) 94.
5. On this last contrast, cf. G. Crane, "Tithonus and the Prologue to Callimachus's Ætia," ZPE 66 (1986) 269–78.

phrasing, as has often been observed, belongs to the language of the Homeric Hymn, the closest parallel being *h. Hom.* 32.18-19 (σέο δ' ἀρχόμενος κλέα φωτῶν / ᾄσομαι ἡμιθέων).[6] One would easily suspect that Apollonius had this hymn in mind, were it not for the fact that the latter could well date to the Hellenistic era,[7] and so in this case it is impossible to say with certainty who is imitating whom. Although an important point may elude us through our ignorance of the interrelationship of these two texts,[8] the parallel is nonetheless instructive: through the striking hymnic phraseology, set conspicuously in the opening lines of the poem, Apollonius makes it clear that he will not be restricted in the exposition of his epic theme by considerations of genre.[9] In sum, although Apollonius may be beginning an epic, the opening of his poem establishes the tone and manner of the more concise and limited hymn form. From Callimachus's thirteenth *Iamb* (fr. 203 Pf.) we learn that there existed purists at this time who eschewed such departures from traditional form. They criticized experimentalists, like Callimachus, who explored a variety of novel combinations in an attempt to revitalize poetry in the third century B.C. The opening words of the *Argonautica* provide a vivid statement about Apollonius's approach to poetic composition, which is in

---

6. Besides the commentators *ad loc.*, cf. Händel 9; E. Bundy, "The Quarrel between Kallimachos and Apollonios, I: The Epilogue of Kallimachos' Hymn to Apollo," *CSCA* 5 (1972) 58; and V. De Marco, "Osservazioni su Apollonio Rodio, 1.1-22," *Miscellanea di studi alessandrini in memoria di A. Rostagni* (Turin 1963) 351-52.

7. Cf. T. W. Allen, W. R. Halliday, and E. E. Sikes, *The Homeric Hymns* (Oxford 1963) 431.

8. Two questions arise: Is it significant that Apollonius begins from Apollo, the sun god, and the hymnist from the moon goddess, Selene, who is often associated with Artemis, Apollo's sister? Does the substitution of ἡρώων for ἡμιθέων, or vice versa depending on the direction of the imitation, affect our understanding of one text or the other?

9. De Marco (supra n. 6) 354 also finds in Apollonius's Proemium the influence of Euripidean prologues; cf. T. M. Klein, "The Role of Callimachus in the Development of the Concept of Counter-Genre," *Latomus* 33 (1974) 229. S. Goldhill, *The Poet's Voice: Essays on Poetics and Greek Literature* (Cambridge 1991) 286-300, offers a fine reading of the Proemium as an instance of the "Kreuzung der Gattungen" (Kroll). P. M. Fraser, *Ptolemaic Alexandria* (Oxford 1972) 1.625, on the other hand, does not hit the mark in saying that "the *Argonautica* was an epic of traditional *form* on a traditional theme" (italics mine).

line with that of his Cyrenian contemporary; with such a beginning, the poet makes it clear that he will employ in his poem the traditional stock in trade of Greek poetry in an original and nontraditional way.

Another surprise in the Proemium is the delaying, and especially the phrasing, of the invocation to the Muses. With the exception of the *Ilias Parva* (fr. 1 Davies), no ancient Greek epic began without mentioning or alluding to one or all of these goddesses.[10] Contrary to the usual practice, Apollonius begins instead from Apollo and addresses the Muses only after first identifying the subject of his poem, the Argonautic expedition, and describing its origin. Moreover, his invocation to the Muses is decidedly understated: Μοῦσαι δ' ὑποφήτορες εἶεν ἀοιδῆς (22). The word ὑποφήτωρ has long been the subject of controversy. Some, following LSJ's interpretation of ὑποφήτωρ as the equivalent of ὑποφήτης, argue that the poet is ascribing a less important role to the Muses, who are, in this view, the poet's interpreters;[11] others, in agreement with Seaton, understand this uncommon noun as a correlative of ὑποφήτης, and conclude that Apollonius asks the Muses not to be his interpreters, but the suggesters or inspirers of his song.[12] The former view seems preferable in two ways. Not only does no other instance of the word support the meaning "inspirer,"[13] but in fact the idea of "interpreter" corresponds with the role that Apollonius appears to assign the Muses

---

10. As Blumberg 7 notes.
11. Cf. A. Gerke, "Alexandrinische Studien (Der Streit mit Apollonios)," *RhM* 44 (1884) 135; Händel 10 n. 2; L. Paduano Faedo, "L'inversione del rapporto Poeta-Musa nella cultura ellenistica," *ASNP* 39 (1970) 377–86; M. Fusillo, *Il tempo delle Argonautiche: Un' analisi del racconto in Apollonio Rodio* (Rome 1985) 363–64, who calls Apollonius's Muses "ministre, collaboratrici"; and most recently, D. C. Feeney, *The Gods in Epic* (Oxford 1991) 90. Feeney's discussion of the role of the Muses throughout the poem (pp. 90–94) is especially insightful.
12. E.g., R. C. Seaton, "Notes on Ap. Rhod. with Reference to Liddell and Scott," *CR* 2 (1888) 83–84; Mooney and Ardizzoni *ad loc.*; and Vian 239 *ad* 22. On these and other Apollonian intrusions in the poem, see A. Grillo, *Tra filologia e narratologia* (Rome 1988) 9–67.
13. In addition to those examples cited by LSJ s.v. ὑποφήτωρ, I would add Eusebius *Præparatio Evangelica* 5.8.7 (= Porphyrius *De Philosophia ex Oraculis* 158.7) and Nonnus *Paraphrasis Sancti Evangelii Joannei* 5.157, cited by *TLG*.

on several occasions in the poem when he asks them to explain what is happening. At 3.1-5 he asks Erato—since she is the expert on love—to explain how Jason took advantage of Medea's love in order to acquire the fleece; at 4.1-5 he asks a Muse, this time unspecified, to explain whether Medea left Colchis out of love or fear; again at 4.552-56 he introduces the description of the Argonauts' journey from the Adriatic to the Tyrrhenian Sea by asking the Muses to tell how it happened. As Vian has noted, this somewhat academic mannerism recalls Callimachus's interview with the Muses in the *Ætia*.[14] It is unnecessary, then, to ascribe to ὑποφήτωρ a meaning that has no parallel. Apollonius does not belittle the Muses with this term, but rather he has in mind for them a function similar to the one they played in the first two books of the *Ætia*.

The role that Apollonius envisages for his Muses, moreover, finds parallel in Aratus's *Phænomena*, which may well have influenced the Argonautic Proemium.[15] Like the *Argonautica*, the *Phænomena* begins with a hymn in which the poet takes his start from the god, in this case Zeus ('Εκ Διὸς ἀρχώμεσθα [*Phæn*. 1]; cf. 'Ἀρχόμενος σέο, Φοῖβε [*Argo*. 1.1]), and concludes with an invocation to the Muses. There also exists a close structural similarity between the two prologues. In the *Phænomena*, a four-line invocation to Zeus (1-4) is balanced at the end of the proemium by a four-line greeting to Zeus and the Muses in which Aratus requests the assistance of the latter (15-18). In between lies the introduction to the topic of the poem, the constellations that Zeus provided in order to mark the seasons and call men to work; in a word, the god's ἀρετή (5-14). In the *Argonautica*, the Proemium is likewise framed with invocations: the first to Apollo, in which he summarizes the topic of the poem—the Argonauts and their expedition to Colchis (1-4)—and the corresponding invocation to the Muses, in which he prepares the reader for the catalogue that is to follow (18-22).[16] The center of the Proemium contains an abbreviated

---

14. Vian 239 *ad* 22, and Vian (3) 147 *ad* 4.2 and 94 n. 2.
15. De Marco (supra n. 6) 350-52 argues this point quite successfully; cf. Fraser (supra n. 9) 635-36 on Apollonius's debt to Aratus.
16. One will observe that ὑποφήτορες εἶεν ἀοιδῆς (*Argo*. 1.22) and τεχμήρατε πᾶσαν ἀοιδήν (*Phæn*. 18) bring their respective sections to a close and that both phrases end with the word ἀοιδή.

version of the incident that was responsible for initiating the expedition: Apollo's warning to Pelias that the man wearing only one sandal would plot to kill him, the appearance of that man, and the commissioning of the expedition to get rid of him (5–17).[17] The central sections of each prologue thus feature gods who call men to work in their respective spheres of activity: Zeus has set the constellations in the sky to summon farmers to the fields, Apollo through his oracle ultimately led Jason to undertake his great contest. In short, as Zeus was the appropriate god for Aratus to celebrate at the beginning of his astronomical poem, so too Apollonius appropriately invokes Apollo not only as the god of poetry, but, more important, as the god of prophecy responsible for providing the oracular response that led to the heroic ἄεθλος celebrated by this poem.[18]

Comparison of the opening of the *Argonautica* with that of the *Phænomena* gives us another perspective from which to see Apollonius's reference to the Muses as ὑποφήτορες. In his concluding prayer Aratus states: ἐμοί γε μὲν ἀστέρας εἰπεῖν / ἧ θέμις εὐχομένῳ τεκμήρατε πᾶσαν ἀοιδήν (17–18).[19] The verb τεκμήρατε (cf. LSJ s.v. τεκμαίρομαι B) shows that Aratus is not asking the Muses to provide him with poetic inspiration but to substantiate the truth of his poem's content. This seems quite appropriate for a poet embarking on the poetic articulation of a scholarly star catalogue. If Apollonius had Aratus's prologue specifically in mind when writing his own, then we can say that the former borrowed not only the hymnal format and tripartite structure but also the academic role he ascribes to his Muses, whom he invites from time to time to comment on the action. If, on the other hand, he was not looking to the *Phænomena*, nonetheless the comparison is useful. For in addition to supporting the more natural sense of ὑποφήτωρ as "interpreter," this parallel with Aratus, in conjunction with the

---

17. Although a minor point, the central sections also begin in a similar fashion: that of Aratus begins τοῦ γὰρ καὶ γένος εἰμέν (5); that of Apollonius, τοίην γὰρ Πελίης φάτιν ἔκλυεν (5).

18. Mooney *ad* 1.1; Blumberg 7; Fränkel *ad* 1.1–4 (3); and others have noted the dual rationale for invoking Apollo.

19. Σ *ad Phæn.* 17–18 noted the ambiguous position of θέμις; J. Martin, *Arati Phænomena* (Florence 1956) *ad* 18 correctly reads ἧ θέμις with εἰπεῖν, comparing Cleanthes *Hymn to Zeus* 37–39.

comparison with Callimachus's Muses made above, brings Apollonius's view of poetry in line with these Hellenistic writers, whose Muses would be more at home in a library than at a fountain thronged by sheep or cattle.[20]

Finally, one other feature of the Proemium associates Apollonius's epic with contemporary attitudes toward the writing of poetry: the poet's refusal—or *recusatio*—to take up a subject that his theme would appear to demand; for Apollonius states explicitly that he will not describe the building of the *Argo*. Moreover, in his description of the topic he will not sing, Apollonius evocatively repeats a unique Homeric clausula:[21]

> Νῆα μὲν οὖν οἱ πρόσθεν ἔτι <u>κλείουσιν ἀοιδοί</u>
> Ἄργον Ἀθηναίης καμέειν ὑποθημοσύνῃσι.
> Νῦν δ' ἂν ἐγὼ γενεήν τε καὶ οὔνομα μυθησαίμην
> ἡρώων δολιχῆς τε πόρους ἁλὸς ὅσσα τ' ἔρεξαν
> πλαζόμενοι·
>
> (18–22)

Earlier <u>poets</u> still <u>celebrate</u> the ship
Argo, which was made under the advice of Athena.
But now instead I shall recount the race and the names of the heroes
the paths of the sea, and as many things as they did
in their travels.

Apollonius reminds us by his use of the Homeric phrase κλείουσιν ἀοιδοί that the building of the *Argo* was one of the most cherished themes of the old bards. The ancient singers and their expected repertoire of tales was in itself an epic topos, which recurs in several well-known Homeric passages. Apollonius here seems

---

20. Cf. Hurst 9–35, who offers an interesting account of this particularly Alexandrian attitude, which he calls the "tentation du mode savant."

21. Cf. Ardizzoni and Campbell *ad loc.*, Vian 51 n. 2, and F. Williams, *Callimachus: Hymn to Apollo* (Oxford 1978) *ad* 18, who have identified the imitation. I follow Vian and others (e.g., Giangrande 1) who retain ἔτι κλείουσιν of the MSS; for a divergent opinion, see A. Ardizzoni, "Riflessioni sul testo di Apollonio Rodio," *GIF* 31 (1979) 261–67. I find it interesting that Athenæus (14.633b–c), when discussing the practices of ancient poets who celebrated the actions of heroes and sang hymns to the gods, recalls, as Apollonius does here, Phemius's choice of topics mentioned at *Od.* 1.337–38 (quoted below).

deliberately to evoke one of the most famous of these bardic scenes—the very scene in which the clausula κλείουσιν ἀοιδοί makes its sole appearance in extant archaic literature. In the first book of the *Odyssey*, Penelope asks Phemius to stop singing the Ἀχαιῶν νόστος (*Od.* 1.326) and to turn to another topic:

Φήμιε, πολλὰ γὰρ ἄλλα βροτῶν θελκτήρια οἶδας
ἔργ᾽ ἀνδρῶν τε θεῶν τε, τά τε <u>κλείουσιν ἀοιδοί</u>·
τῶν ἕν γέ σφιν ἄειδε παρήμενος, οἱ δὲ σιωπῇ
οἶνον πινόντων· ταύτης δ᾽ ἀποπαύε᾽ ἀοιδῆς
λυγρῆς, ἥ τέ μοι αἰεὶ ἐνὶ στήθεσσι φίλον κῆρ
τείρει, ἐπεί με μάλιστα καθίκετο πένθος ἄλαστον.
(*Od.* 1.337–42)

Phemius, you know many other songs to charm human hearts,
songs about the deeds of men and gods, which <u>poets celebrate</u>.
Take your seat and sing one of these, and let the others drink their wine
in silence. But stop singing this grievous
song, which brings constant pain to the heart
within my breast. I cannot forget the suffering that besets me.

Apollonius recalls but playfully inverts a basic notion of this scene. Penelope asks Phemius to sing one of the songs that poets *commonly* sing rather than the νόστος that he was performing. Apollonius, on the other hand, implies that he will not sing about the building of the *Argo* because earlier poets have so worked the topic over that it has become too common.[22] Moreover, inasmuch as Pelias's scheme, the motivation for the expedition, involves depriving the Argonauts of their νόστος (cf. line 17), quite appropriately the poet, unlike Penelope, rejects τά τε κλείουσιν ἀοιδοί in favor of a νόστος tale. In sum, the poet's statement conforms to the advice that Apollo gave Callimachus as a young boy; like Callimachus, Apollonius refuses to follow in the steps of others (cf. *Ætia* fr. 1.21–28). The allusive style and the discriminating choice of topic are vivid indications of the kind of poem that the poet will offer his reader.[23] Thus in his brief, but expressive, Proemium,

---

22. Cf. Bundy (supra n. 6) 46–47, who notes the apologetic tone of the Argonautic lines.
23. Callimachus imitated the same Homeric phrase (κλείουσιν ἀοιδοί) at *H.* 2.18. It is no accident, I am certain, that the line numbers are the same

Apollonius reveals the esthetic principles that underpin his epic: Καλλιμάχου τό τ' ἄεισμα καὶ ὁ τρόπος.[24]

STRUCTURE

There remains another feature of the Proemium that I believe is also programmatic: the structure itself.[25] In lines 1–4, as briefly outlined above, Apollonius begins with an invocation to Apollo and identifies the subject of his poem, the Argonautic expedition. These lines correspond with lines 18–22, where the poet turns to the Catalogue as the starting point for the narrative and ends with an invocation to the Muses. In the central section of the Proemium, lines 5–17, the poet presents in an extremely abbreviated form the *Vorgeschichte* of the expedition.[26] Even this section possesses a unifying structure of its own. Lines 5–7 contain Apollo's prophecy to Pelias that he would die at the hands of the man who wore only one shoe; the next seven lines, 8–14, present the appearance of Jason at Pelias's sacrifice offered to Poseidon and all the gods, except Hera, and Pelias's recognition of the fated man; and lines 15–17 conclude with Pelias's plot to get rid of Jason. The Proemium, then, has the shape outlined on the following page.

We have seen that the hymnic opening, the use of the *recusatio* motif, and the academic role assigned to the Muses all have programmatic implications; they lead us to expect other resemblances in the *Argonautica* to the poetry of Callimachus or of Aratus, thereby advertising, in part, the nature of the narrative the reader is to expect. I find the structure of the Proemium to be

---

or that both passages involve Apollo. The lack of certainty regarding the respective dates of the two poems once again prevents one from knowing who was imitating whom; cf. Williams (supra n. 21) 2.

24. *Pace* Fraser (supra n. 9) 632–33 *et passim*, who insists that although Callimachus and Apollonius share an interest in etiology and employ the same linguistic practice, that typical of Alexandrian writers of the period, temperamentally and stylistically they "face in contrary directions" (633). In my opinion, Fraser (cf. 749–54) trusts too much in the ancient biographical tradition.

25. Cf. Hurst's discussion of this feature of the Proemium (39–44).

26. Fränkel *ad* 1.1–233 provides the most thorough analysis of what Apollonius includes and leaves out in the terse prehistory of the expedition; cf. also Händel 9–14.

The Proemium, 1–22

A. Address to Apollo and Choice of the Subject	(1–4)
B. The Prehistory of the Expedition	(5–17)
a. Pelias's Oracle	(5–7)
b. Appearance of Jason	(8–14)
a. Pelias's Plot	(15–17)
A. Qualification of the Subject and Address to the Muses	(18–22)

no less programmatic in this sense: it furnishes an "example," to use Hurst's term,[27] of the organizational principle that Apollonius will follow for the rest of the poem. The basic building block that can be observed from the analysis of the Proemium and that Apollonius will use in different configurations throughout the poem is ring composition. As I mentioned above in the Introduction, the employment of this structural device will vary from the simple ring (A–B–A), to the ring within the ring, as here in the Proemium (A–B [a–b–a]–A), and to other more complicated variations that suit the content and special focus of an episode or part of an episode. The ring provides a useful way for the poet to organize a vast amount of legendary, mythological, historical, and geographical information and at the same time to call attention to important points that might get lost in what is an extremely involved and learned narrative. In the body of the poem, as in the Proemium, Apollonius consistently gives central position to prominent images, to sudden divine or quasi-divine appearances, and very often to significant allusions that guide and inform our understanding of the section at hand.

By omitting in his introduction much of the prehistory, which—in line with archaic practices—unfolds in the course of the poem,[28] and by articulating his Proemium in the ring format, Apollonius focuses on the ætion of the Argonautic expedition (Apollo's prophecy to Pelias and its fulfillment) and, in particular, on the

---

27. Hurst 43.
28. This is well established by Händel 11–12.

ominous appearance of Jason οἰοπέδιλος, which lies in the center of this central section. The picture given to us by Apollonius, so different from the heroic account of the same scene in Pindar's *Pythian* 4 (70–171), while revealing little about the personality of Jason, nonetheless suggests something about this central figure.[29] Jason will lead the expedition not because of any discernible qualities or ambition on his part, but because he happened to have crossed the Anaurus when he did, thereby losing a sandal. As we learn later on, even Hera's affection for him arises not out of respect for his heroic virtues, but because he was a courteous fellow who once helped an old lady cross a river (*Argo.* 3.61–73). In fact, this rather unspectacular "man of the people" (δημόθεν, 7)[30] will successfully complete his ἄεθλος (15) not through traditional heroic virtues but by being at the right place and knowing and influencing the right people at the right time, especially women. Vian suggests that δημόθεν recalls ξεῖνος αἴτ' ὢν ἀστός at Pindar *P.* 4.78[31] With Pindar's ode in mind, one might well believe that Apollonius was trying to improve on Pindar's version of the oracle by making it more specific. Yet the distinctively unheroic outlook and behavior of the epic's protagonist that the reader will encounter in the course of the poem contrast with Pindar's noble hero. Jason gives no indication of being anything other than a rather ordinary young man[32] who has been thrust into his position by his ingratiating manner and by the accidental loss of his shoe. In short, nothing in the picture of Jason, which the structure of the Proemium sets in relief, leads one to believe that Jason will prove to be a dynamic hero of the Homeric type.

29. Although Apollonius appears to follow Pherecydes' account (*FGrHist* 3 F 105) of the beginning of the Argonautic expedition (cf. Knorr 10–16; J. Brunel, "Jason μονοκρήπις," *RA* 4 [1934] 34–43; and Vian 239 *ad* 17), Pindar's version of the Argonautic story would have been familiar both to Apollonius and his *doctus lector*, as the possible imitation of *P.* 4.78 at line 7 would suggest; see immediately below.
30. So Vian 50 n. 2, *pace* A. Platt, "Apollonius III," *Journal of Philology* 35 (1919) 72.
31. Vian ibid.
32. On δῆμος in the sense of "common man" as opposed to someone of distinction, see LSJ s.v. 2.1 and *TGL* s.v. In *The Herakles Theme* (Oxford 1972) 108, G. Karl Galinsky sums up well this feature of Jason's character: "the *Argonautica* simply is an account of what happens when a Hellenistic burgher is forced to head a mythical expedition."

THE Argonautic program, though subtle, is clear. The reader is led to expect an untraditional epic whose esthetics are Callimachean and whose narrative will be organized in such a way that the most important images and allusions are structurally highlighted. Moreover, in establishing the narrative technique he will use, Apollonius has also given us a suggestive glimpse of the poem's central character, and what we observe might equally be considered programmatic. The "hero" of the epic who undertakes the seemingly impossible ἄεθλος, much as he does in the Proemium, throughout the rest of the poem does not act or create possibilities for action on his own; rather he shows up at the right place and meets the right people at the right time. Thus, Apollonius invites the reader to infer from both the style and content of his Proemium that his epic will not be yet another Homericizing ἄεισμα in many thousands of lines featuring the typical archaic hero.

2

The Argonautic Hero in Question
The Catalogue (*Argo.* 1.23-233)

THE Catalogue of Argonauts might well appear to most modern readers an infelicitous delay of the expedition promised in the opening lines. Apollonius identified the Argonauts and their quest as the subject of his poem (1-4) but instead of going on to describe the building of the *Argo* (18-19), or Jason's trips to different parts of Greece to enlist his crew,[1] the poet immediately launches into a protracted list of all the participants, together with information concerning their families, home towns, and in several cases the reasons for their coming along.[2] The suggestion that Apollonius included a Catalogue because it was a required feature of the epic genre[3] may account for its presence but not its nature or position in the epic.[4] The remarkable success of such Hellenistic catalogue poems as the *Ætia* and the *Phænomena*, which exercised considerable influence on contemporary and subsequent poetry, makes it clear that catalogues were not simply an expected epic conceit but a highly esteemed and desirable art form *per se*, both in Apollonius's day and beyond. Far from being a defect, then, the Catalogue of Argonauts would appear to have been, given Alexandrian sensibilities, an auspicious starting point for the poet.

Homer's Catalogue of Ships (*Il.* 2.484ff.), as one might well imagine, is the primary model for the Argonautic Catalogue. Not

---

1. Apollonius mentions some of the events that occurred prior to the first assembly at Pagasae in the course of the poem; cf. Vian 4 n. 5 for references.
2. E.g., 32-34, 47-48, 97-100, 109-10, 139-41, 149-50.
3. E.g., Blumberg 8.
4. E.g., Händel 15 stated that Apollonius placed the Catalogue at the beginning of the poem so that it would not break up his narrative later on.

only does the prayer to the Muses for their assistance at the conclusion of the Proemium (22) parallel Homer's similar request just before he begins his Catalogue (*Il.* 2.484–93)[5] but, like Homer, Apollonius employs a geographical arrangement in listing the Argonauts.[6] In this regard, the Alexandrian poet even improves upon his archaic model by effecting what Vian styles "un nouvel exemple de 'composition circulaire' ";[7] he begins his survey of Minyan Greece in Thrace[8] with Orpheus and completes it with the Thracian Boreads. Moreover, Apollonius introduces other technical and artistic improvements in his Catalogue: he updates Homeric geography and at times offers clever explanations of controversial names;[9] in line with Hellenistic poiesis, he employs greater variation in the introductions to each entry;[10] he has ensured that the heroic chronology to be inferred from his list of heroes commands plausibility and consistency, the result of eliminating the

---

5. As observed by G. Kaibel, "Sententiarum Liber Quartus," *Hermes* 22 (1887) 511; cf. Blumberg 8.

6. The first to make this observation was R. Walther, "De Apollonii Rhodii Argonauticorum Rebus Geographicis" (diss. Halle 1894); cf. Delage 38–39, and J. F. Carspecken, "Apollonius Rhodius and the Homeric Epic," *YClS* 13 (1952) 38–58. On this and other geographical matters, cf. L. Pearson, "Apollonius of Rhodes and the Old Geographers," *AJP* 59 (1938) 443–59, who discusses Apollonius's debt to Hecataeus and the Ionian logographers.

7. Vian 5.

8. On the association of Pimpleia (25) with Thrace, see Σ *ad* 1.23–25b and Vian 240 *ad* 34.

9. In general, see Delage 39–49. I cite two examples: (1) Homer called the peoples who lived around Elis Epeians (*Il.* 2.619); Apollonius uses the classical name Ἠλεῖοι (found first in Herodotus 8.72; cf. Delage 47), which, given the context, the poet suggests is derived from Ἥλιος, the father of Augeas. (2) When Apollonius states that Asterius and Amphion are the sons of Hyperasius and the grandsons of Pallen (176–77), he provides an etymology for the Homeric towns Hyperasië and Pellene, mentioned by Homer at *Il.* 2.573–74, which lines he imitates; cf. Vian 247–48 *ad* 178. On the controversial phrase Πελλήνης ἀφίκανον Ἀχαιΐδος (177), see A. W. Bulloch, "Apollonius Rhodius *Argonautica* 1.177: A Case Study in Hellenistic Poetic Style," *Hermes* 101 (1973) 496–98. On a related point, G. Zanker, *Realism in Alexandrian Poetry: A Literature and Its Audience* (London 1987) 71–72, when discussing Apollonius's description of the passage of the Acherousian headland in Book 2, states that it is typical of the poet to appeal to "contemporary geographical scholarship in order to give his material scientific credibility, for that accords with his general practice in his use of science" (72).

10. See Händel 16.

many contradictions inherent in earlier traditions;[11] finally, he offers greater variation in his presentation by including several delicately wrought vignettes, which, in a few strokes, provide crisp images of parents responding to their sons' departure on this celebrated expedition.[12] Yet Apollonius's Catalogue of Argonauts is much more than an updated Argonautic version of the Homeric Catalogue. The carefully balanced structure, the poet's emphasis upon certain mythological facts in pivotal sections of the Catalogue, and his allusion to a specific passage of the Homeric Catalogue together pose an important question regarding the nature of the Argonautic hero.

STRUCTURE

Apollonius executes a carefully organized sweep through the Greek world in his listing of the Argonauts, beginning and ending at the same place. As such the Catalogue of Argonauts, like the Proemium, is structured in ring composition. To this carefully balanced list, Apollonius appends the names of two men who ask to come along (224–27): Acastus, the son of Pelias, and Argus, the builder of the *Argo*. These two do not form part of the Catalogue proper, both because they fall outside the geographical ring of the Catalogue and because they put the number beyond the fifty-two crew members needed to drive the ship.[13] That they clearly stand apart from the others as supernumeraries becomes even more evident when they approach the Argonauts, who have already

---

11. See especially Händel 17–26. A good example of the poet's manipulation of legendary material is the case of Nauplius, son of Poseidon and the Danaid Amymone (133–38; cf. Pherecydes *FGrHist* 3 F 4). Apollonius avoided the obvious problem of the generational gap between the age of the Danaids and that of Heracles by having two personages of this name; one the son of Amymone, and the other his Argonautic descendant; cf. Vian 246 *ad* 138. On the issue of relative chronology, cf. M. G. Palombi, "Apollonio e il dodecathlon," *Prometheus* 11 (1985) 126–36, who has shown that Apollonius established the time frame of the Argonautic expedition in relation to the labors of Heracles.

12. E.g., 96–100, 148–50, 163–71, and 193–96; Fränkel's general comments on the Catalogue (pp. 40–54) are particularly enlightening in this regard.

13. The Catalogue up to the Boreads accounts for the 52 men that Jason must have to serve as crew of the *Argo*: 50 to row, one to act as *keleustēs* (Orpheus; for which see Euripides *Hypsipyle* fr. 1.3.8–14 Bond), and one to steer the ship (Tiphys); cf. Vian 13–14 n. 3.

gathered on the beach at Pagasae in preparation for departure; their arrival is greeted with surprise by all (321–23). After this brief addendum, the Catalogue section closes with a digression explaining why the Argonauts as a group were traditionally called "Minyans" (228–33).

One further structural detail requires comment. In addition to the geographical organization, Apollonius also structured the Catalogue proper (23–233) in such a way that it falls into two distinct halves:[14] Orpheus heads the first half, which Talaus, Areius, and Leodocus—the sons of Bias and Pero—bring to a close (23–121); and the second half begins with Heracles and concludes with the Boreads (122–223). Several features in the presentation of the Catalogue point to this bipartite structure. First, only in the cases of Orpheus (μνησώμεθα, 23) and Heracles (πευθόμεθ', 123) does Apollonius introduce an Argonaut in the first person.[15] Second, the length of each section, being very nearly the same (99 lines in the first, 102 in the second), would appear to indicate that Apollonius envisaged these segments as separate and equal halves. Third, common elements also give the impression that each half has its own integrity: both sections have a doomed prophet (Mopsus ≈ Idmon), a helmsman who drives the *Argo* (Tiphys ≈ Ancæus 2), an Iphiclus, whom the poet has set at approximately opposite ends of the Catalogue (fourth from the beginning ≈ fifth from the end), and their own Phœnix figure (Iphiclus 1 for Jason [cf. 45–48] ≈ Laocoön for Meleager [cf. 190–94]).

Thus, two different structural systems operate simultaneously: on the one hand, the geographical ring frames and unifies the various strands of this long list of heroes from all over Minyan Greece, effectively separating the Catalogue proper from the wider section in which it is located; on the other hand, the bipartite structure makes a distinction between an Orphic and a Heraclean

---

14. See Vian 9.
15. A point noted by Blumberg 9. On a more speculative note, it may not be coincidental that both the Catalogue of Argonauts in the *Argonautica* and Callimachus's *Ætia*, framed as it is with Argonautic episodes (*Ætia* fr. 7–21 Pf. ["Argonautorum reditus et ritus Anaphæus"] and fr. 108–9 Pf. ["Ancora Argus navis Cyzici relicta"]) begin their second halves with depictions of Heracles engaged in one of his labors and associated with a nonheroic figure (Molorchus in the *Ætia*; Hylas in the *Argonautica*).

half, which will be seen to introduce a thematic antithesis that the poet sustains throughout the book and that is central to his consideration of the Argonautic hero. The whole Catalogue section thus has the following structure:

THE CATALOGUE, 23–233

A. The Catalogue of Argonauts (23–223)
    a. Orpheus Half: Orpheus to the Sons of Bias and Pero
    b. Heracles Half: Heracles to the Boreads
B. Appendix: Argus and Acastus (224–27)
C. Conclusion: Digression on the Term "Minyans" (228–33)

A. The Catalogue of Argonauts (23–223)

The two-part structure of the Catalogue of the Argonauts, as I have suggested elsewhere,[16] reflects the structure of the entire Catalogue section of *Iliad* 2, which comprises both the Catalogue of Ships (*Il.* 2.494–759) and the Catalogue of the Trojans (ibid. 816–77).[17] The two halves of Apollonius's Catalogue, however, represent not two opposing armies but two opposing types of hero who achieve the goals of their respective quests with antithetical approaches.

Orpheus and Heracles, who introduce each of the two halves, perform comparable tasks through diametrically opposed means; as Lawall has noted, Orpheus brought oak trees from Pieria to Thracian Zone through the power of his music (28–31), while Heracles transported the Erymanthian Boar from Arcadia to Mycenae by virtue of his great strength (124–29).[18] This antithesis is echoed at the end of each half of the Catalogue, where Apollonius has set corresponding stories, stories that do not celebrate the exploits of the respective Argonauts themselves, but events leading to the way in which they were begotten. The Orpheus half concludes

---

16. "A Mythological Thaumatrope in Apollonius Rhodius," *Hermes* 119 (1991) 484–88.
17. The archaic poet arranged the Trojan catalogue too along geographical lines; cf. G. S. Kirk, *The Iliad: A Commentary* (Cambridge 1985) 1.250.
18. Lawall 124 n. 10.

with Talaus, Areius, and Leodocus, whose entry contains a brief reference to the fact that these sons of Bias and Pero owe their existence to Melampus, who was imprisoned in Iphiclus's stables (120–21). The story was well known in antiquity.[19] On behalf of his brother, Bias, the seer Melampus went from Pylos to Phylace to fetch the cattle of Phylacus, which Neleus demanded as the price for the hand of his daughter, Pero. Although caught in the act of taking the cattle and imprisoned by the king, he won his freedom—and the cattle—through his prophetic skills (like Joseph in the Old Testament); the marriage that ensued produced the three Argonauts. At the end of the Heraclean half, Apollonius describes the begetting of Zetes and Calaïs (211–18): Boreas went from Thrace to Attica, where he seized Oreithyia as she danced along the Ilissus River, and, bringing her to the Sarpedonian Rock, there raped her.[20] Both terminal stories, then, involve distant journeys undergone to win a bride. Success in the case of Melampus, like that of Orpheus, results from his skill of communicating with nonhuman life forms;[21] Boreas, on the other hand, wins his bride, just as Heracles secured the Erymanthian Boar (and gained possession of Hylas, who is mentioned in the same entry, 131–32)[22] by brute force.[23]

In the Catalogue itself, then, Apollonius does more than list the Argonauts in a clever geographical arrangement, imitative of the

---

19. For details, see O. Wolf, "Melampus," Roscher 2.1.2567–73; and Pley, "Melampus (1)," *RE* 15.1.394–95. It should be noted that Callimachus alludes to the story in the *Victoria Berenices* (*SH* 260A.5).
20. I discuss the significance of this place name and its relationship with the Homeric Catalogue in the article cited above in note 16.
21. The story goes that Melampus foresaw the collapse of the roof of his prison when he heard the worms talking about how much was left of the beam they were eating; cf. Apollodorus 1.9.12. C. P. Segal, in the preface to his recent collection of articles on Orpheus (*Orpheus: The Myth of the Poet* [Baltimore 1989] xiii), calls Melampus Orpheus's "mythical cousin" since both are able "to hear the music of the world, to know its sights and sounds that others cannot perceive."
22. On the violence exerted in the "winning" of Hylas, cf. 1211–20.
23. Segal (supra n. 21) 18–19 (= "The Magic of Orpheus and the Ambiguities of Language," *Ramus* 7 [1978] 122–23) notes a similar contrast between Orpheus and Heracles in Euripides' *Alcestis*: whereas Orpheus failed to bring Eurydice back through his musical skill, Heracles succeeded in bringing Alcestis back by means of brute force.

Homeric Catalogues. The first half begins and ends with stories involving heroes who achieved their respective feats through their communicative skills; the second half is framed with accounts of heroes who attained the object of their quest through their physical prowess. The Catalogue thus unfolds in such a way that the reader is invited to see the two halves as representative of two types of hero, the man of skill and the man of strength.[24] Not only will this overall heroic antithesis surface in different forms throughout this book and beyond, but more specifically, the quests undertaken by, or leading up to the births of, the Argonauts who begin and conclude both halves of the Catalogue parallel and, to a certain extent, symbolize the Argonautic expedition, which was getting under way: Jason must travel to a distant land in order to fetch a specific item, and, in the course of his expedition, he too will win a bride. The heroic dichotomy of the Catalogue thus raises an interesting question: since Jason must attempt to accomplish what Orpheus, Heracles, Melampus, and Boreas all did in their respective ἄεθλοι, how will he achieve his goal?

B. Appendix: Argus and Acastus (224–27)

The appendix to the Catalogue, in which Apollonius adds the names of Acastus and Argus to the group, likewise does more than list names. As one will fully recognize only when the two

---

24. The parents of the Argonauts could well be another factor in the thematic antithesis between the two halves. Of the twenty-seven Argonauts in the Orpheus half, only in five cases has Apollonius assigned gods as parents (Orpheus [Calliope]; Erytus, Echion, Æthalides [Hermes]; and Phleias [Dionysus]); and of the twenty-five of the Heracles half, the poet associates twelve with divine parentage (Heracles, Castor, and Pollux [Zeus]; Nauplius [indirectly], Euphemus, Erginus, and Ancæus [2] [Poseidon]; Idmon [Apollo]; Palæmonius [indirectly; Hephæstus]; Augeas [Helius]; Zetes and Calaïs [Boreas]). Moreover, in the first half, Apollonius could have made Orpheus the son of Apollo (cf. Σ ad 1.23–25a) and Polyphemus the son of Poseidon (cf. Σ ad 1.40–41), while in the second half, he could have made Idmon the son of Abas (cf. Argo. 2.815) and Augeas the son of Phorbas or Eleius (see Ardizzoni ad 172). It seems possible that the number (three versus six) and the nature of the divine parents who are associated with each half (Calliope, Hermes, and Dionysus, as compared with Zeus, Poseidon, Apollo, Hephæstus, Helius, and Boreas) are also factors that support both the structural and thematic distinction between the halves through the emphasis in the first on human parentage and gods associated with music, and the emphasis in the second on divine parentage and gods often associated with great strength.

heroes join the others at Pagasae (321–26), this addendum mirrors the heroic dichotomy between the man of skill and the man of strength seen in the Catalogue proper. A brief examination of the later passage will reveal that Acastus and Argus represent for Apollonius these two opposite types of hero. The lines in question run as follows:

Ἐς δ' ἐνόησαν Ἄκαστον ὁμῶς Ἄργον τε πόληος
νόσφι καταβλώσκοντας, ἐθάμβησαν δ' ἐσιδόντες
πασσυδίῃ Πελίαο πάρὲκ νόον ἰθύοντας·
δέρμα δ' ὁ μὲν ταύροιο ποδηνεκὲς ἀμπέχετ' ὤμοις
Ἄργος Ἀρεστορίδης λάχνῃ μέλαν, αὐτὰρ ὁ καλὴν
δίπλακα τήν οἱ ὄπασσε κασιγνήτη Πελόπεια.
(321–26)

They noticed Acastus and Argus coming down from the city together, and they were amazed as they saw them
heading their way with all speed contrary to the will of Pelias.
Around his shoulders, Argus, the son of Arestor, wore a bull's hide
black with bristles and stretching to his feet; but Acastus wore an elegant
double-folded cloak, which his sister, Pelopia, gave him.

The conspicuous difference in the attire of the newcomers is significant: Acastus is dressed in an elegant cloak made for him by his sister, while Argus wears a bull's hide. Their arrival immediately precedes the choice of the captain. During this election, Jason, a man who wears a cloak of intricate design, made and given to him by Athena (cf. 1.721ff.), vies against Heracles, a hero famous for his lion skin. To show how Acastus and Argus reflect the thematic antithesis of the two halves of the Catalogue proper, I must for the moment anticipate a point that I shall make at greater length in Chapter 4. Jason and Heracles each represent one of the two types of hero of the Catalogue: Heracles, besides playing an important role in establishing one of the heroic types in the list, is throughout the poem—as everywhere in Greek myth and legend—the consummate man of strength. But Jason, who wins the election upon the insistence of Heracles, believes that the success of the mission depends on the cooperation of the group. For him, it is the skill of a leader who knows how to take care of details and exercise diplomacy that is all-important (332–40). This is in fact how he will proceed in the course of the expedition. Another instance of this sartorial distinction between the two different heroic types is found near the beginning of Book 2 in the boxing match between Polydeuces and Amycus. The former wears a cloak given to him by one of the Lemniades (ἐΰστιπτον θέτο φᾶρος / λεπταλέον, 2.30–31), and the latter is accoutred in rustic attire (ὁ δ' ἐρεμνὴν δίπτυχα λώπην / αὐτῆσιν περόνῃσι καλαύροπά τε τρηχεῖαν / κάββαλε τὴν φορέεσκεν ὀριτρεφέος κοτίνοιο, 2.32–34). In their fight, Polydeuces defeats and kills the much more powerful Amycus through his extraordinary skill (cf. 2.67–97). In these two cases, Apollonius associates the hero dressed in urbane fashion with the man of skill, while the hero in agrestic attire represents the man of strength.[25] Accordingly, Pelias's son, Acastus, and Argus, son of the same Arestor (112) who fathered the other Argus (the fierce, hundred-eyed cowherd slain by Hermes),[26] provide a subtle reflection of the antithetical types of hero seen in the list of the Catalogue.

C. Conclusion: Digression on the Term "Minyans"

After listing individually each of the Argonauts that Jason invited to participate and then adding the names of the two supernumeraries, Apollonius brings the Catalogue section to a satisfying conclusion by explaining the collective name used to refer to the heroes of the Argonautic expedition. The section ends, that is to say, with an etiology: why were the Argonauts as a whole called "Minyans"? The term was a traditional name for the group,[27] and Apollonius suggests a reason for its origin:

> Τοὺς μὲν ἀριστῆας Μινύας περιναιετάοντες
> κίκλησκον μάλα πάντας, ἐπεὶ Μινύαο θυγατρῶν

---

25. On the thematic significance of dress in the *Argonautica*, see A. Rose, "Clothing Imagery in Apollonius' *Argonautica*," *QUCC* 21 (1985) 29–44. It is noteworthy that in vase paintings of the Gigantomachy the (civilized) Olympians wear clothing and carry weapons that are manufactured, while the (barbaric) Giants wear skins and wield clubs; cf. E. Kuhnert, "Giganten," Roscher 1.2.1653–73; and *LIMC* 4.2 s.v. "Gigantes." A similar contrast can be seen in the Gigantomachy featured on the Hellenistic Altar of Zeus at Pergamon; cf. J. J. Pollitt, *Art in the Hellenistic Age* (Cambridge 1986) 97–110.
26. See Vian 244–45 *ad* 112.
27. See Vian 10 n. 2 for references.

οἱ πλεῖστοι καὶ ἄριστοι ἀφ' αἵματος εὐχετόωντο
ἔμμεναι· ὡς δὲ καὶ αὐτὸν Ἰήσονα γείνατο μήτηρ
Ἀλκιμέδη Κλυμένης Μινυηίδος ἐκγεγαυῖα.
(229–33)

Such was the number of men who gathered to assist the son of Æson. The people living in the vicinity called all these heroes Minyans since the majority, and these were the best, boasted to descend from the blood of the daughters of Minyas. Thus, even Jason himself had as mother Alcimede, who was the daughter of the Minyad Clymene.

The explanation that most of the Argonauts were Minyan in origin can hardly be correct. Indeed, the poet records only seven Minyadae among the group.[28] But it is not Apollonius who has blundered.[29] He is not the ultimate source of the faulty genealogical assertion. Rather the poet reports that those who lived in the vicinity of Iolcus (περιναιετάοντες, 229) were responsible for the name. He also informs us of their rationale: the majority of the Argonauts, who also claimed to be "the best," traced their lineage to the daughters of Minyas. The poet here in no way validates the claim either of the Argonauts who vaunt their Minyan lineage and primacy among the heroes or of the Iolcans who thereupon call the group "Minyans." On the contrary, the suggestion is subtly made that the name arose from the boasts of the majority of the Argonauts and from either the credulity or the chauvinism of the Iolcans, who themselves were traditionally called Minyans.[30]

Yet there is more involved here than a passing etiology. The Homeric Catalogue of Ships ends with a question: τίς τ' ἄρ τῶν ὄχ' ἄριστος ἔην, σύ μοι ἔννεπε, Μοῦσα, / αὐτῶν ἠδ' ἵππων, οἳ ἅμ' Ἀτρεΐδῃσιν ἕποντο (Il. 2.761–62).[31] To this inquiry Homer provides his own response: the steeds of Eumelus were the best horses, and Telamonian Ajax was the best of the heroes—that is, as long as Achilles was absent because of his wrath (ibid. 763–79). Lines 229–33 suggest that the origin of the term "Minyans"

---

28. They are Jason, Admetus, Iphiclus, Euphemus, Talaus, Areius, and Leodocus. Vian 10–12 offers a fine analysis of the problem.
29. So Vian 11.
30. For references, see Vian 11 n. 1.
31. Cf. G. Nagy, *The Best of the Achæans* (Baltimore 1979) 27.

for the Argonauts resulted from boasts made by those considered the best among the Argonauts. With the question posed at the conclusion of the Catalogue of Ships in mind, the reader would seem to be invited to ask who the best of the Argonauts is, a question that arises all the more naturally given the arrangement of the Catalogue into two halves representing opposing heroic types. This is in fact a question that Apollonius will explicitly ask twice in the course of the first book in contexts where Jason and Heracles vie for this honor. The first instance occurs in the election (332–50); and the second, in the argument following the abandonment of Heracles (1280–1344).[32] Thus, like Homer in his Catalogue, Apollonius too questions the identity of the "best of the heroes," although in a less direct fashion. The thematic opposition between the man of skill and the man of strength in the Catalogue implies that the answer will involve one of these two types of hero. Finally, one might guess from Homer's answer to his own question that one of the heroes may turn out to be the best only in the absence of the other. The events in Book 1 will bear out the validity of both these suggestions.

IT would be a mistake indeed to consider the Catalogue of Argonauts a mere listing of the *dramatis personæ*, required by the conventions of the genre and placed out front simply to get it out of the way. On the contrary, Apollonius has executed a remarkably original and brilliant adaptation of his Homeric model in such a way that he has not only provided the reader with the names, backgrounds, and in some cases revealing vignettes in the lives of the Argonauts; he has also raised—through the structure, presentation, and allusiveness of the Catalogue—the central question regarding the identity and the very nature of the hero of the *Argonautica*: Who is the best of the Argonauts? Will he bring back the golden fleece by means of some extraordinary skill, or through the exertion of brute strength?

---

32. I shall discuss these passages in detail in Chapters 4 and 8.

3

Unheroic Contrasts

The Departure from Iolcus (*Argo.* 1.234–316)

IN THE first dramatic scene of the poem, Apollonius describes the departure of the Argonauts and Jason from the city of Iolcus to the shore of Pagasae, as well as the reactions to these two separate departures by the Iolcan populace in general and Jason's family in particular.[1] The theme of the departing warrior already appeared in the Catalogue, where several entries focused on the reason why certain Argonauts joined the expedition and/or on the reaction of a parent or other close relative to the hero's participation in the quest.[2] Jason, however, does not have a formal entry in the Catalogue. Rather, Apollonius frames the Catalogue with images of the poem's central character that correspond to both the above-mentioned details: in the Proemium he reveals Jason's reason for forming the expeditionary crew (i.e., Pelias's oracle and his subsequent plot), and in the present episode he describes, at greater length than he does for any other member of the group, the moment when Jason leaves home to embark on this distant and dangerous journey and his parents' highly emotional response to his departure. As I have shown in the previous chapter, the Catalogue raises questions regarding the nature of the Argonautic hero and the identity of "the best" in the group. With this issue in mind, the reader immediately

---

1. Some (e.g., Levin 35–43, Vian 12–17) group this episode with the events that follow at Pagasae. The scene, however, possesses its own integrity in structure and theme, as I trust will become clear from my discussion in this chapter; cf. Hurst 49–52.

2. See Chapter 2, p. 26 n. 2.

encounters a fuller picture of Jason than we have seen up to this point. Regardless of how one will judge Jason in his words and actions in the course of the epic, his traditional role as the leader of the Argonautic expedition and the special focus in the Proemium on his arrival as the man fated to overcome the wicked Pelias lead the reader to expect that he will play a significant role in the successful completion of the quest for the golden fleece. It is important, then, to examine this first extended portrayal carefully to see if the poet will give us some clearer idea of what we can expect in this central figure. The structure of this episode offers much help in making such an evaluation.

STRUCTURE

The episode reveals a fairly common chiastic expansion of the ring-composition format; that is, there is more than one clearly definable section that precedes and follows the central section, and these proceed in reverse order in the second half. The departure of the Argonauts thronged by the Iolcans (A, 234–40a) balances that of Jason similarly surrounded by his townsmen, including the aged Iphias (A, 306–16). Apollonius calls attention to this corresponsion by qualifying each departure with a simile (239a ≈ 307–9).[3] The optimistic reaction of the men of Iolcus to the Argonautic mission (B, 240b–46)[4] matches Jason's optimistic speech to his mother as he is about to depart (B, 295–305). Within these balanced male responses stand a pair of counterpoised female responses to these departures: the fears for the expedition voiced by the women of Iolcus (C, 251–59) correspond to Alcimede's lament (C, 292–94).[5] These corresponding sections leave in the

---

3. On the link between the similes, see F. Stössl, *Apollonios Rhodios: Interpretationen zur Erzählungskunst und Quellenverwertung* (Bern 1941) 62; Levin 38–40.

4. Ardizzoni *ad* 242 offers the best interpretation of line 246 ('Ἀλλ' οὐ φυκτὰ κέλευθα, πόνος δ' ἄπρηκτος ἰοῦσιν), which contains the only negative point in the otherwise enthusiastic speech: the taking of the fleece from Æetes will prove easy; rather it is the trip that is an unavoidable (οὐ φυκτά) and difficult (ἄπρηκτος) task.

5. Beye 81 cleverly summarizes the focusing effect of the contrasting views of the Iolcan men and women: "We move from the *agora* mentality of the men to the *thalamos* mentality of the women and thus Apollonius brings us into the palace and finally to Jason."

central position the portrait of Jason's farewell at Æson's home (D, 261–77). This picture is in essence a triptych in which the poet has captured the pitiable reactions to Jason's departure by members of his household: male and female servants upset by their young master's departure, a gaunt and mournful Æson, and a lachrymose Alcimede, who is compared to a little girl.[6] The contrasts of male–female, young–old, and optimistic–pessimistic that characterize the central panel and the episode as a whole are delicately summarized in the departure of Jason, with which the episode concludes: on his way to the shore, the youthful and enthusiastic hero, who is compared to Apollo, is approached by the old priestess of Artemis, Iphias, who tries to convey some message that remains unspoken as the old woman escapes his notice in the hustle of the crowd (313b–16a). The chiastic structure of the episode and the thematic oppositions mentioned above together suggest that a major concern of the poet in this section, just as in the Catalogue, is contrast. The most important contrast here, however, lies not in the text but in the literary subtext, which will exert a strong impression on how we envisage Jason's heroic stature.

The action can be summarized as follows:

The Departure from Iolcus, 234–316

A. Departure of the Argonauts	(234–40a)
B. Optimistic Speech of the Men of Iolcus	(240b-246)
C. Pessimistic Speech of the Women of Iolcus	(247–60)
D. Æson's Home: Portrait of the Departing Warrior	(261–77)
C'. Alcimede's Pessimistic Speech	(278–94)
B'. Jason's Optimistic Speech	(295–305)
A'. Departure of Jason	(306–16)

---

6. Fränkel *ad* 1.261–306 and Vian 13 have observed that this central portrait harks back to the "departure of warrior" motif popular in art of the classical period. There may be a certain irony in the employment of this motif: Apollonius places Jason in a setting usually allotted to the brave soldier and his noble family; in this episode Jason and his parents will appear less than noble and scarcely heroic.

D. Æson's Home:
Portrait of the Departing Warrior (261–77)

As one can see in the schematic view of the action, the balanced departures and speeches set the portrait of Jason's farewell to his family in relief. In this chapter, differently from subsequent chapters, I have found it expedient to turn immediately to the center of this brief episode, where Apollonius has positioned the first in a series of connected allusions. The scene begins with the poet's striking description of an emaciated Æson, who can do little more than groan pitifully in reaction to his son's departure:

> Ἤδη δὲ δμῶές τε πολεῖς δμωαί τ' ἀγέροντο
> μήτηρ τ' ἀμφ' αὐτὸν βεβολημένη, ὀξὺ δ' ἑκάστην
> δῦνεν ἄχος· σὺν δέ σφι πατὴρ ὀλοῷ ὑπὸ γήραι
> ἐντυπὰς ἐν λεχέεσσι καλυψάμενος γοάασκεν.
> (261–64)

Now the many servants, male and female, gathered,
and also the mother tightly embracing her child. This was a painful sight for each of the women. In their midst, the father, in the grip of
consumptive old age, keeping his bony frame tightly covered in his bed,
was moaning.

As commentators have recognized, Apollonius has in mind the description of Priam lamenting his son's death in Book 24 of the *Iliad*:[7]

> ἷξεν δ' ἐς Πριάμοιο, κίχεν δ' ἐνοπήν τε γόον τε.
> παῖδες μὲν πατέρ' ἀμφὶ καθήμενοι ἔνδοθεν αὐλῆς
> δάκρυσιν εἵματ' ἔφυρον, ὁ δ' ἐν μέσσοισι γεραιὸς
> ἐντυπὰς ἐν χλαίνῃ κεκαλυμμένος· ἀμφὶ δὲ πολλὴ
> κόπρος ἔην κεφαλῇ τε καὶ αὐχένι τοῖο γέροντος,
> τήν ῥα κυλινδόμενος καταμήσατο χερσὶν ἑῇσι.
> θυγατέρες δ' ἀνὰ δώματ' ἰδὲ υυοὶ ὠδύροντο,
> τῶν μιμνησκόμεναι οἳ δὴ πολέες τε καὶ ἐσθλοὶ
> χερσὶν ὑπ' Ἀργείων κέατο ψυχὰς ὀλέσαντες.
> (*Il.* 24.160–68)

---

7. Cf. Mooney, Ardizzoni, and Campbell *ad loc.*

She [sc. Iris] arrived at the home of Priam and came upon the
 sound of moaning.
Sons, seated around their father within the court
drenched their clothing with their tears while their old father lay in
 their midst,
keeping his bony frame tightly covered in his cloak; there was much
 dung around the head and neck of the old man,
which he had heaped upon himself as he rolled on the ground.
His daughters and daughters-in-law were weeping throughout the
 house,
recalling those who, many and noble,
lost their lives, slain at the hands of the Argives.

Like Priam, Æson sits wasting away from sorrow at the thought of his son's absence. In addition to the close rendering of *Il.* 24.162–63 at lines 263–64, since Apollonius makes Jason an only son (287b–89),[8] he has recast Hector's brothers and sisters as the male and female servants of Æson's house.[9] The evocative image thus asks the reader to compare the effect that Jason's departure has on Æson and his whole household with the grief experienced by Priam and his family over the death of Hector.[10] This is not

---

8. The scholiast *ad* 1.287 said that according to Ibycus (fr. 301 *PMG*) Jason had a sister, Hippolyte. Apollonius has suppressed this fact, I believe, on purpose: by having Jason as an only child, he not only provides a situation in which Æson's and Alcimede's excessive grief is all the more plausible, but also sets up a familial arrangement comparable to that of one of its models: Alcimede's plight will be seen to recall that of Andromache and Peleus, both of whom have only one child; see below.

9. The explicit distinction between male and female servants (δμῶές τε πολεῖς δμωαί τ', 261; τῶν μέν ... δμώεσσι δέ, 265–66; cf. Stössl [supra n. 3] 59) parallels the earlier distinction between the male and female citizens of Iolcus. In particular, the women at Æson's house experience grief (262b–63a, 265–66a; cf. 250) while the men, though silent and gloomy, at least take an active role by getting Jason's weapons (267; cf. 240a–41, where the men of Iolcus are fascinated by the Argonauts' weapons).

10. The use of the Homeric *hapax legomenon* ἐντυπάς ("so as to show the contour of his limbs," LSJ; see *TGL* s.v.), which is found before Apollonius only in this Iliadic passage, in conjunction with the other verbal and conceptual points of contact, makes the imitation clear. Apollonius used the adverb again at *Argo.* 2.861, where the Argonauts are in mourning over the deaths of Idmon and Tiphys. In that context, however, there are no other verbal or conceptual links that draw the reader's attention to *Il.* 24.160–68. One should note, nonetheless, that in its second occurrence ἐντυπάς describes the effects of mourning. This adverb is found in only four passages in extant

an isolated reference to the death of Hector and its effect on his family. Apollonius sustains and expands the equation between Hector's death and Jason's departure in what follows with a series of allusions to passages from the *Iliad* and *Odyssey* that pertain to this tragic event.

The poet immediately turns his attention from the decrepit Æson to the almost hysterical Alcimede. She holds on to her son, crying like a girl who clings to her aged nurse:

> Μήτηρ δ' ὡς τὰ πρῶτ' ἐπεχεύατο πήχεε παιδί,
> ὣς ἔχετο κλαίουσ' ἀδινώτερον, ἠύτε κούρη
> οἰόθεν ἀσπασίως πολιὴν τροφὸν ἀμφιπεσοῦσα
> μύρεται, ᾗ οὐκ εἰσὶν ἔτ' ἄλλοι κηδεμονῆες·
> ἀλλ' ὑπὸ μητρυιῇ βίοτον βαρὺν ἡγηλάζει·
> καί ἑ νέον πολέεσσιν <u>ὀνείδεσιν ἐστυφέλιξε</u>,
> τῇ δέ τ' ὀδυρομένῃ δέδεται κέαρ ἔνδοθεν ἄτῃ,
> οὐδ' ἔχει ἐκφλύξαι τόσσον γόον ὅσσον ὀρεχθεῖ·
> ὣς ἀδινὸν κλαίεσχεν ἑὸν παῖδ' ἀγκὰς ἔχουσα
> <u>Ἀλκιμέδη</u>.
>   (268-77a)

Just as his mother had at first thrown her arms around her child,
so she continued to hold him crying constantly, like a girl
who, alone in the world, falls gladly upon her elderly nurse
and sobs. She has no one else to care for her,
but leads a grievous life under a stepmother
who recently <u>scolded her with</u> many <u>abusive taunts</u>;
as she weeps, her heart is imprisoned by her anguish
and she cannot release as much grief as wells up within.
In just this way <u>Alcimede</u> was crying as she held her son in her arms.

The little girl with whom Alcimede is compared in the simile lost her mother and now lacks any other sympathetic family members

---

literature (the fourth being Quintus Smyrnæus 5.529-30: ἡ [sc. Τέκμησσα] δὲ μέγα στενάχουσα φίλῳ περικάππεσε νεκρῷ / ἐντυπὰς ἐν κονίῃσι καλὸν δέμας αἰσχύνουσα). With the exception of the present passage under consideration, all occur in a funereal context (cf. Hesychius s.v., who translates it as πενθικῶς). Since ἐντυπάς would appear to be a rare and colorful poetic adverb delineating the effect of grief for the loss of a loved one, the use of the word in this context suggests that Æson's response to Jason's departure is equivalent to a response to his death.

to care for her.[11] Moreover, her father has remarried and does not prevent his new wife from heaping verbal abuse upon his own daughter.[12] The elderly nurse alone consoles the little girl, who is terrorized by stinging comments from her new maternal guardian. The words that Apollonius has chosen to express this verbal abuse (καί ἑ νέον πολέεσσιν ὀνείδεσιν ἐστυφέλιξε, 273) recall what Andromache feared would happen to Astyanax once Hector was dead:[13]

τὸν δὲ καὶ ἀμφιθαλὴς ἐκ δαιτύος ἐστυφέλιξε,
χερσὶν πεπληγὼς καὶ ὀνειδείοισι ἐνίσσων·
'ἔρρ' οὕτως· οὐ σός γε πατὴρ μεταδαίνυται ἡμῖν.'
δακρυόεις δέ τ' ἄνεισι πάις ἐς μητέρα χήρην,
Ἀστυάναξ.
  (Il. 22.496-500a)

A child, both his parents still alive, thrust him from the banquet,
striking him with his hands and scolding him with taunts:
"Get out of here in your condition! No father of yours shares in
  our feast."
With tears in his eyes he returns to his widowed mother, the child
Astyanax.

11. The scholiast *ad* 1.269-72f compares this to Jason's familial situation; Alcimede has no other children to take care of her.
12. This situation compares with the lot of the young women on Lemnos in Hypsipyle's doctored account of the fate of the male population on the island (*Argo.* 1.809b-17); in particular, cf. 813-15a: οὐδὲ πατὴρ ὀλίγον περ ἑῆς ἀλέγιζε θυγατρός, / εἰ καὶ ἐν ὀφθαλμοῖσι δαϊζομένην ὁρόῳτο / μητρυιῆς ὑπὸ χερσὶν ἀτασθάλου.
13. Cf. Mooney *ad* 1.273. ἐστυφέλιξε, whose sense in each passage is slightly different (cf. LSJ s.v. 1 and 2), in this metrical position is used only twice in the Homeric corpus: here and at *Od.* 17.234 (N.B. it does occur as a *varia lectio* at *Il.* 16.774, but in a martial context). At *Od.* 17.234, Odysseus too is insulted at a feast. Still, Apollonius appears to have his eye chiefly on the Iliadic passage, as can be seen from his contraction of the Homeric ἐστυφέλιξε ... ὀνειδείοισι ἐνίσσων to ὀνείδεσιν ἐστυφέλιξε. The phrase ἠΰτε κούρη in line 269, which introduces the simile, also has a Homeric parallel (cf. Mooney, Ardizzoni, and Campbell *ad loc.*). At *Il.* 16.7, Achilles compares Patroclus to a tearful little girl who cries to be picked up by her mother (N.B. the Homeric age and gender inversion as Patroclus [mature male] is compared to the little girl [young female]). There are, however, no other points of contact with the Argonautic text that I can see. ἠΰτε κούρη is found one other time in Homeric epic at *Il.* 2.872 in a completely unrelated context.

Overcome with anxiety, Andromache envisages Astyanax's future without his father (cf. ibid. 477-514) and imagines her son going to the home of one of Hector's friends to beg for food and clothing (492-95) and returning to her in tears after being cruelly rebuked (499), a situation comparable to the experience of the little girl who runs sobbing to her nurse. This contrast between the text and subtext whereby the abusive treatment imagined by Andromache for Astyanax, her little *boy*, becomes the experience encountered by the little *girl* with whom Alcimede is compared parallels the more explicit contrast that informs the simile: the *elderly* nurse (female) who provides solace is an analogue for the *youthful* Jason (male) and the defenseless *young* girl suffers the plight of the *aging* Alcimede. The role reversals suggested by the poet highlight an uncomfortably realistic fact of life: the elderly are so often reduced to the helplessness of children when encumbered by advanced old age.[14] Apollonius in fact will make reference to the unfortunate effects of aging at the end of the episode in his explanation for the passing-by of the aged Iphias: she was left behind οἴα γεραιὴ ὁπλοτέρων (315-16). In sum, once we presume Æson's almost complete inability to act in any significant way both from his pathetic response to his son's departure and his wife's lack of reference to him as a source of protection or comfort, Alcimede's predicament becomes all the clearer: she will have to endure a difficult lot in her old age, even the outrageous abuse of uncaring guardians, after she is deprived of her only functional and caring κηδεμονεύς. Alcimede herself will address this fear in her speech to Jason.

C. Alcimede's Pessimistic Speech (278-94)

In her plaintive address to her son, Alcimede says that she wants to die and identifies the two greatest fears she has for an old age without Jason: lack of burial by her own son and abandonment in an empty home like a slave because of the loss of the one who provided her with distinction in Iolcan society:

> Αἴθ' ὄφελον κεῖν' ἦμαρ, ὅτ' ἐξειπόντος ἄκουσα
> δειλὴ ἐγὼ Πελίαο κακὴν βασιλῆος ἐφετμήν,
> αὐτίκ' ἀπὸ ψυχὴν μεθέμεν κηδέων τε λαθέσθαι,

---

14. Cf. Levin 42-43, Beye 32-33.

ὄφρ' αὐτός με τεῇσι φίλαις ταρχύσαο χερσί,
τέκνον ἐμόν· τὸ γὰρ οἷον ἔην ἔτι λοιπὸν ἐέλδωρ
ἐκ σέθεν, ἄλλα δὲ πάντα πάλαι θρεπτήρια πέσσω.
Νῦν γε μὲν ἤ τὸ πάροιθεν Ἀχαιϊάδεσσιν ἀγητὴ
δμωὶς ὅπως κενεοῖσι λελείψομαι ἐν μεγάροισι,
σεῖο πόθῳ μινύθουσα δυσάμμορος, ᾧ ἔπι πολλὴν
ἀγλαΐην καὶ κῦδος ἔχον πάρος, ᾧ ἔπι μούνῳ
μίτρην πρῶτον ἔλυσα καὶ ὕστατον· ἔξοχα γάρ μοι
Εἰλήθυια θεὰ πολέος ἐμέγηρε τόκοιο.
Ὤ μοι ἐμῆς ἄτης· τὸ μὲν οὐδ' ὅσον οὐδ' ἐν ὀνείρῳ
ὠισάμην, εἰ Φρίξος ἐμοὶ κακὸν ἔσσετ' ἀλύξας.
                                            (278–91)

Would that I, on that day when I heard King Pelias
uttering the wicked command that would cause me such ruin,
immediately released my soul and lost consciousness of my cares
so that you yourself would have buried me with your own hands,
my son. For this was the only desire I still had
of you; I have long ago received all the other rewards a child owes a
parent. As it is, I, who before was envied by the Achæan women,
will be abandoned like a slave in an empty palace,
wasting away with ill-starred longing for you, because of whom
I had honor and glory in the past, for whom alone
I, first and last, loosened the girdle of childbirth. For
the goddess Eileithyia adamantly forbade my having many children.
O what misery is mine! I did not reckon even in my wildest dreams
that Phrixus's salvation would become my demise.

Commentators have duly observed and recorded the relevant verbal and conceptual echoes in Alcimede's speech (see below), but have not called attention to the fact that the most important of these recall from different angles the effect that the death of Hector had on his family, especially on Andromache.

First of all, Alcimede opens her speech with the wish that she had died when she first heard of the expedition, so that Jason would have been able to bury her; this scenario is all the more desirable since, as far as Alcimede is concerned, Jason has discharged all his other responsibilities (i.e., the θρεπτήρια mentioned in line 283). In the *Iliad*, Andromache similarly wished for death when faced with the prospect of losing Hector (ἐμοὶ δέ κε κέρδιον εἴη /

σεῦ ἀφαμαρτούσῃ χθόνα δύμεναι, Il. 6.410b–11a; cf. 22.481):[15] her desperate wish, similar to that of Alcimede, arises from her lack of κηδεμονῆες; for Achilles had killed Andromache's entire family, leaving Hector as her only protector and source of comfort (cf. Il. 6.411b–30). Second, Alcimede claims that the departure of Jason will result in her being left behind as a slave (δμωὶς ὅπως κενεοῖσι λελείψομαι ἐν μεγάροισι, 285). In her final speech in the *Iliad* (24.725–45), Andromache imagines herself and Astyanax being led off into slavery (731–34), the very thing that Hector feared would happen (cf. Il. 6.447–65), and concludes that her husband's death will result in grievous sorrows being left behind for her to face: ἐμοὶ δὲ μάλιστα λελείψεται ἄλγεα λυγρά (24.742).[16] Similarity of theme (a death wish and the fear of slavery, both resulting from the lack of a κηδεμονεύς) and in the second case verbal reminiscence invite the reader to see Andromache's tragic situation as the literary backdrop for Alcimede's pitiful lament.

Apollonius evidently wants the audience to compare Alcimede's anxiety over the departure of Jason with Andromache's fears for herself and Astyanax in the aftermath of Hector's death. With this in mind the Homeric *hapax legomenon* ἀμφιπεσοῦσα (270) in the previous simile comparing Alcimede to the little girl takes on greater significance.[17] The rare participial form describes the

---

15. Levin 41–42 and Vian 13 and 63 n. 2 both observed the resemblance of Alcimede to Andromache in this wish. M. Fantuzzi, "Varianti d'autore nelle *Argonautiche* d'Apollonio Rodio," *A&A* 29 (1983) 150–52, however, argues that whereas the version in the proecdosis (preserved by Σ *ad* 1.285–86a) recalls the Iliadic lament for Hector, the second version brings the fate of Electra in Sophocles' play of the same name into mind. Although no one will deny the influence of Attic tragedy on the *Argonautica* in general, the similarities between the orphan girl and Sophocles' Electra are only superficial; Electra's fate, as far as I can see, is not at all germane to that of Alcimede.

16. A search of the *TLG* reveals that these are the only instances of the future perfect of this verb in extant hexametric poetry. Prior to Apollonius λείπω in this tense is found three times in Euripides (*Hipp.* 324; *Or.* 1041, 1085) and once in Sophocles (*OT* 1504).

17. This moving image and its specific articulation have been anticipated by the description of Alcimede embracing Jason a few lines earlier: μήτηρ τ' ἀμφ' αὐτὸν βεβολημένη, 262. I follow the text of Vian, who has not, as Ardizzoni and Fränkel (OCT), adopted Herwerden's ἀμφασίῃ. Mooney *ad loc.* rightly observed the tmesis in the phrase ἀμφ' αὐτὸν βεβολημένη. βεβολημένη itself has also proven troublesome to some critics (e.g., E. Livrea, "Apoll. Rh. 1.262," *GIF* 29 [1977] 29–33; cf. R. W. Garson, "Homeric Echoes in Apollonius

little girl's pathetic response to her want of a κηδεμονεύς in the face of a wicked stepmother: she falls crying into the arms of her nurse. ἀμφιπίπτω occurs only once in the Homeric corpus, also in a simile, in which the poet compares Odysseus's crying upon hearing Demodocus's story of the Trojan Horse to a woman lamenting the death of her husband in war:[18]

Ταῦτ' ἄρ' ἀοιδὸς ἄειδε περικλυτός· αὐτὰρ Ὀδυσσεὺς
τήκετο, δάκρυ δ' ἔδευεν ὑπὸ βλεφάροισι παρειάς.
ὡς δὲ γυνὴ κλαίῃσι φίλον πόσιν <u>ἀμφιπεσοῦσα</u>,
ὅς τε ἑῆς πρόσθεν πόλιος λαῶν τε πέσῃσιν,
ἄστει καὶ τεκέεσσιν ἀμύνων νηλεὲς ἦμαρ·
ἡ μὲν τὸν θνήσκοντα καὶ ἀσπαίροντα ἰδοῦσα
ἀμφ' αὐτῷ χυμένη λίγα κωκύει· οἱ δέ τ' ὄπισθε
κόπτοντες δούρεσσι μετάφρενον ἠδὲ καὶ ὤμους
εἴρερον εἰσανάγουσι, πόνον τ' ἐχέμεν καὶ ὀιζύν·
τῆς δ' ἐλεεινοτάτῳ ἄχεϊ φθινύθουσι παρειαί·
ὣς Ὀδυσεὺς ἐλεεινὸν ὑπ' ὀφρύσι δάκρυον εἶβεν.

(Od. 8.521–31)

The celebrated poet [*sc.* Demodocus] sang this song. Odysseus melted, and tears streamed from his eyes down his cheeks.
Just as a woman laments her dear husband, <u>falling down upon him</u>,
who fell before the eyes of his city and people
as he tried to protect his city and children from the piteous day.
Seeing him in the throes of death, she
holds him in her arms, shrieking loudly. Behind her, others
striking her back and shoulders with their spears
lead her into slavery, to a life of pain and lamentation;
her cheeks are sunken from pitiable grief.
Just like this Odysseus shed a pitiful tear from beneath his brows.

Rhodius' *Argonautica*," *CP* 67 [1972] 5); for a defense of this reading, see M. Campbell, "Ap. Rhod. 1.261ff. Again," *GIF* 30 (1978) 288–89.

18. Cf. Mooney, Ardizzoni, and Campbell *ad* 1.270. In extant epic verse, ἀμφιπίπτω is found only in these two passages and at Quintus Smyrnæus 5.444, in a context also involving Odysseus (Ajax, speaking to a slaughtered ram that he believes to be Odysseus, tells his supposedly dead enemy that his wife will not "fall about him"). Furthermore, it occurs always in the same form and metrical position, and in the two non-Apollonian passages, the verb describes a woman falling upon her *dead* husband; cf. the funereal associations of ἐντυπάς discussed above in note 10.

The picture of a woman grieving for her dying husband, whose duty it was to ward off the day of slavery from city and children, closely parallels Andromache's situation at the conclusion of the *Iliad*; so much so that Apollonius well might have seen in the Odyssean text an allusion to the fates of Andromache and Hector. Be that as it may, both the specific references to Andromache's loss of Hector and this allusion to the unidentified woman in the *Odyssey* prompt the reader to associate Alcimede's response to Jason's departure with the grief of a wife for a dead husband, and in particular, of Andromache for Hector.

B. Jason's Optimistic Speech (295–305)

Given that Æson's and Alcimede's reactions to their son's departure recall the lamentation, respectively, of Priam and Andromache for the dead Hector, it should come as no surprise that Jason's response to his mother is a composite of themes and phrases that likewise come from Homeric passages concerning events surrounding the death of this Trojan hero. In his speech, Jason tells Alcimede that excessive lamentation only adds to the present evils that the gods have sent; that she should not worry because he has received sufficient divine and human help to fulfill his mission successfully; and finally that she should go back to her room and not bring bad luck upon the expedition through her pessimistic feelings. His speech runs as follows:

> Μή μοι λευγαλέας ἐπιβάλλεο, μῆτερ, ἀνίας
> ὧδε λίην, ἐπεὶ οὐ μὲν ἐρητύσεις κακότητος[19]
> δάκρυσιν, ἀλλ' ἔτι κεν καὶ ἐπ' ἄλγεσιν ἄλγος ἄροιο.
> Πήματα γάρ τ' ἀΐδηλα θεοὶ θνητοῖσι νέμουσι,
> τῶν <u>μοῖραν</u> κατὰ θυμὸν ἀνιάζουσά περ ἔμπης
> τλῆθι φέρειν· θάρσει δὲ συνημοσύνῃσιν Ἀθήνης
> ἠδὲ θεοπροπίῃσιν, ἐπεὶ μάλα δεξιὰ Φοῖβος
> ἔχρη, ἀτὰρ μετέπειτά γ' ἀριστήων ἐπαρωγῇ.
> Ἀλλὰ σὺ μὲν νῦν αὖθι μετ' ἀμφιπόλοισιν ἔκηλος
> <u>μίμνε δόμοις, μηδ' ὄρνις ἀεικελίη πέλε νηΐ</u>·
> κεῖσε δ' ὁμαρτήσουσιν ἔται δμῶές τε κιόντι.
>
> (295–305)

---

19. On the sense of κακότητος, see Giangrande 2.

Do not for my sake, mother, fill your mind with aching grief
to such extent, since you will not free yourself from suffering
with tears; rather you would only add pain on top of pain.
The gods deal out invisible sorrows to mankind.
Have the courage to endure your <u>portion</u> of these, even though
you grieve in your heart. And find strength in Athena's promise of
  aid;
in the divine oracles, since Phœbus has revealed propitious
signs; and finally in the assistance of the heroes.
<u>Now for your part remain here at home among the servants
free from care, <u>and do not become an inauspicious bird of
  omen for the ship.</u></u>
Our kinsmen and servants will accompany you to your quarters.

When Priam came to the tent of Achilles to ransom the body of Hector, the hero tried to console him, as Jason does here, by pointing out that excessive grief would prove useless and that the gods were ultimately responsible for the misfortunes that all must suffer (*Il.* 24.518–56). Of particular interest are the following two excerpts from this speech:[20]

ἄνσχεο, μηδ' ἀλίαστον ὀδύρεο σὸν κατὰ θυμόν·
οὐ γάρ τι πρήξεις ἀκαχήμενος υἷος ἑῆος,
οὐδέ μιν ἀνστήσεις, πρὶν καὶ κακὸν ἄλλο πάθησθα.
         (*Il.* 24.549–51; cf. *Argo.* 1.295–97)

Endure and do not tear away at your heart with excessive
  lamentation;
for you will not achieve any good by grieving for your son,
nor will you bring him back, but suffer some other evil first.

ὡς γὰρ ἐπεκλώσαντο θεοὶ δειλοῖσι βροτοῖσι,
ζώειν ἀχνυμένοις· αὐτοὶ δέ τ' ἀκηδέες εἰσί.
         (*Il.* 24.525–26; cf. *Argo.* 1.298–300a)

For thus have the gods spun the thread of life for pitiable mortals—
to live a life of grief—while they themselves enjoy a carefree
  existence.

---

20. Cf. Fränkel p. 62 n. 91, Vian 64 n. 1, and Campbell *ad* 1.295ff. Vian and Campbell also point to *Il.* 6.486, where Hector speaks to Andromache.

The sentiment is the same in both speeches: excessive grief does not relieve the evils that the gods send. Although the wording of the Argonautic text does not entail a close imitation of particular words or phrases of the Iliadic, the scholiast nonetheless provides a good indication that Apollonius's audience could have observed the poet's references to this speech. In his comments on lines 296b and 297a, he pointed to *Il.* 24.524 and 551, respectively; the ancient scholar clearly saw that Jason's speech paralleled that of Achilles. Moreover, a point made in the same Iliadic speech to which Apollonius did not allude specifically is germane to the present Argonautic context. In his attempt to assuage Priam's grief, Achilles offered his own father, Peleus, as an example of one who received a mixed lot from the gods. Though Peleus was once fortunate, he now suffered because of the absence of his only child:

ὣς μὲν καὶ Πηλῆι θεοὶ δόσαν ἀγλαὰ δῶρα
ἐκ γενετῆς· πάντας γὰρ ἐπ' ἀνθρώπους ἐκέκαστο
ὄλβῳ τε πλούτῳ τε, ἄνασσε δὲ Μυρμιδόνεσσι,
καί οἱ θνητῷ ἐόντι θεὰν ποίησαν ἄκοιτιν.
ἀλλ' ἐπὶ καὶ τῷ θῆκε θεὸς κακόν, ὅττι οἱ οὔ τι
παίδων ἐν μεγάροισι γονὴ γένετο κρειόντων,
ἀλλ' ἕνα παῖδα τέκεν παναώριον· οὐδέ νυ τόν γε
γηράσκοντα κομίζω, ἐπεὶ μάλα τηλόθι πάτρης
ἧμαι ἐνὶ Τροίῃ, σέ τε κήδων ἠδὲ σὰ τέκνα.
(*Il.* 24.534-42)

And so even to Peleus the gods gave wondrous gifts
from birth, for he surpassed all men
in wealth and riches, and ruled the Myrmidons;
and the gods made a goddess his wife, although he was mortal.
A god, however, inflicted an evil upon him: he did not have
in his home a progeny of sons whose lot it was to rule;
rather he begat one ill-fated son. As it is, I shall not
care for him as he grows old, since very far from my fatherland
I remain in Troy, an anxiety to you and your children.

Like Peleus, Alcimede, though formerly prosperous, now experiences grief over the departure of her only son on a foreign adventure; moreover, she too believes that she can no longer expect either γηροκομία or burial from Jason, a fate comparable to that of Peleus. It is noteworthy that the gender reversal between text and subtext in this instance parallels that between Astyanax and the little girl of the simile.

After trying to encourage his mother by referring to his advice from Athena, as well as to the propitious oracle of Apollo and the assistance of the Argonauts (300-302), Jason dismisses Alcimede rather abruptly, telling her to stay at home with her servants and not to be a bird of ill omen (303-5). Regarding the first point, Hector dismissed Andromache in their last meeting in a similar fashion, the phrasing of which Apollonius has in mind here:[21]

δαιμονίη, μή μοί τι λίην ἀκαχίζεο θυμῷ·
οὐ γάρ τίς μ' ὑπὲρ αἶσαν ἀνὴρ Ἄιδι προϊάψει·
μοῖραν δ' οὔ τινά φημι πεφυγμένον ἔμμεναι ἀνδρῶν,
οὐ κακόν, οὐδὲ μὲν ἐσθλόν, ἐπὴν τὰ πρῶτα γένηται.
ἀλλ' εἰς οἶκον ἰοῦσα τὰ σ' αὐτῆς ἔργα κόμιζε,
ἱστόν τ' ἠλακάτην τε, καὶ ἀμφιπόλοισι κέλευε[22]
ἔργον ἐποίχεσθαι· πόλεμος δ' ἄνδρεσσι μελήσει
πᾶσι, μάλιστα δ' ἐμοί, τοὶ Ἰλίῳ ἐγγεγάασιν.
                    (Il. 6.486-93; cf. Argo. 1.298-304)

My poor distraught wife, do not allow grief for me to tear at your heart.
No one will send me to Hades before my time.
I tell you this: no one has escaped his <u>fate</u>,
neither coward nor hero, once he was born.
<u>But go home and tend to your tasks—</u>
your loom and spindle—and order your <u>servants</u>
to get to work. War will be the concern of all
men born in Ilion, especially me.

As to the second point, Jason's request that his mother not jeopardize his mission by voicing such dire and inauspicious fears prompts the audience to recall what Priam said to Hecuba when

---

21. Cf. Mooney ad 1.303, Vian 64 n. 1. Lines 490-93a of the Iliadic passage are found with only slight variation at Od. 1.356-59a and 21.350-53a. In both passages Telemachus summarily dismisses Penelope. Apollonius may have had these lines in mind as well (in both the Argonautic and the Odyssean passages a son on the verge of manhood dismisses his mother), but this would appear of secondary interest; the relevance of the Iliadic version of this dismissal to Hector's impending death fits the series of references to this tragic event.

22. There could well be a phonetic pun with ἔκηλος of line 303.

she tried to prevent her husband from going on his journey to the Greek camp to fetch Hector's body:[23]

μή μ' ἐθέλοντ' ἰέναι κατερύκανε, <u>μηδέ μοι αὐτὴ
ὄρνις ἐνὶ μεγάροισι κακὸς πέλευ</u>· οὐδέ με πείσεις.
(Il. 24.218–19; cf. Argo. 1.304)

Do not try to stop me from going, which is what I want to do;
<u>and do not
become a bird of ill omen in my house.</u> You shall not persuade
me.

In short, Jason's speech recalls expressions of consolation or impatience uttered by Achilles, Hector, and Priam in response to Hector's death both before and after the fact.

A. Departure of Jason (306–16)

The episode concludes when Jason leaves his home and goes off to Pagasae. Apollonius compares him to the youthful god Apollo as he passes through the crowds at one of his sanctuaries:

Ἦ καὶ ὁ μὲν προτέρωσε δόμων ἐξῶρτο νέεσθαι.
Οἷος δ' ἐκ νηοῖο θυώδεος εἴσιν Ἀπόλλων
Δῆλον ἀν' ἠγαθέην ἠὲ Κλάρον ἢ ὅ γε Πυθὼ
ἢ Λυκίην εὐρεῖαν ἐπὶ Ξάνθοις ῥοῇσι·
τοῖος ἀνὰ πληθὺν δήμου κίεν, ὦρτο δ' αὐτὴ
κεχλομένων ἄμυδις.
(306–11a)

He spoke, and then hastened to depart from the house.
As Apollo goes from his temple, redolent of incense,
through sacred Delos, or Clarus, or Pytho,
or wide Lycia at the streams of the river Xanthus,
just like this he proceeded through the crowds of the city, and the shouting of those bidding him farewell grew loud.

---

23. One should note that this reference, like that to the speech of Achilles to Priam, was first observed by the scholiast *ad* 1.304. Modern commentators have also observed the borrowing: cf. Mooney, Ardizzoni, and Campbell *ad* 1.304, Vian 64 n. 1, and Fränkel p. 62 n. 93. It may not be coincidental that in this last reference to a Homeric passage referring to Hector's death Apollonius looks to the same Iliadic scene that initiated the series of connected allusions (see above, *Argo.* 1.261–64 ≈ *Il.* 24.160–68).

[1.234-316]   UNHEROIC CONTRASTS   53

As he proceeds toward the beach, the young Apollinian male is approached by Iphias—the aged priestess of Apollo's sister, Artemis—whom he leaves behind without notice:

<u>Τῷ δὲ ξύμβλητο γεραιὴ</u>
Ἰφιὰς Ἀρτέμιδος πολιηόχου ἀρήτειρα,
καί μιν δεξιτερῆς χειρὸς κύσεν· οὐδέ τι φάσθαι
ἔμπης ἱεμένη δύνατο προθέοντος ὁμίλου,
ἀλλ' ἡ μὲν λίπετ' αὖθι παρακλιδόν, οἷα γεραιὴ
ὁπλοτέρων, ὁ δὲ πολλὸν ἀποπλαγχθεὶς ἐλιάσθη.
(311b–16)

<u>An old woman met him,</u>
<u>Iphias</u>, the priestess of Artemis, the City Protector,
and she kissed his right hand. But she was not able to say anything,
however much she wanted, because the crowd kept moving forward.
So she was left there on the side of the road, just like an old woman
by the younger generation, as he moved on and into the distance.

As I have observed above, this brief encounter summarizes the thematic oppositions of the episode: male–female, young–old,[24] optimistic–pessimistic.[25] The Iliadic passage that Apollonius is imitating here reveals yet another inversion between text and subtext:[26]

<u>ὁ δὲ ξύμβλητο γεραιός</u>,
<u>Νέστωρ</u>, πτῆξε δὲ θυμὸν ἐνὶ στήθεσσιν Ἀχαιῶν.
(Il. 14.39–40)

<u>The old man met them,</u>
<u>Nestor</u>, and he caused the hearts of the Achæans to flutter within.

The words used to describe the encounter of an enthusiastic Jason with the old Iphias (female) recall the moment that the elderly

---

24. The scholiast *ad* 1.307 noted that the point of comparison between Jason and Apollo was youth.
25. Jason appears to be so full of high spirits and completely wrapped in his thoughts of the adventure before him that he does not even notice the elderly priestess; his optimism, seen in his speech and parallel with the optimistic prognosis of the men of Iolcus (240b–60), is reflected in his godlike demeanor. Accordingly, one would associate Iphias with the pessimistic reactions of the other women of the episode, Alcimede (278–94) and the women of Iolcus (247–60).
26. Cf. Ardizzoni *ad* 311, Campbell *ad* 1.311–12.

Nestor (male) met the wounded Greek leaders at a low point in their struggle near the beginning of *Iliad* 14. A more important difference exists between the two passages than that of gender. Whereas the Greek heroes give evidence of their great respect for the older Nestor, Jason does not even sense the presence of the old priestess, who is abandoned, the poet tells us, just like an old woman by the younger generation. As such, Jason is different from the Homeric heroes: he is too focused on himself and his expedition to take notice of the elderly priestess. In this self-absorption he resembles his parents.

At this point it is possible to make sense of the various threads of this complex set of subtexts. Apollonius compares Æson to Priam as he lamented the death of his son. Priam, on the one hand, shrugged off the paralyzing effects of his grief and went courageously to Achilles' tent to ransom Hector's body. Æson never moves. We are led to believe by the poet's silence that he remained seated, luxuriating in an enervating self-pity. The poet describes Alcimede in terms recalling Andromache. In the passages alluded to, Andromache's fear is that Hector's death will result in the literal enslavement of herself and her son. Alcimede, however, expresses fear not for personal, but for a kind of social enslavement. Up to this time, Apollonius informs the audience, Alcimede derived her status from her son: ᾧ [*sc.* Ἰήσονι] ἔπι πολλὴν / ἀγλαΐην καὶ κῦδος ἔχον πάρος (286b–87). In fact, the women of Iolcus corroborate this statement in advance (Δειλὴ Ἀλκιμέδη, καὶ σοὶ κακὸν ὀψέ περ ἔμπης / ἤλυθεν οὐδ' ἐτέλεσσας ἐπ' ἀγλαΐῃ βιότοιο, 251–52). Comparison with Andromache's serious and, as it would turn out, partially accurate fears shows that Alcimede's reaction to Jason's departure was both excessive and overly egocentric.[27]

---

27. Alcimede gives no indication of any fear that once Jason is gone she and Æson will face any danger at Pelias's hands, although there is a tradition, which Apollonius may have in mind here, that Pelias brought about their suicide when he believed that Jason would not return (cf. Valerius Flaccus *Argo.* 1.777ff., Diodorus 4.50.1, Apollodorus 1.9.27). Her desire to have Jason remain thus does not point to personal fears on her part, but rather ironically parallels a point that Medea made in Euripides' play; there she stated that for a person to have γηροβοσκία and burial from one's sons was enviable (*Med.* 1032–37).

Jason too suffers in comparison with his models. Achilles showed respect for the old and grief-stricken Priam as he thought of his own father; Hector left Andromache and Astyanax to go off to battle only after revealing his great love for them (cf. *Il.* 6.450–81); Priam, despite the danger of his mission, went off in the night to the enemy camp to bring back Hector's body accompanied only by an old man like himself; finally, the Greek heroes all showed great respect for the elderly Nestor. Jason, on the other hand, who begins his expedition with confidence, accompanied by the finest crew in all Greece, evinces little respect or love for his elderly parents or the old priestess. He says nothing to Æson. His reply to his tearful mother is brief, cold, and overly logical;[28] and his lack of response to the aged Iphias trying to speak to him appears insensitive or even callous. In short, Jason shows none of the sensitivities toward his elders and loved ones that characterized his Homeric models. These responses not only anticipate his emotionless and ungrateful farewell to Hypsipyle (1.900–909) as well as his unenthusiastic protection of Medea on his return to Greece (cf. 4.66–97, 338–410, 1031–67, and 1161–69);[29] they also look beyond the scope of the poem to Jason's future abandonment of Medea so brilliantly captured by Euripides.[30]

THE series of related Homeric passages to which Apollonius makes reference exerts a profound impression on our reading of the episode and on our understanding of Jason's character. This rather involved *contaminatio* of diverse elements from both the *Iliad* and *Odyssey* having to do, directly or indirectly, with Hector's death, and how he and his family came to terms with it, gives

---

28. Cf. Fränkel *ad* 1.295–305, *contra* Stössl (supra n. 3) 26 and Vian 13, who believe that Jason had to respond to his mother's frantic lamentation with firmness.
29. See Beye 81–82. Garson (supra n. 17) 5–6, who finds Alcimede's lament hollow and Jason's response unheroic, also observed that Apollonius later on has Medea, in her plea to Jason not to desert her (4.368–69), recall the celebrated words of Andromache to Hector in which she reminds Hector that he is her father, mother, and brother as well as husband (*Il.* 6.429–30); cf. Vian (3) 162 *ad* 369.
30. On the association of Iphias with Medea as priestesses of Artemis, see the recent article by D. P. Nelis, "Iphias: Apollonius Rhodius, *Argonautica* 1.311–16," *CQ* 41 (1991) 96–105.

us a valuable insight into the effect that Jason's departure has on his family and himself. The Argonautic figures clearly suffer in comparison. In particular, we see that even from the beginning of his heroic career, Jason lacks the respect and concern for those who both love and need him. As such, he is the antithesis of Hector, who was the quintessential κηδεμονεύς and who achieved greatness and nobility, in spite of the fact that he was ultimately unsuccessful, by remaining in his home city in defense of his family. Jason, on the other hand, leaves his parents, Iphias, and soon afterwards Hypsipyle. He even considers abandoning Medea in the course of his journey home to secure the success of his mission. Hector and the members of his family provide the measure against which we are to view Jason and his family, and the latter prove to be a weak, shallow, and self-absorbed group, totally unheroic in stature. The initial impression in the Proemium of a Jason who lacks the special qualities that distinguish Homeric heroes was accurate. It remains to see how this rather underwhelming figure from so pathetic a family will approach his formidable ἄεθλος.

4

The Best of the Argonauts Defined
Preparations at Pagasae (*Argo.* 1.317–518)

ALTHOUGH Jason may resemble Apollo as he leaves Iolcus, at Pagasae he is not treated as a divinity by his crew: his welcome at the beach is immediately upstaged by the unexpected arrival of Acastus and Argus,[1] and then, when he asks the group to choose the best among them as their leader, the men without hesitation unanimously elect Heracles, who, however, politely refuses. Thereafter, at the sacrificial banquet in honor of Apollo, the newly elected leader becomes despondent as he envisages the many details of the mission before them. His momentary loss of nerve prompts Idas's hybristic boast, which in turn leads to a disruptive argument between Idas and Idmon. The hero does not, in short, make a very godlike impression, and the expedition would seem to begin on an inauspicious note. Yet a look at the subtext of the episode reveals quite the opposite. Like the propitious omen that Idmon will observe in the sacrificial flame, suggestions made beneath the surface of the text indicate not only that the men will successfully complete their mission, but, even more surprisingly, that Jason may well claim to be the one to carry it off and thus earn the honor of being considered the best of the Argonauts.

STRUCTURE

Apollonius describes the preparations for the journey to Colchis in a more complicated structural format than he has used in the previous episode. Instead of a neatly balanced episode organized

---

1. Beye 24 argues that the late arrival of Argus and Acastus diverts attention from Jason (cf. Collins 34).

around a significant central subsection, the poet has arranged the events at Pagasae in three sections of disproportionate length that do not have a clearly defined structural relationship. In the first (A, 317–30), Jason's welcome by the Argonauts at the beach (a, 317–20; 4 lines) balances his corresponding welcome of Argus and Acastus (*a*, 327–30; 4 lines), in between which lies the suggestive description of their sudden and unexpected appearance (b, 321–26). In the second and slightly longer section (B, 331–62), Jason makes a speech calling for the election of a captain (a, 331–40) and, after finding himself elected only when Heracles refuses the honor (b, 341–50), he gives a second speech (*a*, 351–62) in which he issues detailed instructions for their departure. The third and longest section (C, 363–518) unfolds in a strictly linear movement. The Argonauts, following Jason's instructions, launch the ship and draw lots for seats on board (a, 363–401). After they sacrifice to Apollo (b, 402–47), and while they are partaking of the sacrificial banquet, an argument ensues between Idas and Idmon (c, 448–95). Jason then intervenes and the men forget the tension caused by the argument as they listen to Orpheus's song (d, 496–511). The day and the episode come to a close with a formal sacrifice (e, 512–18).[2]

Although the episode as a whole lacks the A–B–*A* structural formula in simple or expanded form, this is not the case for the first two sections of the episode; in these Apollonius focuses on two important points made in the Catalogue: (1) the contrast between the man of strength and the man of skill, and (2) the nature and identity of the best of the Argonauts. Although the third section is structurally different, one will nonetheless find here, too, clear reflections of both the issues that the poet emphasizes through the central positioning in the first two sections. The overall structure of the episode takes the following shape:

---

2. In his structural analysis of the episode, Hurst 54–57 likewise divides the events at Pagasae into three sections, but identifies the breaks at the occurrences of temporal conjunctions at 317, 394, and 450, which distinguish three themes: *l'homme, le sacré, l'homme et le sacré*. The break at 394, however, does not initiate a new section, but separates the launch of the ship from the apportionment of seats, which clearly belong together, as I shall demonstrate below. Cf. R. Ibscher, "Gestalt der Szene und Form der Rede in den Argonautika des Apollonios Rhodios" (diss. Munich 1939) 8–9.

Preparations at Pagasae, 317–518

- A. Arrival of Argus and Acastus (317–30)
  - a. Welcome of Jason (317–20)
  - b. Appearance of Argus and Acastus (321–26)
  - a. Welcome of Argus and Acastus by Jason (327–30)
- B. Election of the Captain (331–62)
  - a. First Speech of Jason (331–40)
  - b. Election of Jason (341–50)
  - a. Second Speech of Jason (351–62)
- C. Preparations for Departure (363–518)
  - a. Launch and Distribution of Seats (363–401)
  - b. Sacrifice to Apollo (402–47)
  - c. Banquet and Argument of Idas and Idmon (448–95)
  - d. Song of Orpheus (496–511)
  - e. Formal Conclusion of the Banquet (512–18)

A. Arrival of Argus and Acastus (317–30)

In the Proemium, Apollonius underscored the ominous appearance of Jason wearing only one shoe by setting it in a central position. Here too Apollonius accentuates the sudden and, as it turns out, significant appearance of Argus and Acastus by placing it between the Argonauts' welcome of Jason (Aa) and Jason's welcome of the unexpected pair (Aa). In addition to being set off by its central positioning, the description of the two supernumeraries is neatly articulated:

δέρμα δ' ὁ μὲν ταύροιο ποδηνεκὲς ἀμπέχετ' ὤμοις
Ἄργος Ἀρεστορίδης λάχνῃ μέλαν, αὐτὰρ ὁ καλὴν
δίπλακα τήν οἱ ὄπασσε κασιγνήτη Πελόπεια.
(324–26)

Around his shoulders, Argus, the son of Arestor, wore a bull's hide black with bristles and stretching to his feet; but Acastus wore an elegant
double-folded cloak, which his sister, Pelopia, gave him.

The alliteration and line position of δέρμα and δίπλακα, together with their chiastic arrangement (δέρμα ... λάχνη μέλαν ≈ καλὴν / δίπλακα), call attention to the sartorial contrast between Argus and Acastus: the former wears a bull's hide, and the latter a cloak woven by his sister. As I already pointed out in Chapter 2,[3] the two men symbolize in their attire the two kinds of hero that the bipartite structure of the Catalogue highlighted: the animal skin representing the clothing of the man of strength, and the manufactured cloak representing the man of skill. The appearance of these two men so attired right before the election of the captain is not fortuitous. Although Jason throws open the election to all, the slate is effectively limited to himself and Heracles, the man who convened the group of heroes and the foremost hero among the group. The dress of the two candidates, as it happens, resembles that of Argus and Acastus: Jason, as we shall learn later, wears a δίπλαξ (*Argo.* 1.722); Heracles, as one would have expected, joined the expedition dressed in his traditional δέρμα λέοντος (*Argo.* 1.1195).[4]

The clothing worn by Acastus and Argus, then, reflects the theme of the heroic antithesis between man of strength and man of skill. Moreover, the unexpected arrival of the pair carries with it yet another implicit significance. In the Proemium, with its structural focus on Jason's ominous appearance, Apollonius was explicit about why the hero's arrival with only one shoe had so powerful an effect on Pelias and why the latter contrived the impossible mission for the former: Apollo's oracle warned the Iolcan king of the danger the man wearing only one sandal brought. In this instance, however, the poet does not explain why the men marvel at the arrival of Argus and Acastus (ἐθάμβησαν δ' ἐσιδόντες, 322). Lacking any authorial gloss, the audience is left on its own to consider the implications of their presence.

---

3. Supra, Chapter 2, pp. 32–34.
4. Fränkel's suggestion *ad* 1.321–26 that the reason for their manner of dress owes itself to their speed in departing from Iolcus to avoid detection, while plausible, does not account for the vivid difference in the nature of their clothing or the fact that this contrasting form of apparel parallels the dress of Jason and Heracles. For further discussion of this point, see R. Roux, *Le problème des Argonautes* (Paris 1949) 101; Levin 43–44; and recently, A. Rose, "Clothing Imagery in Apollonius' *Argonautica*," *QUCC*, n.s., 21 (1985) 30–31.

The fact that Argus, the carpenter of the *Argo*, has agreed to come along should be read as a propitious sign for the journey. It bespeaks the craftsman's trust in his handiwork. Yet his presence is not as striking as that of Acastus. The reader, aware of the dynastic struggle in Iolcus and Pelias's plan to get rid of Jason through the expedition, must find Acastus's willingness to go along surprising; and this same awareness among the Argonauts might well lie behind their amazement at the sight of Pelias's son coming to Pagasae. The surprise the men register, however, must be of the pleasant sort, since, if Acastus is willing to sail together with the group, he too shows his trust in the workmanship of the vessel: in getting on board he reveals his ignorance of any plans on the part of Pelias to sabotage the *Argo*. In addition to what we can deduce from the text itself, we have the information of the scholiast (*ad* 1.224-26a), who has recorded a rare version of the Argonautic myth attributed to a certain Demagetus:[5] Pelias, according to this source, had ordered Argus to use slender nails in the construction of the *Argo* so that the ship would fall apart at sea. Since Argus saw to the seaworthiness of the ship (cf. 369), both he and Acastus could feel secure in sailing on the *Argo*.[6] For this reason, when Jason sees the two approaching, he need not ask them anything (327-28a). Their desire to sail is an eloquent and auspicious statement in itself, and all the clearer to readers, like the scholiast, who are informed of recondite Argonautic lore.[7]

B. Election of the Captain (331-62)

Two speeches by Jason, the first calling for an election of the best man for captain (B*a*) and the second giving acceptance of this responsibility (B*a*), frame the election proper, in which, although

---

5. On the identification of Demagetus with Timagetus, see F. Gisinger, "Timagetus," *RE* 6.A.1.1071, *FHG* III.316, IV.520; Jacoby (cf. *FGrHist*) tentatively identifies him as the Demaratus mentioned by Σ *ad* 1.145, 1.1289.
6. See Vian 13-14 n. 3
7. Others have seen Jason's silence in a different light. Beye 24 believes that it "takes the narrative from the reader, so that we have a narrative which at times is inaccessible to the reader." Fränkel *ad* 1.327-30, in keeping with many other of his observations wherein he finds solutions in terms of the practical, suggests that Jason did not ask any questions because he was in a hurry to get the expedition under way.

the Argonauts unhesitatingly choose him, Heracles refuses and orders that Jason lead the expedition instead (Bb). The first speech presents something of an anomaly among ancient epics. Jason opens up the leadership of his own mission to the comrade deemed by all to be the best-suited to the job:[8]

Ἀλλά, φίλοι, ξυνὸς γὰρ ἐς Ἑλλάδα νόστος ὀπίσσω,
ξυναὶ δ' ἄμμι πέλονται ἐς Αἰήταο κέλευθοι,
τούνεκα νῦν τὸν ἄριστον ἀφειδήσαντες ἕλεσθε
ὄρχαμον ὑμείων, ᾧ κεν τὰ ἕκαστα μέλοιτο,
νείκεα συνθεσίας τε μετὰ ξείνοισι βαλέσθαι.

(336-40)

But, my friends, our return back to Greece is a matter of common concern
and our journey to the palace of Æëtes is also of common concern.
Accordingly, sparing no one's feelings, elect now the best man
among you as leader. To him will fall the consideration of all the
details: the initiation of conflicts and treaties with foreign peoples.

Although the democratic process, which continues to function throughout the poem,[9] may appear quite strange at first, nonetheless it does suit the stated theme of the poem to some extent. In the opening lines (1-4), Apollonius announced that he would sing not of a man (Jason), but of men (the Argonauts).[10] Moreover, Jason himself had informed Alcimede that he felt confidence in the success of the mission in part because he had the assistance of the finest men of Greece (302). Since none, save Heracles (cf.

---

8. Lines 336-37 recall Hesiod, *Catalogue of Women* 1.6-7 M&W: ξυναὶ γὰρ τότε δαῖτες ἔσαν, ξυνοὶ δὲ θόωκοι / ἀθανάτοις τε θεοῖσι καταθνητοῖς τ' ἀνθρώποις. I have discussed this borrowing in greater detail elsewhere; cf. "Hellenistic Imitations of Hesiod. *Catalogue of Women* Fr. 1.6-7 M&W," *QUCC*, n.s., 36 (1989) 129-40.
9. Fränkel *ad* 1.336ff. notes the other occasions.
10. Although J. F. Carspecken's view ("Apollonius Rhodius and the Homeric Epic," *YCIS* 13 [1952] 41ff., 110ff.) that the group as a whole constituted the hero of the poem goes too far, his argument that the successful completion of the mission depends on the united effort of the group, especially when seen in the context of this speech, hits the mark; cf. Vian 16-17, who calls the harmony of the Argonauts "l'un des leitmotive les plus importants du poème."

1.1161b–64, 2.145–53, 3.1232b–34),[11] who will eventually abandon the group, can hope to achieve the goal of the expedition by himself, the winning of the fleece will require a communal effort. Thus, Jason needs to foster a harmonious atmosphere amidst such a diverse group right from the beginning, and it is apparently for this reason that he invites an election.[12]

Before the vote takes place, Jason defines what he means by the "best" leader (τὸν ἄριστον, 338) : he will be the one who takes care of all the details—in particular, the decisions to initiate conflicts (νείκεα) and treaties (συνθεσίας) with foreign peoples (338–40). Jason thus envisages not a man of strength, but one with a specific skill. Yet the others express their conviction that the best in the group is Heracles by voting him captain. It is obvious that they understand the "best" among the group to be a man of strength. Heracles refuses, however, to accept the honor, and casts his influential vote for the one who assembled the men, Jason.[13]

As I have noted, the structure focuses on the actual election of Jason as captain, and herein lies an important reference to a well-known Homeric text.[14] When Heracles addresses the group, he remains seated:

---

11. Cf. H. Fränkel, "Ein Don Quijote unter den Argonauten des Apollonios," *MH* 17 (1960) 2–3. The loss of Heracles meant that the Argonauts would have to concentrate on working together.

12. The election has also been viewed as Apollonius's way of dealing with the tradition in which Heracles was the leader of the group (cf. Nicander fr. 48 Schneider); cf. M. M. Gillies, *The Argonautica of Apollonius Rhodius Book III* (Cambridge 1928) xxix–xxx; M. Hadas, "Apollonius Called the Rhodian," *CW* 26 (1932) 44; Blumberg 11–12; Levin 45 n. 1; Vian 14. Fränkel *ad* 1.338–50 argues that the election was not necessary, but rather an act of courtesy, especially to Heracles, and a diplomatic ploy to unify the group (cf. F. Vian, "ΙΗΣΩΝ ΑΜΗΧΑΝΕΩΝ," *Studi in onore di A. Ardizzoni*, ed. E. Livrea and G. Privitera [Rome 1978], 1028–29).

13. Hunter (2) 442 appropriately states, "Jason's speech, with its stress on the responsibility of the leader to the group as a whole, suggests why the expedition could not be led by a Heracles, a hero of notoriously solitary and idiosyncratic virtue. Jason is indeed ὁ ἄριστος, if *arete* consists of what is fitting in a particular context." The "particular context" of which Hunter speaks, however, encompasses the whole Argonautic expedition. Although Jason may be "short on heroics," nonetheless he is, as I shall argue, ὁ ἄριστος because he is, as it were, "long on managerial skills."

14. Cf. E. Livrea *apud* Vian 66 n. 1, and Campbell *ad* 1.343–44, who observed the parallel.

"Ὣς φάτο. Πάπτηναν δὲ νέοι θρασὺν Ἡρακλῆα
ἥμενον ἐν μέσσοισι, μιῇ δέ ἑ πάντες ἀυτῇ
σημαίνειν ἐπέτελλον· ὁ δ' αὐτόθεν ἔνθα περ ἧστο
δεξιτερὴν ἀνὰ χεῖρα τανύσσατο φώνησέν τε·
(341–44)

Thus he spoke, and the young members of the crew looked to bold
   Heracles
seated in the middle, and all with one voice
ordered Jason to name him leader. But right from where he sat
he raised high his right hand and spoke.

In an assembly among the Greek forces at Troy, Agamemnon did precisely the same:[15]

"Ὣς ἔφαθ', οἱ δ' ἐχάρησαν ἐυκνήμιδες Ἀχαιοί
μῆνιν ἀπειπόντος μεγαθύμου Πηλεΐωνος.
τοῖσι δὲ καὶ μετέειπεν ἄναξ ἀνδρῶν Ἀγαμέμνων
αὐτόθεν ἐξ ἕδρης, οὐδ' ἐν μέσσοισιν ἀναστάς·
(Il. 19.74–77)

Thus he spoke, and the well-greaved Achæans rejoiced
as the noble son of Peleus renounced his anger.
Then the lord of men Agamemnon addressed them
right from his seat, not even taking his stand in their midst.

The wider context of the Iliadic passage involves the assembly at which Achilles, in the wake of Patroclus's death, accepted recompense from Agamemnon so that he could reenter the war; this event in turn restored harmony within the Greek army. In addition to the similarity, verbal and conceptual, between Agamemnon and Heracles (both Agamemnon and Achilles remain seated, contrary to Homeric parliamentary practice),[16] we can observe several other incidental points of contact between the two passages: both assemblies are at the shore (cf. Il. 19.40–46); Heracles' speech lies between the two speeches of Jason just as Agamemnon's (ibid. 78–144) lies between two speeches of Achilles (ibid. 56–73, 145–53); in their second addresses, both Jason (cf. Argo. 1.351–52) and

---

15. Zenodotus altered line 76 to τοῖσι δ' ἀνιστάμενος μετέφη κρείων Ἀγαμέμνων and expunged line 77 (cf. Σ ad Il. 19.77a). Apparently Apollonius disagreed with Zenodotus on this point.
16. Cf. Vian 66 n. 1.

Achilles (*Il.* 19.148–50) call for immediate action. Both passages, I would add, have to do with the assumption of heroic leadership at a pivotal moment in the course of events.

More important, the culmination of the Argonautic assembly can be seen to parallel that of the Iliadic: the restoration of honor and unity. In the *Iliad*, Achilles left the group because Agamemnon had taken his γέρας (ibid. 89), the girl Briseïs, thus robbing him of his honor (cf. *Il.* 1.503–10). Following the ignominious defeat at the hands of the Trojans, Agamemnon returns Briseïs to Achilles along with many gifts, which restores honor to Achilles and eventually harmony to the group. Heracles, on the other hand, right from the start of the expedition makes it clear that he will not accept the κῦδος (345) that rightfully belongs to Jason. In this way, much like Agamemnon in his reconciliation with Achilles, Heracles restores to Jason the honor that the latter risked and effectively lost in the election. The inversion of the Homeric model is instructive.[17] Because Agamemnon had deprived Achilles of his τιμή, the Greek army risked being pushed back into the sea. In contrast to Agamemnon at the beginning of the *Iliad*, Heracles does not usurp Jason's source of κῦδος, the leadership of the expedition, but rather confers this on the young prince. Reference, then, to the Iliadic scene of reconciliation bodes well for the Argonautic group, who in their very first encounter with each other act in concert. Through Heracles' influential vote, the group avoids the divisive conflict that was so costly to Agamemnon's Trojan expedition. Moreover, Heracles' refusal to act as captain and his insistence on Jason's leadership will result after all in the election of the man Jason described as the best leader. For as soon as he is elected, Jason turns his mind to the details needing attention prior to their departure (351–62, 460–61) and will soon after encounter a conflict (νεῖκος, 492b) that he will settle, not among foreign peoples, but among his own men. As the audience will observe in the course of the expedition, between the man of strength and man of skill, between the man in animal skins and the one in an elegantly manufactured cloak, the captain best suited for accomplishing the

---

17. M. Fantuzzi, "Omero 'autore' di Apollonio Rodio: Le formule introduttive al discorso diretto," *MD* 13 (1986) 93–96, goes so far as to call this assembly "quasi una parodia dei consigli omerici."

shared expedition to and from Colchis (the ξυναὶ κέλευθοι and the ξυνὸς νόστος Jason refers to in his first speech) will prove to be the man of organizational and diplomatic skill.

C. Preparations for Departure (363–518)

In this, the longest section of the episode, the Argonauts follow the orders given immediately after the election in Jason's second speech. They launch the ship, settle on the seating arrangements, sacrifice to Apollo, and enjoy the sacrificial meal that leads to the quarrel between Idas and Idmon. Jason quells the disturbance, and Orpheus's song eases the tension generated by the argument. A coda of seven lines describing the end of the banquet and of the day concludes the episode. The action, as I have observed above, proceeds in a noticeably linear movement. These events—Jason's preparations for departure from Pagasae followed by a banquet at which a celebrated singer performs—recall Alcinous's preparations for Odysseus's departure from Phæacia, which is described near the beginning of Book 8 of the *Odyssey*. A brief comparison between the instructions given by Jason in the *Argonautica* and Alcinous in the *Odyssey* reveals the striking correspondences between these two texts.

Alcinous tells his people of his plans for sending Odysseus home with these words:

ἀλλ' ἄγε νῆα μέλαιναν ἐρύσσομεν εἰς ἅλα δῖαν
πρωτόπλοον, κούρω δὲ δύω καὶ πεντήκοντα
κρινάσθων κατὰ δῆμον, ὅσοι πάρος εἰσὶν ἄριστοι.
δησάμενοι δ' εὖ πάντες ἐπὶ κληῖσιν ἐρετμὰ
ἔκβητ'· αὐτὰρ ἔπειτα θοὴν ἀλεγύνετε δαῖτα
ἡμέτερόνδ' ἐλθόντες· ἐγὼ δ' εὖ πᾶσι παρέξω.
κούροισιν μὲν ταῦτ' ἐπιτέλλομαι· αὐτὰρ οἱ ἄλλοι
σκηπτοῦχοι βασιλῆες ἐμὰ πρὸς δώματα καλὰ
ἔρχεσθ', ὄφρα ξεῖνον ἐνὶ μεγάροισι φιλέωμεν·
μηδέ τις ἀρνείσθω· καλέσασθε δὲ θεῖον ἀοιδόν,
Δημόδοκον· τῷ γάρ ῥα θεὸς πέρι δῶκεν ἀοιδὴν
τέρπειν, ὅππῃ θυμὸς ἐποτρύνῃσιν ἀείδειν.

(*Od.* 8.34–45)

But come now, let us drag a black ship down to the awesome sea, a ship that has never before sailed, and let them choose fifty-two young men from among the people who have long been thought the best.

Then after all of you have bound the oars to the rowlocks
leave the vessel and get ready for a feast right away,
coming to my palace; I shall provide a fine banquet for all.
I give these commands to the young men; as for the other
scepter-bearing kings, you come to my splendid home
so that we might offer hospitality to the stranger in my halls.
Let no one refuse. Also invite the inspired singer,
Demodocus; this one above all others enjoys a god-given talent
  for music,
a sheer pleasure to hear whenever his heart bids him sing.

The Phæacian king orders his men to launch a ship that has never sailed before (35); in the *Argonautica* this is the maiden voyage of the *Argo*. The best fifty-two men in Phæacia were to be selected (35–36); Apollonius's Catalogue lists a crew of fifty-two of the finest heroes of Greece (Argus and Acastus were unscheduled passengers and thus do not figure in this count; cf. 321–28).[18] Once launched, the Phæacians were to secure the oars at their seats (δησάμενοι δ' εὖ πάντες ἐπὶ κνηῖσιν ἐρετμά, 37); Jason orders his men to take lots for the arrangement of their seats after the launch (ὅπλα τε πάντα / ἐνθέμενοι πεπάλαχθε κατὰ κληῖδας ἐρετμά, 357b–58).[19] Alcinous gave a banquet for the Phæacians in honor of Odysseus (38–40); Jason provides the animals for the sacrifice and feast from his own herd (354b–56). At the Phæacian banquet, Demodocus sang his first of three songs in this book, which Homer summarizes as follows:

αὐτὰρ ἐπεὶ πόσιος καὶ ἐδητύος ἐξ ἔρον ἕντο,
Μοῦσ' ἄρ' ἀοιδὸν ἀνῆκεν ἀειδέμεναι κλέα ἀνδρῶν,
οἴμης τῆς τότ' ἄρα κλέος οὐρανὸν εὐρὺν ἵκανε,
νεῖκος Ὀδυσσῆος καὶ Πηλείδεω Ἀχιλῆος,
ὥς ποτε δηρίσαντο θεῶν ἐν δαιτὶ θαλείῃ
ἐκπάγλοις ἐπέεσσιν, ἄναξ δ' ἀνδρῶν Ἀγαμέμνων
χαῖρε νόῳ, ὅ τ' ἄριστοι Ἀχαιῶν δηριόωντο.
ὣς γάρ οἱ χρείων μυθήσατο Φοῖβος Ἀπόλλων
Πυθοῖ ἐν ἠγαθέῃ, ὅθ' ὑπέρβη λάινον οὐδὸν

---

18. See Vian 13–14 n. 3, and above Chapter 2, p. 28.
19. The phrase ἐπὶ κληΐσιν ἐρετμά is unique in the Homeric corpus. One finds ἐρετμά with any form of κληΐς only here, although ἐπὶ κληΐσι(ν) is common in this metrical position; cf. Prendergast and Dunbar s.vv. κληῗσι, κληῗσιν.

χρησόμενος· τότε γάρ ῥα κυλίνδετο πήματος ἀρχή
Τρωσί τε καὶ Δαναοῖσι Διὸς μεγάλου διὰ βουλάς.
(*Od*. 8.72–82)

And when they relinquished their appetite for food and drink
the Muse inspired the poet to sing about the glorious achievements of men,
a part of the story whose fame had reached the wide vault of heaven:
the quarrel of Odysseus and Achilles, son of Peleus.
He sang of how once they argued at an abundant feast of the gods,
using terrible words, and how the lord of men Agamemnon
was happy to see the best of the Achæans arguing.
For Phœbus Apollo had revealed to him that it would be so through his oracle,
pronounced in holy Pytho when the king crossed over the threshold of stone
in order to receive a prophecy. After that the beginning of sorrow unfolded
for the Trojans and Danaans, fulfilling the plans of great Zeus.

Although not specifically invited to perform, Orpheus will sing about cosmic and divine νεῖκος (498) at the Argonautic banquet to ease the tension following the νεῖκος (492) between Idas and Idmon. Apollonius has apparently transformed his model in such a way that the content of Demodocus's song (the argument between Achilles and Odysseus) has become part of the narrative (the argument between Idas and Idmon). This νεῖκος between a man of strength (the braggart Idas who swears by his spear) and a man of skill (Idmon the prophet) neatly parallels the νεῖκος between Achilles, a man of strength, and Odysseus, a man of skill.[20] The Homeric argument takes place between men who vie in their different approaches to heroic action for the honor of being called the

---

20. The contrast between Achilles as a hero of βίη and Odysseus as a hero of μῆτις has been the focus of a recent book-length study by A. T. Edwards, *Achilles in the Odyssey: Ideologues of Heroism in the Homeric Epic* (Königstein 1985). G. Nagy, *The Best of the Achæans* (Baltimore 1979) 15–65, thoroughly discusses this particular scene, examining the contrast between βίη and μῆτις within the context of the νεῖκος and its relevance to the issue of the best of the Achæans. As we have seen, Apollonius positioned reflections of this same thematic contrast at the center of sections A and B.

"best of the Achæans." The Odyssean subtext thus addresses the main issue raised by the Argonautic election, in which Apollonius has Jason ask in effect who the best of the Argonauts is.

In his description of the various phases of the Argonauts' preparations for departure, Apollonius expands the imitation of Alcinous's program for getting Odysseus back home. Through the borrowing of unique words and phrases, the poet alludes to other passages that pertain to the central issues of the episode. Rather than deal immediately with the ramifications that the argument between Achilles and Odysseus has upon our understanding of the events at Pagasae, I shall treat the separate steps in Jason's program for departure in the order of their occurrence.

a. Launch and Distribution of Seats (363-401)

In his account of the launch and mooring of Alcinous's πρωτόπλοος ναῦς, Homer did not present an involved description; rather, he refers to its completion summarily in a few lines (*Od.* 8.50-55). Apollonius, however, does go into considerable detail, accounting for the various stages of the launch in thirty-one verses (363-93) and concluding with the apportionment of the benches (394-401). Fränkel has argued that this launch is in keeping with Apollonius's love of realism and his predisposition toward technical accuracy, a feature of his poetry consonant with contemporary Hellenistic tastes.[21] Yet a unique archaic phrase cleverly incorporated in the narrative refers the reader to a text that suggests that more is going on here than a lengthy and detailed description of the *Argo*'s first launch.

Before the launch of the ship, the men strip off their clothes and set them on a flat stone made smooth from the constant battering of the waves (364b-66). The expression describing this stone (λείῳ ἐπὶ πλαταμῶνι, 365a) looks to *h. Merc.* 128a, the only other recorded instance of this phrase.[22] Although the Homeric

---

21. Fränkel *ad* 1.381-93; cf. Beye 27. An intrinsic feature of Callimachean esthetics entails the avoidance of hackneyed topics. Apollonius mentioned his refusal to describe the building of the *Argo* (see above, Chapter 1, pp. 20-22); I suspect that few, if any, poets treated the launch of the *Argo*.

22. Cf. Mooney, Ardizzoni, and Campbell *ad loc.*; Vian 67 n. 1. πλαταμῶνι alone in this metrical position occurs at Aratus *Phæn.* 993 and πλαταμῶσι also in the same *sedes* at Oppian *H.* 1.121, 5.650. Fränkel *ad* 1.364-66 believes that

hymn might appear an unlikely model for the launch of the *Argo*, an examination of the wider context of the archaic phrase reveals some remarkable correspondences.

On the first day of his life and just after he had invented the lyre, Hermes stole the cattle of his brother, Apollo. He led the herd from Pieria to the river Alpheus. After deciding to sacrifice and roast the meat of two of the cows, the devious god set firewood in a trench (*h. Merc.* 112), slaughtered the two cows (ibid. 116b–19), roasted the meat on spits (121), and then arranged the meat in twelve equal portions on a smooth flat surface (λείῳ ἐπὶ πλαταμῶνι, 126b–29). The launch of the *Argo* involves a procedure whose similarity is remarkable, especially considering the different nature of the two actions. After setting their clothes λείῳ ἐπὶ πλαταμῶνι and securing the ship with ropes, the men dig a trench into which they set logs as rollers; once the ship has been set on the first of these, they reverse the oars in the tholes and use these to shove the vessel forward. The weight of the *Argo* is such that as it moves forward it causes smoke to billow up from the rollers below. After the ship is in the water, the seats are apportioned. In sum, Apollonius has included in his description of the launch analogues to all the basic components of Hermes' sacrifice: trench, wood (= rollers), spits (= reversed oars), roasting meat (= smoke under the ship), portions of meat (= division of the seats). Such a comparison, as unlikely as it may seem at first, finds support not only in the borrowed phrase and similar progression of events but also in the extensive preoccupation with the theme of sacrifice before and after the launch, which deepens the sacrificial overtones in these lines.

In the description of the division of the benches that follows, Apollonius exploits the suggested equation of *Argo* and sacrificial victim in his evocative vocabulary. In the first line, Apollonius says of the men that they took care of each of the details: Αὐτὰρ ἐπεὶ τὰ ἕκαστα περιφραδέως ἀλέγυναν (394).[23] The last two words

---

Apollonius may have had in mind some monument commemorating the launch of the *Argo* in his description of the "smooth, flat surface."

23. Although the phrase αὐτὰρ ἐπεί is ubiquitous in epic verse, αὐτὰρ ἐπεί τὰ ἕκαστα occurs only here and at *h. Merc.* 313; cf. Ardizzoni and Campbell *ad* 1.394. This, unless it is completely fortuitous, would appear to corroborate Apollonius's interest in the hymn in this section.

of this line are used in the *Iliad* and *Odyssey* exclusively in banquet contexts: περιφραδέως occurs only in the phrase ὤπτησάν τε περιφραδέως, and ἀλεγύνω (in the *Odyssey*; it does not appear in the *Iliad*) always has as its object δαῖτα or δαῖτας (1.374, 2.139, 8.38,[24] 11.186, 13.23).[25] Although ἀλεγύνω is used outside the Homeric poems with other objects, even as early as the archaic period (cf. *h. Ven.* 11; *h. Merc.* 361, 476), it clearly has special application to banquets in Homer, of which usage Apollonius is cognizant (cf. 1.979, 2.495).[26] Thus to one intimately familiar with Homeric usage, the direct object of the verb ἀλεγύνω in the expression περιφραδέως ἀλέγυναν would be edible. Second, in describing the selection of seats by lot (κληῖδας μὲν πρῶτα πάλῳ διεμοιρήσαντο, 395), Apollonius uses the verb διαμοιράομαι, which occurs only once in the Homeric corpus (*Od.* 14.434) and which also comes from a banquet context.[27] When Odysseus was staying at the hut of Eumæus, his host butchered and roasted his finest pig, which he divided up into seven portions, setting aside a special piece for the nymphs and Hermes, and saving the piece of honor, the back, for Odysseus:

καὶ τὰ μὲν ἕπταχα πάντα διεμοιρᾶτο δαΐζων·
τὴν μὲν ἴαν νύμφῃσι καὶ Ἑρμῇ, Μαιάδος υἱεῖ,
θῆκεν ἐπευξάμενος, τὰς δ' ἄλλας νεῖμεν ἑκάστῳ·
νώτοισιν δ' Ὀδυσῆα διηνεκέεσσιν γέραιρεν
ἀργιόδοντος ὑός, κύδαινε δὲ θυμὸν ἄνακτος·
(*Od.* 14.434–38)

Cutting up all the food he [*sc.* Eumæus] divided it up into seven portions;
he set aside one portion for the nymphs and Hermes, son of Maia,

---

24. This instance occurs in the context of Alcinous's banquet for Odysseus prior to his departure from Ithaca.
25. Cf. Prendergast and Dunbar s.vv. περιφραδέως, ἀλεγύνω.
26. Other occurrences of ἀλεγύνω in the *Argonautica* without δαῖτα as object are 3.1105 (συνημοσύνας), 3.1198 (ἕκαστα), 4.1203 (absolute).
27. Before Apollonius the only extant instances of this verb are the one in Homer and three in Euripides, who uses it in the sense of "to tear apart" (*Hipp.* 1376; *Hec.* 716, 1977). Hesychius apparently found the sense of partition odd enough to gloss: see s.v. διεμοιρήσαντο. After Apollonius, possibly in imitation of this passage, the form διεμοιρήσαντο in the same metrical position and meaning "to divide up" occurs in Crinagoras *A.P.* 7.645.5 (= 20.5 G&P) and Metrodorus *A.P.* 14.116.2, 119.1, 120.7.

with a prayer, and he shared the other portions with each one.
But he honored Odysseus by giving him the long back
of the white-toothed boar, thus gratifying the heart of his master.

In a similar fashion, the Argonauts reserve a special bench, that in the middle, for Heracles, which he would share with Ancæus (396b–400)—the same two heroes, incidentally, who offer the sacrificial victim to Apollo in the scene that immediately follows.[28] Accordingly, in vocabulary and in the sequence of events, Apollonius prompts the reader to envisage the launch and subsequent apportionment of the benches on the ship as a sacrifice and the *Argo* as a sacrificial victim that, figuratively speaking, they prepare and divide among themselves. An unstated point of contact between the two passages from which Apollonius borrowed such rare vocabulary items (Hermes' sacrifice in the hymn and the banquet at the hut of Eumæus in the *Odyssey*) is potentially significant: it is the god Hermes.

The central story of the Homeric hymn is based upon the age-old expeditionary motif in which the hero goes on a distant trip to bring back some prized object, especially a treasured animal or animals.[29] The two cows that Hermes sacrificed, with which event the launch of the *Argo* is by implication compared, belonged to Apollo's herd, and to steal these cattle the mischievous god had made an extraordinary journey (extraordinary because he was not even one day old!) from Arcadia to Pieria. The Argonautic expedition entails the same motif: Jason must sail to Colchis to retrieve the golden fleece of the ram that rescued Phrixus from the plot of Ino.[30] The Homeric hymn also involves a conflict between the same antithetical types seen in the poem so far: Hermes represents in this poem a god of skill, and Apollo, his older and physically more powerful brother who tries unsuccessfully to overwhelm the infant god with his power, a god of strength. The

---

28. Vian 251 *ad* 400 adds that Heracles' central position on the boat helped stabilize the ship; his weight, in some versions (Σ *ad Argo.* 1.1289–91a, and Apollodorus 1.9.19) jeopardized the navigability of the ship.
29. Cf. S. Thompson, *Motif-Index of Folk-Literature* (Bloomington 1955–58) 1200–1399, 1331–32.6.
30. At the center of the Catalogue Apollonius focused on stories involving the same motif: Melampus's expedition to steal the cattle of Iphiclus and Heracles' capture of the Erymanthian boar (cf. *Argo.* 1.118–32).

conflict, however, is resolved. Although Apollo was furious with his younger brother because of the theft of his cattle, and although his anger showed no sign of abatement, Hermes sang a song about the origin of the universe and the gods to the accompaniment of his newly invented lyre. The song caused Apollo to give up his anger (*h. Merc.* 416a–35). As we have seen, other celebrated arguments underlie the present episode: that between Achilles and Agamemnon in the *Iliad* and that between Achilles and Odysseus in the *Odyssey*. Moreover, there is a disruptive argument about to break out among the Argonauts that, like the dispute between Hermes and Apollo, will ultimately be settled amicably. In fact, the climax of the hymn to Hermes provides a telling parallel to the conclusion of the Argonautic dispute. After Jason puts an end to the shouting match between Idas and Idmon, Orpheus takes up his lyre and sings about the origin of the universe through νεῖκος and about the generations of the gods (496–511). This will have the effect of reestablishing the harmony of the group disrupted by the argument between Idas and Idmon, in which Jason successfully intervened. Just as happens in the Argonautic νεῖκος, the tension arising from conflict between Hermes and Apollo is resolved through the power of theogonic music:

> λύρῃ δ' ἐρατὸν κιθαρίζων
> στῆ ῥ' ὅ γε θαρσήσας ἐπ' ἀριστερὰ Μαιάδος υἱὸς
> Φοίβου Ἀπόλλωνος, τάχα δὲ λιγέως κιθαρίζων
> γηρύετ' ἀμβολάδην, ἐρατὴ δέ οἱ ἕσπετο φωνή,
> κραίνων ἀθανάτους τε θεοὺς καὶ γαῖαν ἐρεμνὴν
> ὡς τὰ πρῶτα γένοντο καὶ ὡς λάχε μοῖραν ἕκαστος.
> Μνημοσύνην μὲν πρῶτα θεῶν ἐγέραιρεν ἀοιδῇ
> μητέρα Μουσάων, ἡ γὰρ λάχε Μαιάδος υἱόν·
> τοὺς δὲ κατὰ πρέσβιν τε καὶ ὡς γεγάασιν ἕκαστος
> ἀθανάτους ἐγέραιρε θεοὺς Διὸς ἀγλαὸς υἱὸς
> πάντ' ἐνέπων κατὰ κόσμον, ἐπωλένιον κιθαρίζων.
> τὸν δ' ἔρος ἐν στήθεσσιν ἀμήχανος αἴνυτο θυμόν.
> (*h. Merc.* 423b–34)

Playing a lovely tune on his lyre
the son of Maia gained courage and took his stand to the left of
Phœbus Apollo. Quick to play a clear-sounding melody
he began to sing—and the voice that issued forth was lovely.
He celebrated the immortal gods and the black earth,

how they first came into being and how each acquired his allotment.
Mnemosyne was the first god he honored in his song,
the mother of the Muses, patron goddess of Maia's son.
The son of Zeus then honored the other immortal gods in order of age,
describing how each of them was born,
telling everything in precise order as he played the lyre cradled in his arm.
Irresistible desire seized his [*sc.* Apollo's] soul.

When we recognize the subtext of the launch of the *Argo* and of the distribution of the seats, one of the central themes of the episode comes more sharply into focus. These actions are a metaphor for a sacrifice. The sacrificial overtones lend a sense that the *Argo*, as a symbolic "victim," is somehow dedicated or sanctified for its goal at the moment of its launching. The apportionment, with its implied sharing of the victim *Argo* by the Argonauts, carries suggestions of the unity—and consequent harmony—that such ritual practice by its very nature represents. More specifically, the details of the scene recall one famous sacrifice by, and another in honor of, Hermes, a young god who ultimately brings about the successful completion of his expedition by calming the νεῖκος between himself and his more powerful brother through his musical skill.[31] The allusion to this sacrifice and the consequent success of Hermes—with its attendant harmony and unanimity achieved through skill—bodes well for the Argonauts and for their leader. Following the launch, our attention is immediately directed to a genuine sacrifice offered to Apollo by Heracles and Ancæus in the scene that follows.

b. Sacrifice to Apollo (402–47)

After the launch, the Argonauts offer sacrifice to Apollo in accordance with Jason's instructions. To summarize the action: the men build an altar to Apollo under his cult titles Actius and Embasius. Attendants then bring two cows and the sacred implements

---

31. I have argued elsewhere that Callimachus also turned to the same Homeric hymn to Hermes as a model in his *Hymn to Zeus*, and that there too the theme of reconciliation in the archaic hymn informed the Hellenistic; cf. "Lies and Allusions: The Addressee and Date of Callimachus' *Hymn to Zeus*," *ClAnt* 5 (1986) 155–70; see especially 169–70.

to the place of sacrifice (402-10). Jason prays to Apollo for a safe return to Greece under his personal guidance, which the god had promised at Delphi, and then vows further sacrifices upon their return (411-24). Heracles and Ancæus each slaughter an animal, the former with his club, the latter with his axe. The men prepare and roast the meat, and Jason pours the libation; and Idmon, who observes the signs in the flame that reveal Apollo's approval (425-38), then announces to all his favorable interpretation, predicting his own death. The Argonauts respond appropriately to the good news with joy but to the bad with grief (439-49).

Vian notes Apollonius's dependence on Homeric sacrificial practice in his presentation of the sacrifice to Apollo, and points out that the passage has special reference to one scene in particular: the sacrifice to Athena celebrated in Pylos at the home of Nestor as described in the *Odyssey*.[32] Two details stand out in particular. First, Apollonius gives a close rendition of three lines:

οἱ δ' ἄρ' ἔπειτα
χέρνιβά τ' οὐλοχύτας τε παρέσχεθον. Αὐτὰρ Ἰήσων
εὔχετο κεκλόμενος πατρώιον Ἀπόλλωνα·
(408b-10)

and the rest
brought holy water and barley meal. Next Jason,
calling on Apollo, the protector of his ancestors, offered prayer:

γέρων δ' ἱππηλάτα Νέστωρ
χέρνιβά τ' οὐλοχύτας τε κατάρχετο, πολλὰ δ' Ἀθήνῃ
εὔχετ' ἀπαρχόμενος, κεφαλῆς τρίχας ἐν πυρὶ βάλλων.[33]
(*Od.* 3.444b-46)

The aged knight Nestor
began the rite with holy water and barley meal, and as a beginning

---

32. Cf. Vian 70 n. 1.
33. Noted (besides by Vian) by Mooney and Ardizzoni *ad* 1.409 and Campbell *ad* 1.408-10. In addition to the expression χέρνιβά τ' οὐλοχύτας τε, which occurs in extant verse only in these two passages, one observes two other verbal points of contact: the name of the one giving the sacrifice at the end of the line (Ἰήσων ≈ Νέστωρ) and the combination of εὔχετο and a middle participle (εὔχετο κεκλόμενος ≈ εὔχετ' ἀπαρχόμενος.)

he <u>offered</u> many a <u>prayer</u> to A̤t̤h̤e̤n̤a̤, tossing the hair of its head into the fire.

Second, the same number of men are involved in the act of killing the animals. In the *Odyssey*, the Pylians sacrifice only one cow, but two men perform the immolation: Thrasymedes strikes it with an axe (the same tool used by Ancæus), and Peisistratus cuts its throat (*Od.* 3.447-54). In the *Argonautica*, there are two cows (the same number of cows slaughtered by Hermes in the Homeric hymn), and Apollonius provides two men to slaughter them, Heracles and Ancæus (425-31). One can add to these two similarities the fact that the Odyssean sacrifice, like its Argonautic imitation, precedes a journey, that of Telemachus to Sparta, where he hopes to learn of his father's fate from Menelaus. These shared features call attention to what I believe is the most important point of contact. At the end of the previous day Athena had advised all to go to sleep after pouring a libation over the tongues (*Od.* 3.332-36), a passage alluded to at the conclusion of this episode (see below). After this, Nestor invites Telemachus and Athena in her disguise as Mentor to stay. Athena refuses, and as she departs transforms herself into a bird (371-73). Nestor responds to this miraculous event by stating:

> ῏Ω φίλος, οὔ σε ἔολπα κακὸν καὶ ἄναλκιν ἔσεσθαι,
> εἰ δή τοι νέῳ ὧδε θεοὶ πομπῆες ἕπονται.
>
> (*Od.* 3.375-76)
>
> O friend, I do not think that you will turn out to be cowardly and weak,
> if in your youth the gods accompany you as your guides.

What marks Telemachus out as special is a sign that the gods personally guide him along his path. It is in response to this sign that Nestor vows the sacrifice of a cow with gilded horns, the sacrifice that Apollonius has in mind when describing that of the Argonauts to Apollo.

Just prior to the slaughter of the two cows, Jason asked specifically for personal guidance from the divinity who commissioned the expedition:

> Κλῦθι, ἄναξ Παγασάς τε πόλιν τ' Αἰσωνίδα ναίων
> ἡμετέροιο τοκῆος ἐπώνυμον, ἔς μοι ὑπέστης

Πυθοῖ χρειομένῳ ἄνυσιν καὶ πείραθ' ὁδοῖο
σημανέειν, αὐτὸς γὰρ ἐπαίτιος ἔπλευ ἀέθλων·
αὐτὸς νῦν ἄγε νῆα σὺν ἀρτεμέεσσιν ἑταίροις
κεῖσέ τε καὶ παλίνορσον ἐς Ἑλλάδα.

(411–16a)

Hear, O Lord, you who dwell in Pagasae and the city of Æsonis,
named after our father; you who promised when I consulted your oracle
at Pytho to reveal to me how I would accomplish the goals
of my journey; you who were responsible for this expedition:
you yourself now guide the ship there and back again to Greece
with my comrades unharmed.

Apollonius reveals in two ways, directly and indirectly, that Apollo has heard and assented to Jason's prayer. The poet has Idmon explicitly confirm his father's consent with his reading of the murky flame, which he characterizes as ἐναίσιμον (438). But the good will of the god is also to be inferred from the clear reference to the Odyssean sacrifice that Nestor offered to a divinity who acted as personal guide for the youthful Telemachus. In short, Jason prayed for personal guidance, and the sacrifice following this prayer alludes to a sacrifice offered in response to a god's personal guidance. The explicit sign was for Jason; but there is an implicit sign, as well, and this sign is for the *doctus lector*.

In the course of his travels to Colchis and back, Jason will in fact receive personal assistance from several divinities, among whom Apollo will play an important role, especially in his celebrated epiphany to the Argonauts near the island of Anaphe.[34] At Anaphe a thick mist will envelop the heroes during the night, and Apollo will appear in person to illuminate their way to safety (cf. 4.1694–1730). This will be the climactic obstacle to the completion of their νόστος. Callimachus dealt with the same episode

---

34. In addition to Apollo, several other gods intervene personally in the action to aid the expedition: Hera (2.864–68; 3.7–112, 210–14, 250, 818, 919–23, 1131–36; 4.507–10, 576b–80a, 640–48, 753–865, 956–67, 1151b–52, 1183b–85a, 1199–1200); Aphrodite (3.25–111; cf. 2.423–25, 3.540–54); Eros (3.275–98); Hephæstus (4.760b ff.); Thetis (4.758ff.); Athena (1.18–19, 109–10, 721–24; 2.537–614; 3.7–112; 4.956–60); and Apollo (1.439; 2.674–84a; 4.529–32a [cf. 1547–49], 1701b–30).

near the beginning of Book 1 of the *Ætia* (fr. 7–21 Pf.). As Pfeiffer noted (*ad* fr. 18.6–15), Apollonius in this passage is imitating Jason's vow to sacrifice to Apollo on his return in Callimachus's poem:[35]

Σοὶ δ' ἂν ὀπίσσω
τόσσων ὅσσοι κεν νοστήσομεν ἀγλαὰ ταύρων
ἱρὰ πάλιν βωμῷ ἐπιθήσομεν· <u>ἄλλα δὲ Πυθοῖ,
ἄλλα δ' ἐς Ὀρτυγίην ἀπερείσια δῶρα κομίσσω.</u>

(416b–19)

For you thereafter
we shall offer again on this altar as many splendid bulls
in sacrifice as there are those of us who have returned. <u>I shall
bring countless other gifts to Pytho, still others to Ortygia.</u>

]τε .τ[Τυ]νδαρίδαι
].μνησ[   ]ς Δία πρῶτον ἵκ[ο]ντο
].ἄλλους ητεσαν ἀ[θ]ανάτους
ἀοσ]ητῆρας ἐυστείρ[....].ελέ[.]ο[.]·
ἀλλ' ὅγ' ἀνι]άζων ὃν κέαρ Αἰσονίδης
σοὶ χέρας ἤέρ]ταζεν, Ἰήιε, <u>πολλὰ δ' ἀπείλει
ἐς Πυθὼ πέ]μψειν, πολλὰ δ' ἐς Ὀρτυγίην,</u>
εἴ κεν ἀμιχ]θαλόεσσαν ἀπ' ἠέρα νηὸς ἐλάσσης·
].ὅτι σήν, Φοῖξε, κατ' αἰσιμίην
πείσματ'] ἔλυσαν ἐκ[λ]ηρώσαντό τ' ἐρετμά
]πικρὸν ἔκοψαν ὕδωρ·

---

35. Cf. C. Corbato, *Riprese calimachee in Apollonio Rodio* (Trieste 1955), who likewise concluded that Apollonius was imitating Callimachus and not the other way around: "e non sarà difficile constatare che Apollonio reprende chiaramente la massa iniziale di Callimaco" (20), and later: "dai passi che abbiamo fin qui esaminati e dai confronti che abbiamo instaurato fra Callimaco e Apollonio Rodio mi pare si possa concludere, chiaramente e senza dubbi, che Apollonio, scrivendo questi versi, aveva dinanzi agli occhi l'equivalente luogo di Callimaco e che ad esso faceva referimento" (22). Although Corbato is talking here about the relationship between fr. 18 and *Argo.* 4.1701–5, he includes *Argo.* 1.418–19 (p. 20 n. 55); cf. G. O. Hutchinson, *Hellenistic Poetry* (Oxford 1988) 87–88. T. B. L. Webster, "Chronological Problems in Early Alexandrian Poetry," *WS* 76 (1963) 76–78, on the other hand, argues for the possibility that Callimachus had access to Apollonius's first two books through their contact in the library. The lack of specific information regarding the dates of these works does not allow for certainty in this instance, as in others.

]..ἐπώνυμον 'Εμβασίοιο
]...εν..Παγα[σ]αῖς[36]
(Ætia fr. 18.1-13 Pf.)

>the Tyndaridae
>they approached Zeus first
>they asked the other immortals
>who would help the ship of excellent keel
>But the son of Æson, with anguish in his soul
>raised his hands to you, Ieius, <u>and promised to send
>many gifts to Pytho</u>, <u>and many to Ortygia</u>,
>if you dispersed the murky cloud from the ship.
>that, in accordance with your oracle, Phœbus,
>they untied the cables and divided up the oars
>they struck the bitter waters
>named after the god of embarkation
>at Pagasae

If Apollonius is in fact the imitator here and wants the reader to recall his model, then just as happens in the reference to Nestor's sacrifice to Athena in *Odyssey* 3, the allusion has the effect of confirming Apollo's acceptance of Jason's prayer. The verbal reminiscence of the Anaphe episode in Callimachus's *Ætia* causes the reader to think of the climactic moment of the expedition, when Apollo provided his personal assistance. Moreover, Apollonius will repeat his imitation of these Callimachean lines just before Apollo will make good his promise to assist Jason in person (4.1704-5).

c. Banquet and Argument of Idas and Idmon (448-95)

While the men are eating, drinking, and conversing in the latter part of the day, Jason broods over the details of the journey and gives the appearance of one who lacks self-confidence (460-61). This elicits from Idas, who is well along in his cups (472-74a), a hybristic speech in which, while trying to encourage Jason, he claims that they will accomplish the goal of the expedition through the power of his spear, the source of his preeminent χῦδος,

---

36. Vian (3) 207 *ad* 1705 has observed several other verbal points of contact in this episode with this same Callimachean passage: 358 ≈ fr. 18.10; 404 ≈ fr. 18.12-13; 401 ≈ fr. 18.4 (N.B. these are the only two instances of εὐστείρης in extant literature); 423 ≈ fr. 18.9-10. One should now consult *SH* 250-51 on these lines.

even if Zeus should be against their success.³⁷ Mention of κῦδος (467) recalls Jason's acceptance of his election as leader of the expedition, which he identified as a κῦδος (351). Prior to the vote Jason defined the best leader as the one who would take care of all the details (ᾧ κεν τὰ ἕκαστα μέλοιτο, 339b). Here we encounter the newly elected captain working through the details mentally (πορφύρεσκεν ἕκαστα, 461).

Idas's blasphemous comments meet with the disapproval of the rest of the group (cf. 474–75), and in particular the prophet, Idmon, who warns Idas against dishonoring the gods, citing the Aloadae as a negative exemplar of such behavior (476–84). He does, however, recognize that Jason requires encouragement: Ἄλλοι μῦθοι ἔασι παρήγοροι οἷσι περ ἀνὴρ / θαρσύνοι ἕταρον (479–80a).³⁸ Idmon's chastisement elicits a second speech from Idas, who scorns the seer's prophecy as idle and even threatens him with violence (487–91). At this point, the harmony of the group temporarily succumbs to the νεῖκος between Idas and Idmon (492), but the dispute soon comes to an end: as the men shout down the disputants, Jason intervenes and puts a stop to the argument (αὐτός τ' Αἰσονίδης κατερήτυεν, 494). In this Apollonius gives us a second indication that Jason fits his definition of the best of the Argonauts: he deals successfully with νείκεα. It is after Jason's intervention that Orpheus, like Hermes in the hymn, eases the residual tension by singing a theogonic song (496–511).

The present Argonautic νεῖκος involves a man of strength (Idas) and a man of skill (Idmon). Vian compares this argument with the celebrated altercations between Typheus and Amphiaraus and between Hector and Polydamas;³⁹ but given the imitation of the preparations for Odysseus's departure from Phæacia, it now proves more instructive to think of the argument between Achilles and Odysseus, about which Demodocus sang at Alcinous's banquet.

Demodocus's song in *Odyssey* 8 told of Agamemnon's joy when he observed the argument between Odysseus (a man of skill) and

---

37. The best study of Idas in this passage and in the rest of the poem is that of Fränkel (supra n. 11).
38. Cf. Hunter (2) 443.
39. Vian 72 n. 3.

Achilles (a man of strength); for he had learned from Apollo at Delphi that a νεῖκος between these two at a banquet would signal the beginning of their victory over the Trojans (*Od.* 8.73–82).[40] Jason too consulted Apollo at Delphi (412–14), and now at a sacrificial banquet in honor of Apollo a νεῖκος between two comrades of opposite natures was occurring. The scholiast on the Odyssean passage (Σ *ad Od.* 8.75 and 75 HQV) informs us that Achilles and Odysseus were arguing over how Troy would be taken, by force or strategem.[41] The dispute in the *Argonautica* begins when Idas claims that his weapon will bring success to the mission; he states this at the very time that Jason reveals his characteristic form of leadership: thoughtful consideration of all the details. The antithesis of skill and strength comes explicitly into play when the prophet, Idmon, counters Idas's reliance on brute force with reverence toward the gods (476–84). Jason, like Agamemnon, watches a man of vision quarrel with a man of strength.[42] By implication, the argument, like the appearance of Argus and Acastus and the sacrifice to Apollo, is a good sign.

This conflict between a man of strength and a man of vision finds reflection in another Homeric argument to which Apollonius alludes; in this case the opponents are a man of strength and a man whose vision is not internal but ocular. As mentioned above, the quarrel in the *Argonautica* comes to an end through the intervention of Jason:

Χώετ' ἐνιπτάζων· προτέρω δέ κε νεῖκος ἐτύχθη,
εἰ μὴ δηριόωντας ὁμοκλήσαντες ἑταῖροι
αὐτός τ' Αἰσονίδης κατερήτυεν. Ἂν δὲ καὶ Ὀρφεὺς
λαιῇ ἀνασχόμενος κίθαριν πείραζεν ἀοιδῆς.

(492–95)

Such were his angry taunts. The quarrel would have gone farther unless the comrades had shouted down the disputants

---

40. On this passage, see now A. Heubeck, S. West, and A. J. Hainsworth, *A Commentary on Homer's Odyssey* 1 (Oxford 1988) 349–52.
41. Cf. Nagy (supra n. 20) 45–46.
42. Händel 71 is surely wrong in seeing Idas's speech as a mere psychological detail lacking in any effect on the narrative. Fränkel (supra n. 11) 7–8 argues along similar lines.

and unless the son of Æson himself had restrained them. Orpheus too,
taking up his lyre in his left hand, gave his music a try.

At Patroclus's funeral games in the *Iliad*, Idomeneus and Ajax son of Oileus argued about who would win the chariot race. From his vantage point, Idomeneus could see that Diomedes was in the lead and confidently predicted his victory (*Il.* 23.450-72). Ajax rejected his prediction and impugned his vision (ibid. 473-81). Idomeneus responded with insults, calling Ajax νεῖκος ἄριστε (ibid. 483), at which point the dispute was about to get out of hand:[43]

"Ὣς ἔφατ', ὄρνυτο δ' αὐτίκ' Ὀιλῆος ταχὺς Αἴας
χωόμενος χαλεποῖσιν ἀμείψασθαι ἐπέεσσι·
καί νύ κε δὴ προτέρω ἔτ' ἔρις γένετ' ἀμφοτέροισιν,
εἰ μὴ Ἀχιλλεὺς αὐτὸς ἀνίστατο καὶ φάτο μῦθον·
(*Il.* 23.488-91)

Thus he spoke, and the swift son of Oileus hastened
in his anger to reply with fierce words.
And the dispute would have gone farther for both
unless Achilles himself had stood up and said the following words.

In this case, the man of physical vision, Idomeneus, proved accurate in his prediction of Diomedes' victory (ibid. 499-500).[44]

I return to the argument between Achilles and Odysseus. Agamemnon rejoiced when he witnessed the argument between the best of the Achæans (ὅ τ' ἄριστοι Ἀχαιῶν δηριόωντο, *Od.* 8.78)

---

43. Vian 73 n. 1 and Campbell *ad* 1.492-94 note the parallel.
44. That Idas encountered no punishment in the *Argonautica* for his blasphemy and his treatment of Apollo's son has been an issue that scholars have found necessary to explain. Some examples: Zeus eventually punished Idas by killing him with the thunderbolt (Fränkel *ad* 1.476-78; Vian 16, 72 n. 2); this altercation sets up an irony in Book 2 (830b-31) when Idas kills the boar that gored Idmon (Lawall 141ff., Fränkel *ad* 1.485-92, Vian 16); Idas's behavior is at least consistent with tradition (Σ *ad* 1.468, Blumberg 13, Fränkel [supra n. 11] 8); Idas is punished in his failure to succeed in his plan of action at Colchis (3.558-68) and in his embarrassment when his sword proves useless against Jason's spear treated with Medea's potion (3.1252-54; Lawall 141ff., Levin 54-55). Although all are true to a certain degree, these explanations do not explain what lies behind the argument; once the reader identifies the beginning of *Odyssey* 8 as the model for events at Pagasae, it becomes clear that the Argonautic argument is a transmogrified version of that between Achilles and Odysseus as sung by Demodocus.

because this was a sign that the troubles for the Greeks and Trojans were coming to an end (ibid. 81–82). As any reader of the *Argonautica* knows well, Odysseus was ultimately proved correct: Troy was taken not by Achilles' βίη, but by Odysseus's μῆτις. It is significant that Apollonius incorporates a reference to this argument in a context where the best of the Argonauts is in question, both as to the nature of this hero (man of strength or man of skill) and as to his identity (Jason or Heracles). As in the taking of Troy, the successful completion of the Argonautic expedition will ultimately be achieved not through the strength of a Heracles, but through the skill of a Jason. What emerges as truly remarkable is that the skill identified here—the taking care of details and in particular the handling of conflicts and contracts— not only is not the traditional skill one associates with heroes like Odysseus, Hermes, Idmon, and the like (who generally show more resourcefulness and courage than does Jason in the course of the poem) but is quite circumscribed and for this reason unique in the epic tradition. Moreover, what makes Jason the best of the Argonauts—his concern for the details—also reduces him to ἀμηχανίη (460) for the first of many times in the poem.[45] Jason is often depicted as a man in the grip of depression and helplessness. But it will become clear at the end of the book, when Heracles has been lost to the expedition, that Jason has the uncanny ability to chance upon timely assistance, often divine, and knows how to snatch victory from the jaws of defeat, especially in the manner in which he deals with νείκεα.

d. Song of Orpheus (496–511)

In adapting his model of the preparations for departure from Pagasae, as I argued above, Apollonius substituted a theogonic song for Demodocus's abridged version of the quarrel of Achilles and Odysseus.[46] The reconciling power of theogonic poetry celebrated in the hymn to Hermes seems to have suggested this. In the latter, Hermes' song assuaged his brother's anger over the theft of his cattle; in the *Argonautica*, Orpheus's theogony has

---

45. See 1.1286; 2.410, 623, 885; 3.336, 423, 432, 504; 4.1318.
46. On the significance of the creation theme in an epic context, cf. D. M. Gaunt, "The Creation-Theme in Epic Poetry," *CompLit* 29 (1977) 213–20.

the same effect of charming its audience and easing the hostile tension generated by the νεῖκος.

Apollonius presents Orpheus's song in two clearly defined parts, each introduced by the expression ἤειδεν δ' ὡς (496, 503). In the first half, the singer tells of how the present world order arose out of conflict (νείκεος ἐξ ὀλοοῖο, 498a); Apollonius has Empedoclean theory in mind in Orpheus's brief cosmogony.[47] This, as the scholiast *ad* 1.496–98a observed, represents on the cosmic scale the restored unity of the Argonauts following the νεῖκος of Idas and Idmon. In the second half, the topic changes from a cosmogonical to a succession myth. Apollonius contaminates Empedoclean creation theory with the theogony of Pherecydes:[48] Cronus and Rhea replace Ophion and Eurynome, and will eventually be replaced by Zeus, who, in Orpheus's song, is still a young boy in the Cretan cave.[49] Apollonius alludes to the ultimate resolution of the dynastic struggle among the gods by observing that in the future Zeus will receive the thunderbolt. Through this weapon the youthful deity will in time achieve his κῦδος (511). Like Zeus, as well as Hermes and Telemachus, the youthful Jason wants to win κῦδος (cf. 351); and like Zeus, he does not yet have his weapon. For the completion of the Argonautic mission his "weapon" will prove to be Medea, whose magic will make Jason, even if momentarily, immensely powerful. In fact, Apollonius would appear to have this subtle parallel in mind when, after Jason has prepared himself with Medea's drugs for his great ἄεθλος, the poet likens the gleam of his hero's armor to flashes of lightning:[50]

> Φαίης κεν ζοφεροῖο κατ' αἰθέρος ἀίσσουσαν
> χειμερίην στεροπὴν θαμινὸν μεταπαιφάσσεσθαι
> ἐκ νεφέων, ἅ τ' ἔπειτα μελάντατον ὄμβρον ἄγωνται.
> (3.1265–67)

---

47. Cf. Vian 252–53 *ad* 502.
48. Cf. Vian 253 *ad* 511.
49. One might well think of the young Jason who grew up in Chiron's cave (cf. Pindar *P.* 4.102–3, Hesiod *Catalogue of Women* 40 M&W), which the poet recalls when Chiron and his wife, holding the infant Achilles, wave goodbye to the Argonauts as they leave the Gulf of Pagasae (1.553–58).
50. Hunter *ad loc.* notes the comparison between Jason and Zeus in these lines.

You would say that the thunder flash of a wintry storm, streaking down through the dark sky, darted constantly this way and that from the clouds that bring in their wake a most black storm.

The song of Orpheus thus provides a mythic reflection of the immediate context, the establishment of harmony out of νεῖκος, and hints at Jason's future attainment of κῦδος.

e. Formal Conclusion of the Banquet (512–18)

Orpheus's song works like a charm (κηληθμῷ and θελκτύν, 515). The bad feelings generated by the vicious argument would appear to have vanished upon the completion of the music, and the unity of the group is now completely restored. The eventful day and the banquet come to an end with the pouring of a libation over the tongues of the victims:

Οὐδ' ἐπὶ δὴν μετέπειτα κερασσάμενοι Διὶ λοιβάς
ᾗ θέμις, ἑστηῶτες ἐπὶ γλώσσῃσι χέοντο
αἰθομέναις, ὕπνου δὲ διὰ κνέφας ἐμνώοντο.
(516–18)

Not long thereafter, mixing libations in honor of Zeus, as is customary,
they stood over the blazing tongues and poured their offering;
they then turned their thoughts to sleep in the darkness of night.

Such a ceremony occurs only once among the Homeric texts, in the same section of *Odyssey* 3 to which the poet made reference shortly before; and the Odyssean ceremony took place at the conclusion of the day, as it does in the *Argonautica*. Just prior to her epiphany, Athena had recommended ending the sacrificial banquet with the libation over the tongues:[51]

"Ὣς ἔφατ', ἠέλιος δ' ἄρ' ἔδυ καὶ ἐπὶ κνέφας ἦλθε.
τοῖσι δὲ καὶ μετέειπε θεὰ γλαυκῶπις Ἀθήνη·
'"Ὦ γέρον, ἦ τοι ταῦτα κατὰ μοῖραν κατέλεξας·
ἀλλ' ἄγε τάμνετε μὲν γλώσσας, κεράασθε δὲ οἶνον

---

51. Cf. Vian 74 n. 1, who notes all the individual verbal points of contact. As the ceremony of pouring libations over the tongues was offered to Hermes as well as Zeus Teleios (cf. Athenæus 1.16b), Apollonius may also have had the former in mind given the subtextual presence of this divinity in the launch and division of the seats.

ὄφρα Ποσειδάωνι καὶ ἄλλοις ἀθανάτοισι
σπείσαντες <u>κοίτοιο μεδώμεθα</u>· τοῖο γὰρ ὥρη·
ἤδη γὰρ φάος οἴχεθ' ὑπὸ ζόφον, <u>οὐδὲ ἔοικε
δηθὰ</u> θεῶν ἐν δαιτὶ θαασσέμεν, ἀλλὰ νέεσθαι.'
(*Od.* 3.329-36)

Thus he spoke and the sun set as <u>darkness</u> approached.
The goddess then addressed them, owl-eyed Athena:
"Old man, these words of yours were spoken as is right.
But come now, cut the <u>tongues</u> and <u>mix the wine</u>
so that after we pour libation to Poseidon and the other
gods, we might <u>turn our thoughts to sleep</u>; for the hour has come.
Already the light has receded into the darkness, and it is <u>not</u>
    proper
to sit <u>for a long time</u> at the feast of the gods, but to depart."

Accordingly, Apollonius brings the episode to an end with a second reference to the Odyssean scene in which Nestor recognized Telemachus's divine favor through the personal guidance he received from Athena. Jason too has been promised such assistance by Apollo. The preparations for the Argonautic expedition thus come to an auspicious conclusion.

THE analysis of Apollonius's narrative of the events on the beach at Pagasae once again reveals a complex *contaminatio* of several models of diverse provenience. All the significant imitations are of passages that reflect crucial moments of the episode. Apollonius presents vivid contrasts between men of physical power and violence (Argus, Heracles, Idas) and men of poise and vision (Acastus, Jason, Idmon). He refers his reader to similarly opposed pairs celebrated in Greek literature: Apollo and Hermes, Achilles and Odysseus, and Idomeneus and Ajax. The explicit indication in the text that the mission will succeed (Idmon's reading of the sacrifice to Apollo) is corroborated at the subtextual level in several ways: first, through the reference to Telemachus; next, the evocation of Apollo's epiphany at Anaphe in the *Ætia*; and then through the argument between Idas and Idmon, which corresponds to that between Achilles and Odysseus and signals the beginning of success. Finally, as Jason implies in his first speech, the success of their mission depends on the recognition of their interdependence (336-37). Discord threatens to undermine their ability to cooperate; the dispute between Idas and Idmon could have ended the venture right there at Pagasae. Jason, however, like Achilles in the *Iliad*, intervenes and puts a stop to the disruptive νεῖκος.

The importance of harmony, which underlies Jason's view of the best of the Argonauts—and thus the need for reconciliation—finds resonance in the cases of Achilles and Odysseus, of Hermes and Apollo, and in Orpheus's song, which takes up this theme and offers the reconciliation of cosmic and divine νεῖκος as a backdrop for the restoration of harmony among the Argonauts. As Apollonius indicated at the beginning of the poem, the Argonautic expedition depends not upon one man, but upon a group of individuals, many of whom possess celebrated talents in their own right and have had, have, or will have challenging exploits of their own. As Jason sees quite accurately, the leader must keep so large and diverse a group of talented men together and united in purpose through a careful management of the many details that the journey will require, and above all through the dextrous handling of what will prove to be at times a temperamental crew. Such a leader will prove to be the best among this group.

5

The Wrath of Thetis

Journey from Pagasae to Lemnos (*Argo.* 1.519-608)

APOLLONIUS'S description of the departure of the Argonauts from the Gulf of Pagasae (519-79) is considered one of the most picturesque scenes of the epic.¹ The vivid narrative includes many details of sight and sound: the thunderous noise emitted by the harbor and by the *Argo* itself;² the frothy wake of the ship; the appearance of the gods and the nymphs of Pelion as divine spectators of the event; the arrival of the centaur Chiron with his wife and the infant Achilles; the schools of large and small fish swimming after the ship in response to Orpheus's music. The author's presentation of these marvels, however, is not a self-indulgent exercise in verbal portraiture. Rather, critics have failed to observe that these lovely details play a significant role in the first of two structurally distinct, but thematically related, phases of the journey from Pagasae to Lemnos.

Apollonius organized the first phase of the journey, the departure from the Gulf of Pagasae (519-79), in ring format, which sets in relief a portrait of divine and semidivine observers watching as the *Argo* sails out of the gulf. An inference to be drawn from this centrally positioned vignette will explain the cause and significance of the delay at Aphetae Argous, which follows in the second

---

1. See A. Lesky, *Thalatta: Der Weg der Griechen zum Meer* (Vienna 1947) 267; Blumberg 14; Händel 78-79; Fränkel *ad* 1.(517-)579; and E. Phinney, "Hellenistic Painting and the Poetic Style of Apollonius," *CJ* 62 (1967) 145-49.

2. On Apollonius's treatment of the *Argo* here and throughout the whole poem, see D. M. Gaunt, "Argo and the Gods in Apollonius Rhodius," *G&R* 19 (1972) 117-26.

phase, the journey from the southern end of the Magnesian Peninsula to island of Lemnos (580–608).[3] This inference will provide a revealing parallel for Jason in his future dealings with Hypsipyle and especially with Medea. For the legendary and historical subtext of the *Argo*'s first encounter with trouble asks the reader to look beyond the temporal confines of the expedition. For it is at that time that the one who can claim to have been the best of the Argonauts will learn that parental concerns—a central motif of the present episode—far outweigh heroic skills, accomplishments, and the κῦδος they bring.

STRUCTURE

The first phase, departure from the Gulf of Pagasae (A, 519–79), unfolds in two distinct stages.[4] The first of these stages begins at dawn on the day following the launch of the ship and the sacrifice to Apollo (a, 519–46; 28 lines).[5] After Tiphys gives the order to board the ship, the men take their seats as previously arranged, and, when the *Argo* starts to move away, Jason sheds a few tears (aα).[6] As the ship moves steadily through the gulf, Apollonius

---

3. See E. Livrea, "Da Pagasai a Lemnos," *SIFC* 51 (1979) 146–54, and especially 152 (Tav. II).
4. On the structure of this section, see Hurst 57–58; Fränkel *ad* 1.(519–)579; and Vian 255 *ad* 579.
5. In the proecdosis (*apud* Σ *ad* 1.516–18c), the Argonauts left Pagasae on the third day. At present I do not see what benefit the poet derives from such a change. Hunter (2) 439 compares the *Argo*'s departure from Pagasae to that of the Athenian fleet from Piraeus on its way to Sicily as described by Thucydides 6.30–32; the similarity is striking.
6. Some have seen this as unheroic behavior on Jason's part: cf. Blumberg 13 and H. Faerber, "Zur dichterischen Kunst in Apollonios Rhodios' *Argonautica* (Die Gleichnisse)" (diss. Berlin 1932) 101. Fränkel *ad* 1.533–35 and Vian 253–54 *ad* 535 offer a more positive interpretation of these tears. See also F. Grajew, "Untersuchungen über die Bedeutung der Gebärden in der griechischen Epik" (diss. Königsberg 1934) 40–41. It is important to observe that Jason's reaction (αὐτὰρ Ἰήσων / δακρυόεις γαίης ἀπὸ πατρίδος ὄμματ' ἔνεικεν, 534–35) has been modeled on that of Odysseus's men when, in *Od*. 10.48–49 (τοὺς δ' αἶψ' ἁρπάξασα φέρεν πόντονδε θύελλα / κλαίοντας, γαίης ἄπο πατρίδος), they open the bag of winds given to Odysseus by Æolus, which results in their being blown away from home. On the one hand, the men weep as they lose the chance of returning home after many years abroad; on the other hand, Jason's tears well up the moment he leaves home for the first time. The contrast between the two texts is noteworthy. In the *Odyssey*, Odysseus's

highlights the regularity of their rowing and its effect on the water in two similes: he compares the rhythmic movements of the men, for whom Orpheus sets the beat with his lyre, to youths at a dance in honor of Apollo (aβ). The white seafoam that is stirred up by the oars is likened to a road in a verdant plain (aγ). Several details of the second stage (a, 559–79; 21 lines) correspond to elements in the first. After Tiphys has successfully steered them out of the gulf and the mast is raised, they no longer row, but proceed under sail (aα) along Cape Tisae, a promontory stretching in an east-west direction at the southern end of the gulf. Orpheus sings a hymn to Artemis (aβ), the female counterpart of Apollo, which has the effect of compelling many fish of various sizes to follow. Description of the sailing stage in this first phase concludes, like the rowing, with a simile (aγ): the fish are compared to sheep following a shepherd who pipes his way home. The correspondence of these similes is highlighted by the fact that each compares a maritime scene with a terrestrial image. These two neatly balanced stages of the journey out of the Gulf of Pagasae thus frame the central subsection, in which Apollonius describes two groups of divine and semidivine spectators who admire the Argonauts (b, 547–58): the gods and nymphs of Mount Pelion from above (bα, 547–52; 6 lines),[7] and Chiron, Chariclo, and Achilles from land (bβ, 553–58; 6 lines).

The second phase (B, 580–608) comprises the journey from just outside the Gulf of Pagasae along Cape Tisae to the island of Lemnos and contains two halves of equal length.[8] In the first (a, 583–93, 580–82; 14 lines), the Argonauts are forced to land near the tomb of Dolops after they encounter stiff headwinds. Here they offer sacrifice to the deceased hero's ghost, after which the winds subside. People will accordingly call this place

---

men unwittingly bring about the loss of their νόστος because of jealousy over their leader's gift. Jason's men, however, their unanimity confirmed through Orpheus's song, row away from Iolcus in unison to the coxswain's rhythm.

7. Fränkel *ad* 1.(519–)579 points out that the reader's view of the ship was the same as that of the gods: from above.

8. I follow Livrea's transposition of lines 580–82 to follow 591 (see supra n. 3). On the geographical problems in this section, see Delage 74ff., and F. Vian, "Notes critiques au chant I des 'Argonautiques' d'Apollonios de Rhodes," *REA* 72 (1970) 89–90.

Aphetae Argous: that is, the place where the *Argo* left. After a delay of two days, they sail past Sepias Acte and stormy Melibœa. As scholars have recognized,[9] all these places figured in Herodotus's description of the disastrous storm that sank many of the Persian ships in 480 B.C. on their way south to support their army against the Greeks at Thermopylae (7.183ff.). As I shall point out below, a significant number of shared details reveal that Apollonius has this historical event in mind. In the second half of this phase (b, 594–608; 15 lines), which begins with dawn and ends at nightfall of the next day (ἅμ' ἠελίοιο βολαῖς, 607),[10] the *Argo* sails from Melibœa to Lemnos, skirting Cape Canastræon on the Pallene Peninsula and Mount Athos on the Acte Peninsula. This stage of the journey to Lemnos also parallels a celebrated itinerary; namely, Hephæstus's fall to Lemnos. The structure of the episode thus looks as follows:

JOURNEY FROM PAGASAE TO LEMNOS, 519–608

A. First Phase: Journey out of the Gulf of Pagasae   (519–79)
   a. First Stage:
      α. Rowing the *Argo* through
         the Gulf
      β. Orpheus's Music Compared to
         Hymn for Apollo
      γ. Concluding Simile   (519–46)
   b. Spectators:
      α. Gods and Nymphs
      β. Chiron, Chariclo, and Achilles   (547–58)
   a. Second Stage:
      α. Sailing along Cape Tisae
      β. Orpheus's Hymn in Honor of
         Artemis
      γ. Concluding Simile   (559–79)

---

9. Delage 76–79; cf. Vian (supra n. 8), Livrea (supra n. 3).
10. On the time of arrival, see Vian 18–19 n. 2; cf. Livrea (supra n. 3) 147 n. 3.

B. Second Phase: From the Gulf of Pagasae
   to Lemnos (580–608)
   a. Cape Tisae to Meliboea (583–91)
   b. Meliboea to Lemnos (601–8)

A. First Phase:
Journey out of the Gulf of Pagasae (519–79)

In the first phase of their journey from Pagasae to Lemnos, the Argonauts board the ship at dawn and head out of the Gulf of Pagasae on the first leg of their journey to Colchis. As indicated above, elements in the first subsection (a) balance comparable elements in the third (a), thus creating a ring (rowing ≈ sailing; song in honor of Apollo ≈ song in honor of Artemis; concluding simile comparing the wake of the *Argo* to a path in a plain ≈ concluding simile comparing fish sailing behind *Argo* to sheep following after a shepherd). Before looking at the portrait framed by these two stages of the first phase, I would call attention to two details of the framing sections that hark back to earlier themes, the second pertaining to one of the principal focal points of the episode.

Close examination of the portrayal of Heracles in the first subsection (a) with that of Tiphys in the second (a) reveals that Apollonius has once again reintroduced the thematic antithesis of the man of strength versus the man of skill. In the former, Ancæus and Heracles, the latter with his celebrated club beside him, sit in the middle of the ship:

Μέσσῳ δ' Ἀγκαῖος μέγα τε σθένος ‘Ηρακλῆος
ἵζανον, ἄγχι δέ οἱ ῥόπαλον θέτο· καί οἱ ἔνερθε
ποσσὶν ὑπεκλύσθη νηὸς τρόπις.

(531–33)

In the middle, Ancæus and the <u>extremely powerful</u> Heracles took their seats; the latter set his club at his side, and below his feet the ship's keel sank beneath the waves.

As scholars have observed, the sinking of the keel under the hero's feet refers to the tradition that Heracles was abandoned at

Aphetae Argous because of his excessive weight.[11] In addition to this clever allusion to an alternative version of Heracles' abandonment, the brief description of the massive Heracles at his seat with his club at hand parallels in the second subsection the sketch of Tiphys, who skillfully wields the rudder as he steers the ship out of the harbor:

Οἱ δ' ὅτε δὴ λιμένος περιηγέα κάλλιπον ἀκτὴν
<u>φραδμοσύνῃ μήτι τε</u> δαΐφρονος Ἁγνιάδαο
Τίφυος, ὅς ῥ' ἐνὶ χερσὶν ἐΰξοα <u>τεχνηέντως</u>
πηδάλι' ἀμφιέπεσκ', ὄφρ' ἔμπεδον ἐξιθύνοι.
(559-62)

After they left the harbor's curving beach
following the <u>instructions</u> of Hagnias's son,
Tiphys, who <u>with great skill</u> was maneuvering the polished
rudder in his hands in order to keep the vessel on a steady course.

Apollonius calls attention to this antithetical corresponsion by mentioning the respective virtues of both men (σθένος Ἡρακλῆος ≈ φραδμοσύνῃ μήτι τε δαΐφρονος ... Τίφυος ... τεχνηέντως) and by associating both with their respective instruments (ῥόπαλον ≈ πηδάλια). The focus on Heracles in the rowing section is appropriate because his propelling the ship by oar requires power, whose effect on the water Apollonius elegantly accentuates:[12]

Ἀφρῷ δ' ἔνθα καὶ ἔνθα κελαινὴ κήκιεν ἅλμη
δεινὸν μορμύρουσα ἐρισθενέων μένει ἀνδρῶν.
(542-43)

Here and there the dark brine was churned into foam,
boiling furiously from the strength of the mighty heroes.

---

11. See Mooney ad 1.533; Blumberg 13; Faerber (supra n. 6) 93; Vian 251 ad 400. Σ ad 1.1289-91a attributed this version to Antimachus in the Lyde (fr. 58 Wyss [= B. Gentili and C. Prato, *Poetae Elegiaci Pars II* (Leipzig 1985) s.v. "Antimachus" fr. 4]; cf. Pherecydes FGrHist 3 F 111, Apollod. 1.9.19); in this he was followed by Posidippus, identified, incidentally, as one of the Telchines by the diegesis on the opening lines of the *Ætia* (*Schol. Flor. ad Ætia* 1-12 Pf.).

12. As they leave Cyzicus later on in the book, Heracles will even row the *Argo* by himself (cf. 1.1153-71).

On the other hand, through Tiphys's skill and direction, the men need not work; rather, taking advantage of the wind, they travel at ease: Τισαίην εὔκηλοι ὑπὲρ δολιχὴν θέον ἄκρην (568; "They ran leisurely past the long Tisæan headland"). The difference between Heracles' and Tiphys's contribution to the driving of the ship compares quite closely with the different heroic styles of Heracles and Jason. The former always depends on his great strength for success, while the latter achieves his goals by skilfully manipulating people and circumstances. It is essential to note that right here, at the beginning of the expedition, we can observe how φραδμοσύνη and μῆτις can be just as effective as σθένος.

In addition to their comparable importance in the driving of the *Argo*, Apollonius may have associated Heracles and Tiphys at the moment of the *Argo*'s departure because, as it will turn out, neither will complete the journey to Colchis. When Heracles in Mysia rushes off in search of Hylas, Tiphys's call to sail will result in Heracles' abandonment (1.1273ff.). Not long after this, the Argonauts will also lose the services of Tiphys when he dies among the Mariandyni (2.851–57).[13] Moreover, the loss of each Argonaut threatens the continuation of the mission because of the resulting discord and despair among the group (1.1280–1309, 2.859–63); but in both cases, thanks to divine intervention (Glaucus at 1.1310–25, Hera at 2.864–66a), the others pull themselves together and the journey continues.

Second, the corresponsion between Apollo in the rowing (aα), and Artemis in the sailing section (aα) also recalls an earlier contrast. In his description of the departure of Jason and the Argonauts from Iolcus, discussed in Chapter 3, Apollonius emphasized in structure and content the different reactions to the departure of the men and women of Iolcus, of the male and female slaves

---

13. It is noteworthy that the episode in which Tiphys dies contains a reference back to the abandonment of Heracles in Mysia. When Heracles had visited these very people earlier, after securing the girdle of Hippolyte (see 2.775–85), he arrived on the occasion of Priolaus's funeral. The latter had died in battle with the Mysians, which resulted in the celebration of an annual dirge in his honor. At the funeral games, Heracles defeated in a boxing match Titias, whom in one account (Nymphis *FGrHist* 432 F 5b) nymphs carried off while he was fetching water, and for whom the local peoples performed an annual search while singing dirges; see Vian 277–78 *ad* 785. The parallels with Hylas's fate are obvious (cf. 1.1221–39, 1345–57).

at the home of Æson, of Jason and Alcimede, and of Jason and Iphias. He completed this extended contrast in gender by comparing Jason, who encounters the aged priestess of Artemis, to Apollo (306-16).[14] In the present episode, the close relationship between Jason and Apollo is viewed once again in a simile.[15] In this case, Apollonius compares the rhythmical rowing of the Argonauts accompanied by Orpheus to the dance of Apollo's devotees at one of his cult sites (536-39). Because the group of rowers resemble the god's worshippers, the captain would appear to be the nautical analogue of the god.

In the corresponding section, Orpheus sings a hymn to Artemis (569-72). One recalls the mention of Iphias, her Iolcan priestess, not only because of the similar juxtaposition of Apollo and the functionary of Artemis, but because in both passages, Apollonius highlights the protective function of the female divinity (πολιηόχου, 312 ≈ Νηοσσόον, 570). As we saw, the Apollinian Jason coldly left behind the Artemisian Iphias without saying a word; she could only manage to kiss his hand. Such behavior toward a woman who has apparently outlasted any importance or usefulness she may have had (cf. ἀλλ' ἡ μὲν λίπετ' αὖθι παρακλιδόν, οἷα γεραιὴ / ὁπλοτέρων, 315-16) will prove consonant with Jason's future dealings with the two important women he encounters in the *Argonautica*, both of whom have Artemisian associations and offer Jason their protection.

Hypsipyle resembles this goddess in that when the Argonauts arrive she is a virgin queen ruling over an all-female society. After the love-struck young woman provides Jason and his men with the use of her harbor, city, and citizens—including herself—for an unspecified period of time on Lemnos (cf. 1.861-64), her guest will cooly abandon her in pursuit of his mission. In particular, in her farewell to Jason, Hypsipyle, like Iphias, holds his hands when, among other things, she asks to be remembered:[16]

---

14. One should note that Iphias is a syncopated form of Iphianassa, a name with Artemisian associations; cf. Vian 64-65 n. 3.
15. J. F. Carspecken, "Apollonius Rhodius and the Homeric Epic," *YClS* 13 (1952) 96-97, concluded that Jason and Apollo were so closely linked that it would be impossible to think of one without being reminded of the other.
16. The reminiscence in these lines of Nausicaa, another woman associated with Artemis, will be discussed in the next chapter.

'Ὡς δὲ καὶ Ὑψιπύλη ἠρήσατο χεῖρας ἑλοῦσα
Αἰσονίδεω, τὰ δέ οἱ ῥέε δάκρυα χήτει ἰόντος.
. . . .
'Μνώεο μήν, ἀπεών περ ὁμῶς καὶ νόστιμος ἤδη,
Ὑψιπύλης.'

(1.886-97a)

Hypsipyle too offered this prayer, clasping the hands
of Æson's son; she began to cry, realizing her loss in his departure.
. . . .
"Remember, then, both while you are away from home and when
you return,
Hypsipyle."

After a brief response, Jason is the first on the ship (1.910). In the case of Medea, Apollonius explicitly compares her to Artemis when the Colchian maiden goes to meet Jason at the temple of Hecate (3.876-84); and her assistance to, and protection of, Jason are what will ultimately give him the ability to achieve the goal of his mission. Moreover, like Hypsipyle she too will hold Jason's hand as she asks to be remembered for her favor:[17]

Ἀντῳῷ δέ μιν ἄντην
ἐξαῦτις μύθῳ προσεφώνεεν, εἷλέ τε χειρὸς
δεξιτερῆς· δὴ γάρ οἱ ἀπ' ὀφθαλμοὺς λίπεν αἰδώς·
'Μνώεο δ', ἢν ἄρα δή ποθ' ὑπότροπος οἴκαδ' ἵκηαι,
οὔνομα Μηδείης·'

(3.1066b-70a; cf. 3.1109-11)

Looking him directly in the eye,
again she gave voice to her painful feelings, taking his right
hand—for shame had by now left her eyes.
"Remember, if ever you make it back to your home,
the name of Medea."

Within the poem, Jason wavers in his protection of Medea, especially when handing her over would appear to ensure the success of his mission (4.338ff.). Beyond the conclusion of the poem, Jason will abandon Medea, once again to further his own interests. Thus

---

17. Vian 24 n. 2 observed these and other comparisons between the experiences of Hypsipyle and Medea.

the Apollo-Artemis pairing would seem to represent an emblem of Jason's infelicitous relationships with the women of his life. Moreover, this suggestive pairing frames an appropriate picture within; for implications that can be drawn from the personages described in the central panel point to another famous male-female relationship that, like Jason's with Medea, turned sour, that of Peleus and Thetis. This relationship not only adds another perspective from which to view Jason's future abandonment of both Hypsipyle and Medea, but it also ties in closely with the action of the second phase of the journey to Lemnos.

In the central position of the first phase of the journey from Pagasae to Lemnos (Ab), Apollonius sketches an idyllic scene in two parts. In the first (bα), all the gods from the sky and the nymphs from the peaks of Mount Pelion look down in admiration on both the ship and the Argonauts. Apollonius refers to the Argonauts as the ἡμιθέων ἀνδρῶν γένος (548).[18] The epithet ἡμίθεος in this context confirms what we learned in the Catalogue; namely, that many of the Argonauts are the sons of gods and mortals. In the second part of the central panel (bβ), we see Chiron at the edge of the sea bidding the Argonauts farewell. Next to him, his wife, Chariclo, holds the infant Achilles, whom she shows to his father, Peleus. Thus both parts of the picture involve parents, divine and mortal, looking at their sons. Since Chiron and Chariclo are caring for Achilles, one must assume that Peleus and Thetis have already separated. In the fourth book, Apollonius corroborates this assumption with an explicit account of their marital rift and its cause (4.865–79): Peleus had earlier interrupted Thetis's attempt to make Achilles immortal when she held him in a fire at night and anointed him with ambrosia during the day. Because of this, Thetis immediately abandoned her husband and son, at

---

18. Although it is true that this is the only passage in the text where Apollonius refers to the Argonauts as ἡμίθεοι (Vian 75 n. 4), Phrixus's son, Argus, identifies the Argonauts as the sons and grandsons of the gods at 3.365-66, and Apollonius clearly identifies the age of the Argonautic expedition as that of the ἡμίθεοι when describing Talos (4.1641–44). Apollonius had earlier associated the Argonauts with the age of the ἡμίθεοι in an allusion to Hesiod *Catalogue of Women* 1.6-7 M&W at lines 336-37 (see Chapter 4 n. 8); the Hesiodic lines were axiomatic for the age when gods and mortals communed and had children.

which point Chiron and Chariclo stepped in to help Peleus raise Achilles.[19]

The interest shown by the gods in their children and by Chiron in showing Peleus his infant son recalls an earlier motif. In the Catalogue, Apollonius gave several touching sketches of parental concern for the well-being and success of their sons (69–70, 97–100, 115–17, 146–50, 164–71, 190–96); immediately after the Catalogue, Apollonius focused in greater depth on Jason's departure from his home and the reactions of his parents. As the group of ἡμίθεοι leave Greece, Apollonius brings this theme to a dramatic climax by having all the gods witness the departure of the young heroes, many of them their semidivine children. The theme of parental concern, however, has another side in this tableau. Peleus and Thetis divorced over an incident involving the well-being of their son, and as a result the father gained control of the child. This experience ominously parallels Jason's future parental experiences. When Jason leaves Hypsipyle, he will instruct her that if he should not return to Greece and she should give birth to a son, she should relinquish the child and send him to his own parents to support them in their old age (1.904–9).[20] Similarly, as in the Euripidean play, when Jason divorced Medea he wanted her to relinquish control of their sons, purportedly for their benefit. Both women thus face the unhappy prospect of giving up their sons. Allusion to the divorce of Peleus and Thetis in a centrally placed section depicting parental concern holds a special signifcance for Jason as he begins his celebrated journey to Colchis, where he will meet Medea; such a reference is surely inauspicious.[21]

Finally, although the rearing of heroic children by Chiron was a well-known motif, Apollonius invites the reader to see a similarity in the fates of Medea and Thetis through an imitation of

---

19. On the divorce of Peleus and Thetis, see Vian (3) 178 *ad* 879, and N. J. Richardson, *The Homeric Hymn to Demeter* (Oxford 1974) 237–38 *ad* 237ff. On Thetis's anger with Peleus, see Σ *ad* 4.816, Livrea *ad* 4.816, 868.

20. This, however, will not come to pass; for Jason does return to Greece, and we find a son of Jason and Hypsipyle, Euneus, ruling at Lemnos during the Trojan War (*Il.* 7.467–69, 23.745–47).

21. The comparison between the experiences of Peleus and Thetis and Jason and Medea is similar to the more explicit association of the experience of Theseus and Ariadne to that of the latter pair made later in the poem; cf. 3.997–1007, 1074–76, 1096–1108; 4.424–34.

a pertinent text. Χείρων Φιλυρίδης, as Apollonius calls Chiron at line 554, is the phrase used by Hesiod to refer to the centaur who cared for Medeius, the son of Jason and Medea:[22]

καί ῥ' ἥ γε δμηθεῖσ' ὑπ' Ἰήσονι, ποιμένι λαῶν,
Μήδειον τέκε παῖδα, τὸν οὔρεσιν ἔτρεφε Χείρων
Φιλυρίδης· μεγάλου δὲ Διὸς νόος ἐξετελεῖτο.
(*Theog.* 1000–1002)

And she [*sc.* Medea], submitting to Jason, shepherd of his people, gave birth to a son, Medeius, whom Chiron, the son of Philyra, raised in the mountains. In this way the will of Zeus was fulfilled.

The reference to the eponymous hero of the Medes[23] anticipates the trouble the Argonauts encounter in the second phase of the journey.[24]

B. Second Phase:
From the Gulf of Pagasae to Lemnos (580–608)

The second phase of the episode entails the journey from Cape Tisae to the island of Lemnos. As mentioned above (see note 8), I follow Livrea's intelligent solution to the geographical and textual problems of lines 580–93 and so read lines 580–82 after 591.[25] The transferral of the lines, among other advantages, places Aphetae Argous at the southern tip of the Magnesian Peninsula, where both Herodotus (7.193) and Strabo (9.436) located it. Delage has added the convincing observation that Apollonius modeled the journey from Cape Tisae to Meliboea on a well-known historical event (see note 9). In 480 B.C., the Persian fleet descended from

---

22. See Ardizzoni and Campbell *ad* 1.554, and Vian 76 n. 1. A search of the *TLG* reveals that the phrase occurs only in these two passages.

23. See M. L. West, *Hesiod: Theogony* (Oxford 1966) *ad* 1001.

24. Another connection between Medea and Thetis exists in their methods of conferring youth or immortality. Medea had in some accounts rejuvenated Æson by boiling him in a pot (cf. *Nostoi* 6 Davies) and murdered Pelias by tricking his daughters into attempting to do the same, with disastrous results (see J. G. Frazer, *Apollodorus: The Library*, 2 vols. [London 1921] 1.121–22 *ad* Apollodorus 1.9.27). Thetis, like Demeter in the Homeric Hymn (*h. Cer.* 237–41), placed Achilles in the fire (4.865–79). Both the roasting of children and the boiling of elderly were strategies meant to counter mortality; cf. Frazer ibid. 2.362.

25. I also accept Livrea's reading of ἀκτή (D) in place of ἀκρή (Ω) at 582 and his retention of lines 592–93.

Therma to assist the army that was about to engage the Greeks at Thermopylae. Their first stop was the beach (αἰγιαλόν) between Casthanea and Sepias Acte on the eastern coast of the Magnesian Peninsula; some vessels had landed at a small island near Sciathus (Herodotus 7.183). A gale-force wind arose and destroyed many ships, some at Sepias Acte and Melibœa (ibid. 7.188). The storm lasted for three days and was allayed on the fourth after an offering of propitiatory gifts (ἔντομά τε ποιεῦντες; it is not stated to whom) and a sacrifice to Thetis because she had been raped by Peleus at Sepias Acte (ibid. 7.191). The Persian fleet then put in at Aphetae, where Heracles had been abandoned (ibid. 7.193).

Apollonius's account of the *Argo*'s journey, which proceeded in a direction opposite to that of the Persians, reveals several explicit points of contact with the Herodotean account. The Argonauts experience bad winds (585–86), for which they sacrifice ἔντομα (587) at the tomb of Dolops at Aphetae Argous (591), which is located on the Magnesian Peninsula (584);[26] a period of two days follows in which the wind prevents their sailing (588–89); they then pass Sepias Acte, Sciathus (582–83), and finally the windy αἰγιαλόν of Melibœa (592–93). Apollonius, like Herodotus, also suggests an etymology for the name Aphetae Argous (591).

I would add two less explicit points of contact between the narratives. First, Herodotus explicitly referred to Heracles' abandonment at 7.193: ἔστι δὲ χῶρος ἐν τῷ κόλπῳ τούτῳ τῆς Μαγνησίης, ἔνθα λέγεται τὸν Ἡρακλέα καταλειφθῆναι ὑπὸ Ἰήσονός τε καὶ τῶν συνεταίρων ἐκ τῆς Ἀργοῦς ἐπ' ὕδωρ πεμφθέντα, εὖτε ἐπὶ τὸ κῶας ἔπλεον ἐς Αἶαν [τὴν Κολχίδα]· ἐντεῦθεν γὰρ ἔμελλον ὑδρευσάμενοι

---

26. According to the scholiast, Apollonius borrowed this feature of his story from the *Argonautica* of Cleon of Curion (see Σ *ad* 1.587). Why this son of Hermes should be involved is not clear. Livrea (supra n. 3) 151–52 suggests that possibly this Dolops is the brother of Chiron (cf. Hyginus *Fab. Praef.* 14) and that "gli onori dovuti all'immortale maestro di Giasone sono qui resi sotto forma di ἔντομα μήλων alla sua mortale ipostasi, l'eroe Dolope." I would not be surprised to discover that among those who received ἔντομα from the Persians was this Dolops; no information, however, exists to my knowledge that confirms or even suggests that this is the case. M. D. Petrusevski, "Perewote—Doroqo Sowote," *ZAnt* 15 (1965–66) 201, argues that the Mycenaean phrase "Doroqo Sowote" is the name of a locality synonymous with Δόλοπος σῆμα (cf. Orph. *A.* 464). Surely more lies behind this cryptic reference to what might be a very ancient monument than is readily apparent.

ἐς τὸ πέλαγος ἀφήσειν, ἐπὶ τούτου δὲ τῷ χώρῳ οὔνομα γέγονε
Ἀφέται. ("There is a place within this gulf in Magnesia where it
is said that Heracles was abandoned by Jason and his companions, sent away from the *Argo* for water when they were sailing
to [Colchis in] Asia in search of the fleece. After taking on a sup-
ply of water, they intended to depart from here for the open sea,
and for this reason the place acquired the name Aphetae" [i.e.,
place of departure].) Apollonius, on the other hand, alludes to the
same event in the first phase of the journey to Lemnos when he
states that the keel of the ship was sinking under Heracles' weight
(531–33), a purported reason for the hero's abandonment. Second, and of greater importance, Herodotus expressly mentioned
that the Persians sacrificed to Thetis, whom they believed they
had angered by their presence near Sepias Acte, the spot where
she had been raped by Peleus. At the center of the first phase,
Apollonius alludes to another unhappy event in Thetis's life, her
bitter divorce from Peleus. It would appear that the poet would
have us recall the Persian disaster along the Magnesian Peninsula while reading about the Argonauts' problem with the strong
headwinds in this same region.[27] In the Herodotean narrative the
Persian Magi concluded that the wrath of Thetis was responsible for the winds that destroyed the Persian ships. By having the
Argonauts retrace in reverse the path of the Persians, Apollonius
invites the reader to see the wrath of Thetis as operative here too
in the obstructive headwinds that delay the expedition. Imitation
of the phrase Χείρων Φιλλυρίδης from *Theogony* 1001–2 in the central panel of the first section of the episode now comes into better
focus: like Achilles, Medeius, the son of Jason and Medea, will
be reared by Chiron; and like Jason, his descendants, the Medes,
will experience difficulties with the winds along the Magnesian
Peninsula.

---

27. Such winds were a common problem in the area; cf. Vian 77 n. 4, and
p. 89 of his article cited in note 8 above. H. Fränkel, "Das Argonautenepos
des Apollonios," *MH* 14 (1957) 3–8, discusses Apollonius's precision in his
articulation of the details of the journey; Fränkel has shown that the poet took
into consideration such particulars as the constant need for provisions, local
terrain, and meteorological phenomena like the ἀπηλιώτης or Ἑλλησποντίης
wind off the coast of Magnesia.

In the second half of the second phase (just before the Argonauts arrive at Lemnos) Apollonius makes reference to a Homeric passage describing a journey that likewise parallels that of the *Argo*.[28] The last leg of their trip to the island extended from the beach at Melibœa to Lemnos and lasted two days. The second day finds the Argonauts sailing from Cape Canastræon at the southern end of the Pallene Peninsula to Mount Athos at the southern tip of the Acte Peninsula and from there to Lemnos. During the entire day, the Argonauts have Mount Athos in sight: it appears to them at dawn providing a marker toward which they sail; and, after reaching it, they follow its shadow, which stretches all the way to Lemnos. We are, moreover, told that the distance from Mount Athos to Lemnos was equal to the distance covered by a well-equipped merchant ship (εὔστολος ὁλκάς) in half a day. Thus the Argonauts spend half of the day sailing from Cape Canastræon to Mount Athos, and like the ὁλκάς spend the second half of the day traveling to Lemnos. The description of this journey recalls the famous passage in the *Iliad* in which Hephæstus tells of his own trip to Lemnos:[29]

> Ἦρι δὲ νισομένοισιν Ἄθω ἀνέτελλε κολώνη
> Θρηικίη, ἣ τόσσον ἀπόπροθι Λῆμνον ἐοῦσαν
> ὅσσον ἐς ἔνδιόν κεν εὔστολος ὁλκὰς ἀνύσσαι,
> ἀκροτάτῃ κορυφῇ σκιάει καὶ ἐσάχρι Μυρίνης.
> Τοῖσιν δ' αὐτῆμαρ μὲν ἄεν καὶ ἐπὶ κνέφας οὖρος
> πάγχυ μάλ' ἀκραής, τετάνυστο δὲ λαίφεα νηός.
> Αὐτὰρ ἅμ' ἠελίοιο βολαῖς ἀνέμοιο λιπόντος
> εἰρεσίῃ κραναὴν Σιντηίδα Λῆμνον ἵκοντο.
> Ἔνθ' ἄμυδις πᾶς δῆμος ὑπερβασίῃσι γυναικῶν
> νηλειῶς δέδμητο παροιχομένῳ λυκάβαντι.
>
> (601–10)

---

28. I discuss this imitation at greater length elsewhere; cf. "Two Curious Reflections in the Argonautic Looking-Glass (*Argo*. 1.577 and 603)," *GIF* 41 (1989) 198–206.

29. Delage 84, Mooney and Arcizzoni *ad* 1.608, and Vian 256 *ad* 608 cite besides *Il*. 1.594 also *Od*. 8.294, where Homer mentioned the Sintians, who aided Hephæstus. None have seen that more is involved than a learned use of Σιντηίδα; Vian 18–19 n. 2 did, however, observe that ἅμ' ἠελίοιο βολαῖς was modeled on Homer's ἅμα δ' ἠελίῳ καταδύντι. The Odyssean passage, on the other hand, has no other verbal indications to suggest that Apollonius had this passage in mind, *pace* Levin 59.

At dawn, Mount Athos rose up before them as they traveled;
a Thracian landmark, which, being as far away from Lemnos
as it takes a well-equipped freighter to sail by noon,
casts the shadow of its highest peak all the way to Myrine.
<u>On this very same day</u> a brisk wind blew constantly
until dusk, fully extending the ship's sail.
But when the wind gave out <u>at the same time as the rays
of the sun</u>,
they reached the rugged island of <u>Sintian</u> Lemnos under power
of oars.
Here the entire male citizenry in one moment was pitilessly
cut down in the previous year through the crime of the <u>women</u>.

<u>πᾶν δ' ἦμαρ</u> φερόμην, <u>ἅμα δ' ἠελίῳ καταδύντι</u>
κάππεσον ἐν Λήμνῳ, ὀλίγος δ' ἔτι θυμὸς ἐνῆεν·
ἔνθα με <u>Σίντιες ἄνδρες</u> ἄφαρ κομίσαντο πεσόντα.
(*Il.* 1.592–94)

<u>All day long</u> I [*sc.* Hephæstus] fell downward and <u>at the same
time as the sun set</u>
I landed on Lemnos; there was only a little bit of life left in me.
There the <u>Sintian men</u> immediately cared for me after my fall.

In addition to the obvious verbal echoes, one observes that both Hephæstus and the Argonauts spend an entire day in traveling to Lemnos and arrive at sunset; both travel to Lemnos from a mountain (Athos and Olympus); and both are cared for by the Sintian people. Homer, however, expressly states that the Sintian men (ἄνδρες) cared for the ailing god, whereas the hale Argonauts will be welcomed and entertained by the Sintian women (γυναικῶν). The witty *oppositio in imitando* provides a fine transition to the Lemnian episode. By describing the Argonautic journey in a way recalling that of Hephæstus and by having the female inhabitants entertain their guests, Apollonius brings to mind the favor that the Sintian men performed for Hephæstus when he fell to their island. As it turns out, the Argonauts will repay the earlier favor by playing a part in the restoration of the Sintian men through the intervention of Hephæstus's wife, Aphrodite, who encourages the sexual encounters between the Argonauts and the Lemnian women:

Καὶ δ' αὐτοὺς ξεινοῦσθαι ἐπὶ σφεὰ δώματ' ἄγεσκον
ῥηιδίως· Κύπρις γὰρ ἐπὶ γλυκὺν ἵμερον ὦρσεν
Ἡφαίστοιο χάριν πολυμήτιος, ὄφρα κεν αὖτις
ναίηται μετόπισθεν ἀκήρατος ἀνδράσι Λῆμνος.
(849–52)

Easily the women led them back to their homes
to entertain them; for Cypris had cast pleasant desire upon them
as a favor for Hephæstus, so that once again in the future
Lemnos would be made whole with the restoration of its male population.

As in the imitation of the Herodotean narrative, the allusive reference to Hephæstus's fall to Lemnos provides the background for the action about to unfold: Hephæstus would be pleased by Aphrodite's favor (i.e., the restoration of the Sintian men) because they nursed him back to health after his fall to the island.[30]

DESPITE the structural asymmetry of the episode, the two phases of the journey to Lemnos are connected by an extremely fine subtextual thread, the anger that Thetis harbors toward her husband, Peleus.[31] This is the unexpressed contact between the focal point of the first phase and the problem with the winds in the first part of the second. Fränkel, commenting on the sacrifice to Dolops's shade, observed in passing that the sacrifice of Iphigeneia was the

---

30. Reference to the fall of Hephæstus within a larger context involving Thetis brings to mind the alternative version of this story according to which Thetis played a part in the rescue of Hephæstus after his fall from Olympus (*Il.* 18. 394–405; cf. also *h. Ap.* 317–21, Apollodorus 1.3.5 [the latter passage implies that Thetis saved Hephæstus near Lemnos]; on Thetis in general, see Roscher 5.785–99, s.v. "Thetis"). If Apollonius intended the reader to recall Thetis's role in the saving of Hephæstus, one might infer that he wanted to suggest two different aspects of Thetis, one who saves and one who, when angered, is very dangerous. Such a dual nature not only suits the Lemnian women, who both have killed the entire male population of their island and will soon offer hospitality to Jason's crew, but even more to the point, I believe, the equally benevolent and malevolent Thetis parallels the other woman Jason will encounter in the poem, Medea, who will prove as useful when wanted as deadly when scorned.

31. In this regard, I find L. M. Slatkin's explanation for the wrath of Thetis alluded to by Homer most intriguing (see "The Wrath of Thetis," *TAPhA* 116 [1986] 1–24); she identifies the "primary cause of her suffering" as her forced marriage with the mortal Peleus. As chance would have it, I selected the title of this chapter before reading Slatkin's article.

best-known example of a sacrifice forced on travelers experiencing problems with the winds.[32] There is more than a general similarity to the sacrifice of Iphigeneia here. I would suggest that Apollonius wanted the reader to envisage Jason's problem with the winds at Aphetae Argous as the Argonautic analogue to the famous delay at Aulis. As the audience knew well, the Greeks could not leave Aulis because of the lack or adversity of the wind, a situation resulting from the anger of the goddess Artemis. To remedy this impasse, Agamemnon sacrificed his own daughter. The Argonauts too encounter a problem with the winds, the strong headwinds that plagued sailors in this area. Through his suggestive narrative, Apollonius prompts the reader to see an angry goddess behind the Argonauts' problem with the winds. This goddess would have prevented the *Argo* from sailing and thus from creating another situation comparable to her own. But sacrificial offerings calm the obstructing winds, and history is allowed to repeat itself. For, like Agamemnon upon his return to Greece, Jason will encounter future problems with his wife over their children. These parallels, unlike those observed in the episode at Pagasae, do not bode well for leader of the Argonautic expedition.

Finally, the poet has even provided an ingenious verbal indication that he had the delay at Aulis in mind. The first phase of the journey concluded with Orpheus's song to Artemis and a simile comparing the effect of his song (the attraction of fish who follow the ship) to a shepherd leading his sheep back to his tent; their progress suddenly comes to a halt because of the winds, and they pull into the site that will later be called Aphetae Argous. As it happens, while the Argonauts are heading toward Aphetae Argous, the shepherd and his flock are going εἰς αὖλιν (577).[33]

---

32. Fränkel 87 n. 163.
33. For a more detailed analysis of this point, cf. "Two Curious Reflections" (supra n. 28) 196–98. If I am correct in my suggestion that the Apollo-Artemis pairing represents the various relationships Jason has with women, then the subtextual presence of the angry Artemis constitutes another significant connection with the first half of the episode.

6

ἢ νῆσος ἢ νόστος

Sojourn on Lemnos (*Argo.* 1.609–909)

AFTER leaving their "Aulis," the Argonauts sail to the island of Lemnos and encounter the first foreign threat to the expedition, the Lemnian women. The Argonautic sojourn on Lemnos was a popular story before Apollonius, and several different versions survive, both *in toto* and in fragmentary form; most noteworthy are those of Pindar's *Pythian* 4, Æschylus's *Lemniades* and *Hypsipyle*, Euripides' *Hypsipyle*, and the *Argonautica* of Cleon of Curion.[1] None of these versions, however, has had as much influence on Apollonius's rendition of this story as Odysseus's comparable encounters with women living on islands in the *Odyssey*. After choosing to place the stopover on their way to Colchis (as in Euripides *Hypsipyle* fr. 64.93 Bond) and not on their way back (as in Pindar *P.* 4.252ff.), through subtle imitation of select Homeric texts Apollonius casts Hypsipyle in the roles of Calypso, Nausicaa, and Circe; and like these Odyssean heroines, the Lemnian queen's love for Jason and her desire to have him remain as her husband threatens the continuation of his mission, even before the *Argo* leaves the Ægean Sea. In the creation of this remarkable

---

1. Apollonius's dependence on these earlier accounts has received considerable attention; cf. Blumberg 15; H. Faerber, "Zur dichterischen Kunst in Apollonios Rhodios' *Argonautica* (Die Gleichnisse)" (diss. Berlin 1932) 8off. (Pindar); F. Stössl, *Apollonios Rhodios: Interpretationen zur Erzählungskunst und Quellenverwertung* (Bern 1941) 26ff.; W. Bahrenfuss, "Die Abenteuer der Argonauten auf Lemnos bei Apollonios Rhodios (Argo. 1.601 bis 909), Valerius Flaccus (Argo. 2.72 bis 430), Papinius Statius (Theb. 4.746 bis 5.498)" (diss. Kiel 1951) 242; A. Ardizzoni, "Echi pitagorici in Apollonio Rodio e Callimaco," *RFIC* 63 (1965) 261ff.; and Vian 25–28.

contaminatio, Apollonius has also interwoven several other subsidiary themes (the contrast between male and female and that between the man of strength and the man of skill) and referred to other texts, which render the episode unusually complex.

In the present chapter I shall consider the first of three episodes —the sojourns on Lemnos, in Cyzicus, and in Mysia—that comprise, roughly speaking, the second half of Book 1. Since Heracles will leave the group in the final episode of the book, these are the only opportunities the reader will have for comparing Heracles and Jason in action at the same time and place. In each episode Apollonius continues his focus on the contrast between Jason's and Heracles' approach to the expedition. How they operate will ultimately decide the identity and nature of the best of the Argonauts.

STRUCTURE

The structure of this episode is the most complex seen thus far.[2] Nonetheless, it should become clear to anyone reading this section of the first book, even for the first time, that the description of Jason's cloak lies at the center of the Lemnian narrative and accordingly cuts the episode into two parts of roughly comparable length (609–720, 112 lines; 774–909, 136 lines: the central section of the episode thus extends from 721 to 773, 53 lines).[3] As we have seen in the earlier episodes of Book 1, elements in the first half are reechoed in the second. In the first half (A), after the Argonauts arrive at Lemnos, the women (who in the previous year had killed all the men of the island) decide in assembly to take advantage of their presence and use them to restore the male segment of their population. As the episode begins we are given an account of the murder of all the men on the island at the hands of the women (a, 609–39). This subsection itself assumes the ring format with balanced pictures of the male (α) and female (α) warriors of Lemnos bracketing mention of Hypsipyle's rescue of her father, Thoas, from the general slaughter (β). After a brief description of the women rushing out of the city to ward off the Argonauts,

---

2. I owe many of the corresponsions recorded in this summary to Hurst 58–62.
3. Besides Hurst 58, see also Blumberg 17.

whom they believe to be Thracian invaders (b, 633–39), which description lies at the center of this first half, Apollonius gives us a picture of the Lemnian women in assembly (a, 640–720). The narrative of the assembly, like that of the Lemnian slaughter (a), also exhibits a ring-composed structure: the embassy of the Argonaut Æthalides, whose μῦθοι are not reported (α), balances the embassy of Iphinoë, whose μῦθοι are repeated almost verbatim (α). In between comes the actual assembly (β), at which the elderly Polyxo argues that the women must act by seducing the Argonauts, since in the future, when all the women are old, the cattle will not plow the fields by themselves (αὐτόματοι βόες).

The two tripartite subsections of the first half (Aa and Aa) correspond in two significant ways. First, both central sections are framed by male-female oppositions (male warriors–female warriors in the first; male messenger–female messenger in the second); and second, the central panel of each section has as its focus the theme of salvation through marriage: in the first subsection Apollonius recounts the salvation of Hypsipyle's father, Thoas, who marries the Næad Œnoeë; at the heart of the second subsection, Hypsipyle's nurse, Polyxo, suggests marriage with the Argonauts as the way to save their people.

The second half (A) unfolds in the extended ring format. The arrival of Jason in the city (a) corresponds with his departure (a);[4] a conversation with Hypsipyle in which the queen gives her account of the Lemnian crime and offers Jason her kingdom (b) is balanced by a second conversation, in which she reiterates her offer and Jason repeats his refusal (b); the procession of the Argonauts into the city of Myrine (c) is echoed by their departure from the city, on which occasion the Lemnian women rush out after them (c). In the center is the assembly of the Argonauts (d), at which Heracles urges the Argonauts to act by leaving Lemnos and continuing with the journey to Colchis; for, he argues, the gods will not on their own present the Argonauts with the fleece (αὐτόματον

---

4. Although mention of Jason's departure appears to belong to the next section of the book in that there is no clear division between his and the Argonauts' embarkation (910b–12a) and the following journey to Samothrace, which certainly belongs to the next episode, nonetheless his sudden withdrawal from Hypsipyle clearly balances his slow and ceremonious arrival.

κῶας). The corresponsion between the two halves of the episode (A ≈ A) now becomes clear: in each there is an account of the Lemnian crime (that of Hypsipyle and that of the narrator), the women are seen to rush out of the city (once to ward off and once to retain the Argonauts), and finally there is an assembly (that of the Lemnian women and that of the Argonauts) in which a featured speaker (Polyxo, Heracles) urges the group to action because the animal associated with their goals (draught oxen in one case and the golden fleece of Phrixus's ram in the other) will not function independently of them.

In the center of the episode lies the ecphrasis on Jason's cloak (B). This too reveals a carefully balanced structure. Jason's taking up of the cloak (a) and of his spear (a) frame the description of the seven scenes on the cloak (b), which Apollonius has arranged in an extended ring. The first scene (α: the Cyclopes) and the last scene (α: Phrixus and the ram) accentuate visual and aural qualities of the artistic creations of Hephæstus and Athena, respectively. Amphion and Zethus (β) are balanced by Apollo and Tityus (β) in that both scenes entail the victory of skill over strength. Aphrodite with Ares' shield (γ) and the corresponding scene depicting Pelops's race with Œnomaus to win the hand of Hippodamia (γ) are both concerned with the power of love. In the middle Apollonius has set an instance of the quest motif, the Mycenæans' expedition to get back cattle they believe to be rightfully theirs from the sons of Electryon (δ).

The structure of the episode as a whole, then, runs as follows:

Sojourn on Lemnos, 609–909

A. Arrival and Prelude to the Encounter (609–720)
   a. Account of the Lemnian Crime (609–32)
      α. Lemnian Warriors (Male)
         Reject Aphrodite
      β. The Saving of Thoas
      α. Lemnian Warriors (Female)
         Reject Athena
   b. The Women Rush out of the City (633–39)

      a. Assembly of Women   (640–720)
         α. Embassy of Æthalides: Unreported μῦθοι
         β. Assembly: Speech of Polyxo: αὐτόματοι βόες
         α. Embassy of Iphincë: Reported μῦθοι

B. Jason's Cloak   (721–73)
    a. Jason Dons his Cloak   (721–29)
    b. Ecphrasis on the Cloak   (730–67)
         α. Cyclopes: Visual Quality Emphasized
         β. Amphion and Zethus: Brawn Versus Skill (Lyre)
         γ. Aphrodite with Ares' Shield: Love
         δ. The Teleboan Expedition: The Quest
         γ. Pelops and Hippodamia: Love
         β. Apollo-Tityus: Brawn Versus Skill (Bow)
         α. Phrixus and the Ram: Aural Quality Emphasized
    a. Jason Takes Up His Spear   (768–73)

A. The Encounter and Departure   (774–909)
    a. Jason Arrives   (774–92)
    b. Conversation between Jason and Hypsipyle: Second Account of the Lemnian Crime; Offer and Refusal of the Kingdom   (793–841)
    c. The Argonauts Go to Myrine   (842–60)
    d. Assembly of the Argonauts: Speech of Heracles: αὐτόματον κῶας   (861–74)
    c. The Argonauts Leave Myrine; the Women Rush out of the City   (875–85)
    b. Conversation between Jason and Hypsipyle: Second Offer and Refusal of the Kingdom   (886–909)
    [*a.* Jason Departs   (910a)]

A. Arrival and Prelude to the Encounter (609-720)

The episode begins with an account of the murder of the Lemnian men (a). Apollonius fashioned this introductory material in a way that places special emphasis on the one exception to the slaughter: Hypsipyle's rescue of her father, Thoas, by setting him adrift in a chest (λάρναξ).[5] To expand slightly on what was said above, in the first section (α), Apollonius describes the situation leading up to the murder of the men (609-19; 11 lines): the Lemnian warriors (male), smitten with a harsh love (τρηχὺν ἔρον, 613) for their captive Thracian women, fell at the hands of their jealous wives as a punishment for dishonoring Aphrodite.[6] In the third section (α), he describes the result of that murder: the women, rejecting the tasks associated with Athena, have taken on the jobs previously reserved for men—tending the flocks, plowing the fields, and waging war. At the sight of the *Argo*, the Lemnian warriors (now female), expecting an attack from Thracian invaders (627-39; 13 lines), instead encounter the Argonauts, who will soon enter their town and their bedrooms in peace. In the central position lies the description of Thoas's rescue, escape, and marriage with Œnoëë (β, 620-26). As we have seen at the end of the previous chapter, the poet's imitation of Hephæstus's fall to Lemnos in the description of the *Argo*'s journey from mainland Greece to the island called to mind the god's rescue by the Lemnian men. This clever inversion of gender is an appropriate transition to the present episode, at the beginning of which Apollonius depicts the Lemnian women assuming masculine roles; for the exchange of role is neatly reflected in the manner in which Hypsipyle saved her father, the central focus of the first subsection.

All accounts of the Lemnian crime are unanimous in making Thoas the only man to escape the general slaughter of the male population of the island. But there is disagreement among the

---

5. Vian's beginning of a new paragraph at 633 is confusing. In the presentation of these lines, Fränkel (OCT) and Ardizzoni more correctly, I believe, see lines 633-39 as closely connected with the introductory material; cf. Fränkel *ad* 1.630b-39.

6. See Blumberg 15-16 and Vian 26-27, who argue convincingly that Aphrodite was angry with the Lemnian men, and not the women as supposed by Σ *ad* 1.609-19a, Ardizzoni *ad* 614, Levin 62, and, most recently, B. Pavlock, *Eros, Imitation, and the Epic Tradition* (Ithaca 1990) 46.

several extant versions of this story about what happened to Thoas after Hypsipyle saved him.⁷ Either the Lemnian women discover and kill him (Apollodorus 3.6.4, Herodotus 4.145, hypothesis *ad* Pindar *Nem.*, p. 424 Boeckh) or he escapes from the island in a vessel of some sort (Apollonius, Val. Flac. 2.242–310, Statius *Theb.* 5.284–91). In the latter case, he either goes to the land of the Taurians (Val. Flac., Hyginus 120), to Sikinos (Apollonius, Xenagoras *FGrHist* 240 F 31; cf. Σ *ad* 1.623–26a), or to Chios (Statius). According to one version in which Thoas was discovered and killed, Hypsipyle had hidden him in a chest (κιβωτός; cf. hypothesis *ad* Pindar *N.*), which the Lemnian women then threw into the sea. It would thus appear that Apollonius combined two contradictory accounts: Thoas escapes successfully to Sikinos, but not in a boat; instead his daughter sets him adrift in a chest, significantly described here as a λάρναξ:

> Οἴη δ' ἐκ πασέων γεραροῦ περιφείσατο πατρὸς
> ῾Υψιπύλεια Θόαντος ὃ δὴ κατὰ δῆμον ἄνασσε·
> λάρνακι δ' ἐν κοίλῃ μιν ὕπερθ' ἁλὸς ἧκε φέρεσθαι,
> αἴ κε φύγῃ.
>
> (620–23a)
>
> Of all the women, Hypsipyle alone spared her old father,
> Thoas, who held sway over the people.
> She set him adrift over the sea in a hollow chest
> with the hope that he might escape.

In all likelihood, Apollonius was influenced by the story of Danaë and Perseus. Danaë's father, Acrisius, likewise set her and her infant son, Perseus, adrift in a λάρναξ (cf. λάρνακι ἐν δαιδαλέᾳ, Simonides *PMG* 543.1–2), and the two were rescued by fishermen on the island of Seriphos (cf. Æschylus, *Dictyulci* fr. 464 Radt). Like Danaë and Perseus, Thoas survived the perilous journey and, after being rescued by fishermen, married the nymph after whom the island was named prior to the birth of their son, Sicinus:⁸

> Καὶ τὸν μὲν ἐς Οἰνοίην ἐρύσαντο
> πρόσθεν, ἀτὰρ Σίκινόν γε μεθύστερον αὐδηθεῖσαν

---

7. Cf. Immisch, "Thoas (1a)," Roscher 5.803–8.
8. Pavlock (supra n. 6) 46 sees another gender reversal in the renaming of the island Sicinus (male) from Œnoeë (female).

νῆσον, ἐπακτῆρες, Σικίνου ἄπο, τόν ῥα Θόαντι
Νηιὰς Οἰνοίη Νύμφη τέκεν εὐνηθεῖσα.
(623b-26)

     And fishermen pulled him ashore
onto an island, formerly Œnoëë, afterwards called Sikinos
from the Sicinus whom the naiad Œnoëë bore
to Thoas after the young woman went to his bed.

  The question now arises: Was Hypsipyle's motive completely honorable? Fathers traditionally exposed children in chests on the sea, especially unmarried daughters discovered to be pregnant. The motive was to escape the pollution of parricide while at the same time to do away with their children.[9] Consonant with the Lemnian women's role reversal, Hypsipyle assumes here the role of a father who refuses to kill his own child but acquiesces in the inevitability of its death. In mythic accounts of such exposures it is usually sexual indiscretion and the birth of illegitimate children that occasion the abandonment to death. And it is precisely such indiscretion and illegitimacy that Hypsipyle reports as reasons for the absence of men on Lemnos when she recounts the story to Jason in the second version of the Lemnian crime (cf. 798-826). The suggestive inversion of the exposure motif at the very least brings Thoas's innocence into question. Moreover, Hypsipyle confirms her usurpation of her father's role when she dons his armor (637-38), sits on his throne (667), and offers his kingdom (827-29). As a result of the Lemnian crime, women now perform the functions of men. A daughter even appears to expose her father for his sexual encounters.

  After the introductory triptych explaining the absence of the Lemnian men, Apollonius briefly depicts the panic among the Lemnian women as the *Argo* approaches (b). The women rush down to the shore (προχέοντο, 635), dressed in armor like Thyades because they imagine that the Argonauts are Thracians come to invade the island. This event is echoed in the second half of the episode, when the Lemniades once again rush down to the shore (προχέοντο, 883), but this time to bid the Argonauts farewell (*A*c).

---

9. See *TGL* s.v. λάρναξ: "Puellas vitiatas cum adulteriis vel infantibus in λάρνακι in mare proiectas."

In their first rush to the shore, the women are portrayed in a traditionally male role as they prepare to ward off the Argonauts; in the corresponding section, they will be seen to have reverted to their earlier female roles when Apollonius subtly suggests that they will become the mothers of the Argonauts' children.

In the third section of the first half (a), Apollonius sets the scene for the encounter between Jason and Hypsipyle. The Argonauts send their herald, Æthalides, a son of Hermes endowed with an imperishable memory, to ask permission to stay the night. The next day, however, the opposing north winds prevent them from leaving (α, 640–52; 13 lines).[10] The women then meet in assembly. On the advice of Polyxo, they decide to invite the men into the city in the hope of reestablishing the male community. Hypsipyle thereupon instructs Iphinoë to approach the leader of the group, inviting him to speak with her in Myrine while the rest of the Argonauts have her permission to avail themselves of the island (β, 653–708). Iphinoë delivers Hypsipyle's invitation, and the Argonauts happily accept (α, 709–20; 12 lines). The embassy of Æthalides clearly corresponds with that of Iphinoë,[11] and the assembly of the Lemnian women falls in the central position between them.

In addition to the contrast between male and female in the framing elements, which parallels the format of the introductory narrative (a), Apollonius, as mentioned above, records each herald's embassy in a contrastive fashion. He does not report Æthalides' speech to Hypsipyle and the Lemnian women (Ἀλλὰ τί μύθους / Αἰθαλίδεω χρεώ με διηνεκέως ἀγορεύειν; 648–49) but focuses instead on the imperishable memory of the Argonaut.[12] On the other

---

10. *Pace* Σ *ad* 1.652, who sees them remaining despite the blasts of the north wind; see Mooney *ad* 1.651–52, Vian 257 *ad* 652, and A. Ardizzoni, "'Trappole' e infortuni apolloniani," *GIF* 30 (1978) 276–78. Cf. Stössl (supra n. 1) 31ff., who sees this as one of the seams that reveals Apollonius's model, Æschylus's *Hypsipyle*.
11. It may not be coincidental that the name Ὑψιπύλη occurs in both sections (α and α) three lines from the end.
12. Ardizzoni (supra n. 1) 264 puts too much emphasis on this phrase. Like Stössl, he believes that Apollonius's model was Æschylus's *Hypsipyle*; the interruption, he concludes, is an allusion to a speech by this character in the play. Yet once again the Homeric and not the Æschylean model appears to be of greater importance, given the fact that Apollonius describes Æthalides' fabulous memory in terms reminiscent of both Tiresias (644–45 ≈ *Od.* 10.490–95; cf. Vian 257 *ad* 646) and the Dioscuri (647–48 ≈ *Od.* 11.302–4; cf.

hand, he has Iphinoë repeat Hypsipyle's message almost verbatim. After the assembled women decide to welcome the Argonauts into the city with the hope of luring them into their beds (cf. 695), the poet continues:

Ἡ ῥα καὶ Ἰφινόην προσεφώνεεν ἆσσον ἐοῦσαν·
'Ὄρσο μοι, Ἰφινόη, τοῦδ' ἀνέρος ἀντιόωσα
ἡμέτερον δὲ μολεῖν ὅς τις στόλου ἡγεμονεύει,
ὄφρα τί οἱ δήμοιο ἔπος θυμηδὲς ἐνίσπω·
καὶ δ' αὐτοὺς γαίης τε καὶ ἄστεος, αἴ κ' ἐθέλωσι,
κέκλεο θαρσαλέως ἐπιβαινέμεν εὐμενέοντας.'
(702-7)

She [*sc.* Hypsipyle] said this and then addressed Iphinoë, who was close at hand:
"Go quickly, Iphinoë, and ask the man
who leads this expedition to come to our home so that
I might announce to him the decision of our people, which I am sure will
please him; and tell the others they can disembark without fear and
come into the city, if they so desire and their intentions are friendly."

Iphinoë's embassy provides one of the few instances in which Apollonius repeats several lines of text.[13] Iphinoë gives a close, but not perfect, rendition of Hypsipyle's message:

Κούρη τοι μ' ἐφέηκε Θοαντιὰς ἐνθάδ' ἰοῦσαν
'Ὑψιπύλη καλέειν νηὸς πρόμον ὅς τις ὄρωρεν,
ὄφρα τί οἱ δήμοιο ἔπος θυμηδὲς ἐνίσπῃ·
καὶ δ' αὐτοὺς γαίης τε καὶ ἄστεος, αἴ κ' ἐθέλητε,
κέκλεται αὐτίκα νῦν ἐπιβαινέμεν εὐμενέοντας.
(712-16)

Mooney *ad* 1.647, Vian 80 n. 3, and Campbell *ad* 1.647ff.) as described in the Nekyia. Like Tiresias, Æthalides retains his memory even in Hades; like the Dioscuri, he lives now in Hades and now among the living. There may be a lighthearted passing reference to the quasi-technical phrase Πυθαγορικοὶ μῦθοι (as Ardizzoni ibid. 264 n. 1), but this gives way to the narrator's interest in reported μῦθοι in the episode; see below.
13. See G. W. Elderkin, "Repetitions in the *Argonautica* of Apollonius," *AJP* 34 (1913) 198-201.

Hypsipyle, the daughter of Thoas, has ordered me to come here
to summon the captain of the ship, whoever he is, so that she
might announce to him the decision of our people, which she is
    sure will
please him; and to tell you others to disembark right now and
come into the city, if you so desire and your intentions are friendly.

The female herald, whose name implies strength or force of mind, slightly edits her message, unlike, it would seem, her male counterpart in the first embassy. In place of θαρσαλέως, Iphinoë states that the Argonauts are invited to come αὐτίκα νῦν. Iphinoë, then, like Hypsipyle in her version of the Lemnian slaughter, speaks μύθοισι αἱμυλίοισι (cf. 792) in order to encourage the Argonauts to enter the city as soon as possible.[14]

Hypsipyle opens the assembly, which these two contrasting embassies frame in the center of the subsection (β), by inviting a discussion on the problem of what to do with the Argonauts, who are as yet unaware of the situation on Lemnos. After suggesting that they keep them away from the city by giving them supplies for their journey, she concludes by inviting other suggestions:[15]

ὑμέων δ' <u>εἴ τις ἄρειον ἔπος μητίσεται</u> ἄλλη,
ἐγρέσθω· τοῦ γάρ τε καὶ εἴνεκα δεῦρο κάλεσσα.
                              (665–66)

If <u>any</u> other among you <u>can come up with a better idea</u>,
let her stand up; for this reason I summoned you here.

The scholiast *ad* 1.665 noted that Hypsipyle's openness to other proposals was modeled after a similar request made by Agamemnon in the *Iliad*:[16]

---

14. Fränkel *ad* 1.709–20 (cf. also p. 98 n. 188) suggests that the repetition serves Hypsipyle's ruse; she did not want Jason to know too much, but wanted to give him her own explanation for the absence of the men. E. George, "Poet and Characters in Apollonius Rhodius' Lemnian Episode," *Hermes* 100 (1972) 57, argues that Apollonius wanted to underscore the nervousness of the Lemnian women in their invitation by having Iphinoë slightly confuse the message.

15. See Giangrande 11 on the sense of ἐγρέσθω in 666.

16. None of the commentaries acknowledge this imitation. Yet Apollonius has not only echoed the idea of the Iliadic passage, but has also played with the sound of his model: εἴ τις ≈ εἴη ὅς τῇσδε; ἄρειον ≈ ἀμείνονα; ἔπος ≈

νῦν δ' εἴη ὃς τῆσδέ γ' ἀμείνονα μῆτιν ἐνίσποι
ἢ νέος ἠὲ παλαιός· ἐμοὶ δέ κεν ἀσμένῳ εἴη.
(*Il.* 14.107–8)

I wish someone would now come up with a better idea than this, either young or old. This would please me.

When Agamemnon invited anyone, young or old, to suggest a plan in the wake of their defeat at the hands of Hector, Diomedes, first excusing his youthfulness (ibid. 110–27), advised immediate action. Polyxo similarly calls for immediate action in the case of the unexpected arrival of the Argonauts (693–96). Not only does Hypsipyle's elderly nurse contrast with Diomedes in gender and age, but even in the nature of her advice; she speaks of surrendering themselves and their homes to the Argonauts, while Diomedes advocates a more aggressive approach in their war against the Trojans. The change of advice from an immediate attack in the battlefield to immediate submission in bed is as striking as it is suggestive of the importance that love will play in the present episode and in the epic in general.

The inversion of this Iliadic model parallels the adaptation of an Odyssean text that immediately follows. Once Hypsipyle sits down on her father's throne after her brief address to the assembly, the elderly Polyxo rises to speak, surrounded by four aging maidens:[17]

Ὣς ἄρ' ἔφη καὶ θῶκον ἐφίζανε πατρὸς ἑοῖο
λάινον. Αὐτὰρ ἔπειτα φίλη τροφὸς ὦρτο Πολυξώ,
γήραϊ δὴ ῥικνοῖσιν ἐπισκάζουσα πόδεσσι,
βάκτρῳ ἐρειδομένη, πέρι δὲ μενέαιν' ἀγορεῦσαι·
τῇ καὶ παρθενικαὶ πίσυρες σχεδὸν ἑδριόωντο
ἀδμῆτες, λευκῇσιν ἐπιχοάουσαι ἐθείραις.

ἐνίσποι; μητίσεται ≈ μῆτιν. In the last two cases, Apollonius has inverted the syntax by making a noun of the Homeric verb and a verb of the Homeric noun.

17. G. Giangrande, "Polisemia del linguaggio nella poesia alessandrina," *QUCC* 24 (1977) 98–99, however, has argued that the λευκῇσιν ... ἐθείραις (672) of these women refer not to their gray hair, but to the crests of their helmets; that is, they are still dressed in their armor. Ardizzoni (supra n. 10) 280 countered that the use of ἔθειραι in the sense of human hair (found in the Homeric corpus only at *h. Ven.* 228) is an example of an "*unicum* semantico dell' 'Omero minore.'" As Ardizzoni stated, the presence of graying virgins here has an important symbolic value.

Στῆ δ' ἄρ' ἐνὶ μέσσῃ ἀγορῇ, ἀνὰ δ' ἔσχεθε δειρὴν
ἦκα μόλις <u>κυφοῖο</u> μεταφρένου ὧδέ τ' ἔειπε.
(667-74)

Thus she spoke, and <u>she sat down on her father's seat</u>
of stone. Then Polyxo, her beloved nurse, arose,
moving haltingly on legs twisted <u>from age</u> and
leaning on her cane; she was most eager to address the assembly.
Alongside her sat four young women,
unmarried girls whose hair was beginning to turn gray.
She stood in the middle of the assembly and could barely hold
her neck up, her back was so badly <u>crippled</u>. She said the
    following.

The scholiast *ad* 1.669 was the first to observe that Apollonius had a specific Homeric passage in mind, in this case from the second book of the *Odyssey*:[18]

<u>ἕζετο</u> δ' ἐν <u>πατρὸς θώκῳ</u>, εἶξαν δὲ γέροντες.
τοῖσι δ' ἔπειθ' ἥρως Αἰγύπτιος ἦρχ' ἀγορεύειν,
ὃς <u>δὴ γήραϊ κυφὸς</u> ἔην καὶ μυρία ᾔδη.
καὶ γὰρ τοῦ φίλος υἱὸς ἅμ' ἀντιθέῳ Ὀδυσῆι
Ἴλιον εἰς εὔπωλον ἔβη κοίλῃς ἐνὶ νηυσίν,
Ἄντιφος αἰχμητής· τὸν δ' ἄγριος ἔκτανε Κύκλωψ
ἐν σπῆϊ γλαφυρῷ, πύματον δ' ὁπλίσσατο δόρπον.
τρεῖς δέ οἱ ἄλλοι ἔσαν, καὶ ὁ μὲν μνηστῆρσιν ὁμίλει,
Εὐρύνομος, δύο δ' αἰὲν ἔχον πατρώϊα ἔργα·
(*Od.* 2.14-22)

He [*sc.* Telemachus] <u>sat down on his father's throne</u> and the elders
    yielded.
The hero Ægyptus was the first to speak among them,
a man who was <u>crippled from age</u> and knew countless things.
For his own dear son went together with godlike Odysseus
to horse-rich Ilion in the hollow ships,
the warrior Antiphus. The savage Cyclops killed him
in his cavernous home, the one whom he ate last.
Yet there were three other sons, and one associated with the
    suitors,
Eurynomus, while the other two stayed on their father's farm.

---

18. Noted among modern commentators by Campbell *ad* 1.667ff. Moreover, κυφός is a Homeric *hapax legomenon*.

In the Homeric passage, Telemachus called the first assembly held in Ithaca since the departure of Odysseus for Troy twenty years earlier. As Telemachus sits on his father's throne, the aged Ægyptus, who was the father of four sons, asks the reason for the assembly. He imagines that there must be the threat of an invading army (ibid. 25–34).[19] Here we can observe several points of contact with the Argonautic text:

- Hypsipyle, the daughter of the king, calls an assembly just as does Telemachus, the son of Ithaca's king, Odysseus.
- Both Telemachus and Hypsipyle are portrayed as seated on their fathers' thrones.
- The aged Polyxo is the female counterpart of the aged Ægyptus.
- The four maidens with Polyxo parallel the four sons of Ægyptus.
- Invading armies are the apparent concern of both assemblies.

Moreover, both assemblies take up the issue of prospective marriages: the Lemnian women debate marriage with the Argonauts, while in the Ithacan assembly, marriage with Penelope lies at the heart of the problem for which the people were convened. In both this and in the previous Iliadic reference, Apollonius contrasts the Lemnian women with Homeric males, a contrast that reflects the gender opposition of the surrounding frame (Æthalides-Iphinoë).

By counterposing Lemnian and Argonautic men with Lemnian women in the structure of the subsections, and by inverting the gender of the exposure motif and the Homeric models, Apollonius pits male against female in the first half of the episode. The gender antithesis neatly reflects the role reversal of the Lemnian women, which lies at the heart of the story. These armed warriors, highlighted at the center of the first half, will threaten the continuation of the Argonautic mission. As will become clear in the second half of the episode, the poet will imply through allusion to well-known Homeric texts that the Argonauts are in danger of becoming less than men because of their association with the masculine women of Lemnos.

---

19. Cf. W. B. Stanford, *The Odyssey of Homer* (London 1950) vol. 1 *ad* 2.30.

B. Jason's Cloak (721–73)

Apollonius frames the elaborate description of Jason's cloak, which lies at the center of the episode, with balancing descriptions of Jason taking up his cloak (a) and his spear (*a*). Two elements confirm the corresponsion of these subsections, which thereby create a ring. In the first line of the first paragraph (a), Apollonius identifies the cloak as the work of Itonian Athena—θεᾶς 'Ιτωνίδος ἔργον (721). These words are echoed in the first line of the second paragraph (*a*) with the phrase θεᾶς Ἰτωνίδος ἦεν Ἀθήνης (768). Second, in each of the corresponding subsections Apollonius mentions that the items that Jason takes up are gifts: Athena gave him the cloak (τήν οἱ ὅπασσε / Παλλάς, 722–23), and Atalante the spear (ὅ ῥ' Ἀταλάντη / Μαινάλῳ ἔν ποτέ οἱ ξεινήιον ἐγγυάλιξε, 769–70). As Vian has pointed out, Jason's preparations to meet Hypsipyle not only recall the typical Homeric arming scene but possibly have special reference to the lines in which Agamemnon prepared himself for battle at the beginning of *Iliad* 11.[20] The neatly balanced enclosure for the ecphrasis thus prompts the reader to imagine that Jason is arming himself for battle. Indeed, the ecphrasis by itself suggests the same thing.

Apollonius modeled his ecphrasis on the famous description of the shield that Hephæstus made for Achilles in *Iliad* 18. Not only does Apollonius employ the formulaic ἐν μέν ... ἐν δέ that characterizes the description of the Iliadic shield,[21] but he also includes an allusive reference to its creator. Hephæstus was busy working on one of his projects the moment Thetis arrived seeking armor for her son,[22] and, in the very first scene of the cloak, Apollonius reminds the reader of this visit in his suggestive vignette of the Cyclopes at work on a thunderbolt that needs only one ray to be finished:

Ἐν μὲν ἔσαν Κύκλωπες ἐπ' ἀφθίτῳ ἥμενοι ἔργῳ,
Ζηνὶ κεραυνὸν ἄνακτι πονεύμενοι· ὃς τόσσον ἤδη
παμφαίνων ἐτέτυκτο, μιῆς δ' ἔτι δεύετο μοῦνον

---

20. Vian 83 n. 2, 86 n. 3.
21. See Mooney *ad* 1.730–68, Ardizzoni *ad* 730ff., Vian 84 n. 2, and Campbell *ad* 1.730ff. As Vian points out, the Hesiodic *Aspis* employs this same cataloguing technique.
22. See Mooney *ad* 1.731, Vian 258 *ad* 734.

ἀκτῖνος, τὴν οἵ γε σιδηρείης ἐλάασκον
σφύρῃσιν, μαλεροῖο πυρὸς ζείουσαν ἀυτμήν.
(730-34)

On it there were Cyclopes engrossed in their immortal work of forging a thunderbolt for Lord Zeus. Its brilliance had already been achieved, though it still needed only one more ray; this, a seething blast of raging fire, they were in the act of hammering out with their iron mallets.

In the *Iliad*, Hephæstus was working on twenty tripods, which similarly still needed their handles:

τὸν δ' εὗρ' ἱδρώοντα ἑλισσόμενον περὶ φύσας
σπεύδοντα· τρίποδας γὰρ ἐείκοσι πάντας ἔτευχεν
ἑστάμεναι περὶ τοῖχον ἐυσταθέος μεγάροιο,
χρύσεα δέ σφ' ὑπὸ κύκλα ἑκάστῳ πυθμένι θῆκεν,
ὄφρα οἱ αὐτόματοι θεῖον δυσαίατ' ἀγῶνα
ἠδ' αὖτις πρὸς δῶμα νεοίατο, θαῦμα ἰδέσθαι.
οἱ δ' ἤτοι τόσσον μὲν ἔχον τέλος, οὔατα δ' οὔ πω
δαιδάλεα προσέκειτο· τά ῥ' ἤρτυε, κόπτε δὲ δεσμούς.
(*Il.* 18.372-79)

She found him [*sc.* Hephæstus] sweating as he moved about the bellows
in haste. He was making tripods, twenty in all,
to stand around the wall of his well-built hall;
he set golden wheels on the base of each
so that they might enter the assembly of the gods on their own[23]
and come back to his home, a marvel to behold.
They were finished up to this point, but the elegantly crafted handles
had not yet been added. He was getting these ready and was hammering the rivets.

There are, it is true, two instances of cloaks embroidered with various scenes in the *Iliad* (for δίπλακα πορφυρέην, 722, see *Il.*

---

23. We may be invited through the recollection of this passage to observe the contrast between Hephæstus's tripods with golden wheels, which move on their own (αὐτόματοι) and the Lemnian oxen as viewed by Polyxo (686) and, more to the point, the golden fleece as viewed by Heracles (871), which do not.

3.125–28, 22.440–41), but it seems clear from Apollonius's inclusion of a forged implement just short of completion in the passage that the poet had Achilles' shield specifically in mind in providing a lengthy, scene-by-scene description of Jason's cloak. The effect of this reference, like the frame of the ecphrasis itself, encourages us to envisage Jason as a warrior going off to battle, and in particular, as a counterpart to Achilles. For Achilles took up his fabulous shield to face Hector and to achieve his greatest victory on the field of battle. What ensues, of course, is quite different.

Apollonius continues the comparison between Achilles and Jason in the beginning of the next section (A), to which I now turn briefly. The poet draws a comparison between Jason's approach to Hypsipyle's palace at Myrine and a star that appears to brides in their chambers or to a maiden awaiting the return of her fiancé who is out of the country. The simile neatly parallels the situation at hand: the Argonauts will soon visit the chambers of the Lemnian women, and Jason, coming from a foreign land, will encounter the virgin Hypsipyle. Three times in the *Iliad*, Homer compared a warrior approaching his opponent to a star, the point of comparison being both its brilliance and its harmfulness (cf. *Il.* 5.4–6, 11.62–64, 22.25–32).[24] The last example is especially relevant to Jason: there Achilles, dressed in his new armor, approached the city of Troy to do battle with Hector.[25] Apollonius has thus set the scene for the meeting between Jason and Hypsipyle in such a way that the reader envisages a climactic military clash between opposing warriors. But instead of such an encounter, we find the well-dressed and urbane Iolcan prince sweeping the young Lemnian queen off her feet.[26] The vivid contrast between the reader's expectations and the actual event is significant. Jason is not an Achilles, who succeeds by virtue of his martial prowess. On the contrary, making young women fall in love with him will prove to be this hero's most potent skill, one

---

24. Cf. A. W. James, "Some Examples of Imitation in the Similes of Later Greek Epic," *Antichthon* 3 (1969) 79–80 (*ad* 3.956ff.); and R. W. Garson, "Homeric Echoes in Apollonius Rhodius's *Argonautica*," *CP* 67 (1972) 8.

25. Noted by Mooney *ad* 1.774, Vian 86 n. 3, and Campbell *ad* 1.774–75.

26. Σ *ad* 1.721–22 has noted the appropriateness of Jason's attire as he goes to meet Hypsipyle.

that will play an important role in establishing him as the best of the Argonauts.²⁷

Before turning to the "heroic" match featured in the second half of the episode, I shall first examine at greater length the individual scenes on the cloak, which Apollonius arranged in an extended ring. These scenes view both the Argonautic expedition and Jason's role in it through a series of icons that reflect salient events ahead for the Argonauts.²⁸

In the first scene (730–34), the Cyclopes are about to finish one of Zeus's thunderbolts, and, as I noted, the poet here deliberately evokes the image of Hephæstus at the time of Thetis's arrival just prior to his forging of Achilles' new armor. Mention of the Cyclopes and of Zeus's weapon picks up where Orpheus's song

---

27. It should not be overlooked that when Odysseus first encountered Nausicaa, a figure with whom Hypsipyle will be compared in this episode, he emerged from the bushes "like a mountain-bred lion"; in this way, says Homer, Odysseus was about to associate with well-tressed young women (*Od.* 6.130–36). Similes such as this normally describe a warrior about to engage in armed conflict.

28. One of the best interpretations of the cloak is still that of Lawall 154ff. I do not, however, fully accept his conclusion that the cloak has a didactic function; for Lawall argues that the cloak teaches Jason piety, charm, the power of love, the tragedy of war, and the effectiveness of intelligence and treachery (154). The poet does not suggest, nor does one ever sense, that Jason understands the significance of the scenes of his cloak. Beye 91–92 and "Jason as Love-Hero in Apollonius' *Argonautica*," *GRBS* 10 (1969) 53, finds in the scenes the rhythm of love and hate that permeates the epic. Levin 68–69 and "Δίπλαξ πορφυρέη," *RFIC* 98 (1970) 17ff., believes that the cloak symbolizes the reliance on persuasion and a more civilized approach in general. Collins 55–85 tried to show how the scenes of the cloak pertained to both the Lemnian episode and the poem as a whole (cf. J. K. Newman, *The Classical Epic Tradition* [Madison 1986] 77–80, who also offers an allegorical interpretation of the scenes). On the other hand, H. A. Shapiro, "Jason's Cloak," *TAPhA* 110 (1980) 263–86, argued, unconvincingly, against reading the scenes in a symbolic or allegorical fashion; he holds that Apollonius was concerned only with representing a work of impressionistic art based on contemporary ideas; cf. Blumberg 18 and Fränkel *ad* 1.725-67(b), who dismiss the possibility of a unifying theme or close interrelationship between the scenes. The two are in no way exclusive. G. O. Hutchinson, *Hellenistic Poetry* (Oxford 1988) 142, while not providing a reading of all the individual scenes, asserts quite correctly that the scenes of the cloak have "an emblematic significance for the whole poem"; cf. Pavlock (supra n. 6) 34, who claims that the ecphrasis is a "symbol of the poem as a whole, [and] reflects the poet's attempt to captivate through style." I would like to explore the relevance of the cloak to the whole poem more closely in what follows.

(496–511) left off: there Zeus did not yet have his thunderbolt, the source of his κῦδος (cf. 509–11). In the scene on the cloak, we observe that Zeus is about to gain possession of the weapon by which he will hold sway in Olympus. The young Zeus in Orpheus's song was seen to parallel the young Jason, who would soon have his first taste of κῦδος as leader of the Argonautic expedition. The parallel between god and hero continues in this first scene on the cloak: as Zeus is about to be armed with the thunderbolt, his special weapon, Jason assumes as his special weapon the cloak that makes him so strikingly handsome to Hypsipyle. She is, after all, the "opponent" whom Apollonius leads us to expect by describing Jason's preparation for and arrival in Myrine in terms of Achilles' arming and his approach to meet Hector in battle. Both weapons, moreover, are brilliant: Zeus's thunderbolt is παμφαίνων (732), while the cloak too is as blinding as the sun:

> Τῆς μὲν ῥηίτερόν κεν ἐς ἠέλιον ἀνιόντα
> ὄσσε βάλοις ἢ κεῖνο μεταβλέψειας ἔρευθος·
> (725–26)
>
> More easily would you cast your eyes into the rising
> sun than gaze upon the cloak's ruddy brilliance.

The two, man and god, are now armed and dangerous. Zeus attains his κῦδος by vanquishing his enemies with his flashing thunderbolt; Jason will succeed in his coming ἀριστεία through his radiant appearance and attire.

The second scene (735–41) features an episode in which the antithesis of strength versus skill once again emerges. In the building of Thebes, the strongman Zethus struggled to lift boulders the size of a mountain peak on his shoulders, whereas Amphion through the sound of his music caused rocks twice as large to move by themselves. The image recalls the contrast between Orpheus and Heracles in the Catalogue: the former had led trees from Pieria to Thracian Zone through the power of song (28–31), while the latter was carrying the Erymanthian boar on his shoulders at the moment that he heard of the Argonautic expedition (124–29). This scene nicely parallels the way in which Jason succeeds in this expedition. For unlike Heracles in his attainment of the golden apples of the Hesperides, Jason will ultimately secure the object of his quest not by virtue of his physical strength, but through Medea's magic, acquired from the impressionable young girl through his physical attractiveness and verbal dexterity.

The sensual portrait of an Amazon-like Aphrodite occupies the third scene (742–46). Part of the goddess's tunic has slipped off her arm, exposing her breast as she uses Ares' shield as a mirror. The goddess of love in the likeness of an Amazon anticipates the two warrior maidens Jason will encounter in the poem: the armed Hypsipyle (637–38) in the present episode and the even more dangerous Medea, who successfully takes on Talos, the last of the Bronze Race, in the final book (4.1636–72). The image of the love goddess on Jason's cloak is highly significant because, as Phineus will later tell Jason, his mission will succeed through the help of Aphrodite (2.423–25), who will provide the hero with the means for achieving his goal by sending Eros to make Medea fall in love with him. In fact, Aphrodite's role in the *Argonautica* so closely parallels Medea's that the goddess in a way can be seen as an Olympian analogue of the Colchian maid. For both women give the self-centered young men of their lives golden objects: Medea, the fleece to Jason; Aphrodite, the golden ball to Eros.[29]

In the fourth and central scene (747–51), the Teleboans, also called Taphian pirates (750), have the upper hand in a battle with the sons of Electryon over cattle. The scholiast *ad* 1.747–51b recalls Herodorus's explanation for this battle: the Teleboans are the grandchildren of Hippothoë, herself the granddaughter of Perseus and Andromeda, who went to Mycenae to demand from Electryon their inheritance, the cattle that they insisted rightfully belonged to them.[30] The story parallels the Argonautic expedition

---

29. This point is made by T. M. Klein, "Apollonius Rhodius, *Vates Ludens*: Eros' Golden Ball (*Arg.* 3.113–50)," *CW* 74 (1980–81) 225–27. As Collins 73 pointed out, Aphrodite's possession of Ares' shield implies a tryst with the god of war. The marital strain and threat of divorce that this affair caused, celebrated by Demodocus in *Odyssey* 8, could well be another implication we are meant to draw from the vignette. Such a theme would parallel the subtle comparison between Medea and Thetis made in the previous episode and the failed marriages of the Lemnian people. D. C. Feeney, *The Gods in Epic* (Oxford 1991) 70, aptly describes this scene as a "representation in words of a representation in cloth of a representation in marble of a goddess—and her reflection."

30. Cf. E. Livrea, "L'épos philologique: Apollonios de Rhodes et quelques homérismes méconnus," *AC* 49 (1980) 150–52.

quite closely. Like the Argonauts, the Teleboans made a long journey (from the island of Taphos, near Acarnania, to Argos) in order to retrieve something that they believed was theirs; while they sought a herd of cattle, Jason travels to Colchis in search of the hide of an animal that belonged to his ancestor, Phrixus (who together with the ram appears on the last scene of the cloak). As we have seen at the center of the Catalogue, the motif of the journey made in quest of special animals becomes a symbol in Apollonius for the Argonautic expedition.

The fifth scene, like the third, has to do with the realm of love (752-58). While Pelops rides together in a chariot with Hippodamia, her father, Œnomaus, and the charioteer, Myrtilus, follow them in fast pursuit. The story clearly anticipates Jason's future experience in Colchis. Like Pelops, he will take up the father of the bride's challenge—although not in a chariot race, but in the yoking of fire-breathing bulls with which he will plow a field and sow the dragon's teeth. Jason will then escape with Medea on the *Argo*, and through betrayal and deceit kill not the father of the bride, Æëtes, but as a most cruel substitute, his innocent brother-in-law, Apsyrtus.

The sixth scene (759-62) balances the second by focusing once again upon the antithesis of strength versus skill. The youthful and smaller Apollo (βούπαις, οὔ πω πολλός, 760)[31] shoots his bow at the huge Tityus (Τιτυὸν μέγαν, 761), who tries to rape Leto. The correspondence with Amphion and Zethus is all the closer in that the instruments used by the respective men of skill are both stringed: the lyre and the bow. The close association between Jason and Apollo that we have seen in previous episodes turns Apollo's success over the monstrous Tityus into a hint of Jason's future success, both over the powerful and menacing Æëtes and also over Pelias, whose reign in Iolcus threatens Jason and his family. Moreover, another archer, Eros, will cause Medea, through whom the Argonauts will gain possession of the fleece, to fall desperately in love with Jason (cf. 3.275-98).

---

31. R. L. Hunter, "Apollo and the Argonauts: Two Notes on Ap. Rhod. 2.669-719," *MH* 43 (1986) 53 n. 22, suggests that Apollonius is alluding to the etymology of Apollo's name from πολλός.

In the seventh and final scene (763–67), Phrixus listens as the ram speaks. The workmanship of the marvelous cloak is so exquisite that the narrator exclaims:

Κείνους κ' εἰσορόων ἀκέοις ψεύδοιό τε θυμόν,
ἐλπόμενος πυκινήν τιν' ἀπὸ σφείων ἐσακοῦσαι
βάξιν, ὅτευ καὶ δηρὸν ἐπ' ἐλπίδι θηήσαιο.
(765–67)

Looking at these you would fall silent and deceive yourself
in the expectation of hearing some intelligible message from them;
you would spend a long time hoping to see something.

The embroidery is so spellbinding, the narrator seems to say, that the viewer feels drawn into the scene and even expects to hear some πυκινὴ βάξις. Apollonius has thus raised—but significantly gives no answer to—the question, What does the ram say to Phrixus? The reader is left to ponder the message that the ram imparts. The scholiast *ad* 1.763–64b suggests that the ram was encouraging Phrixus by telling him that Zeus had guaranteed his safety. By this the ancient commentator must have in mind Phrixus's escape from Ino's plot and his safe arrival and eventual welcome in Colchis. This interpretation, even if not exactly what the poet had in mind, is nonetheless instructive; for it points the way toward seeing the close parallel that exists between the experiences of Phrixus and those of Jason. Like Phrixus, Jason will arrive safely in Colchis. He will also travel on a vessel that has the magical ability to speak.[32] Moreover, Jason, like Phrixus, travels from Greece to Colchis as the result of a plot against his life, and both marry daughters of Æëtes. Thus the heroic achievements of the two have close similarities, and the success that Phrixus experienced in his journey to Colchis, foretold quite possibly in the πυκινὴ βάξις of the ram, bodes well for the success of Jason's expedition. A final point: this last scene corresponds by way of contrast with the first, and neatly brings the ecphrasis to a close—whereas in the first the accent was on the visual quality of the scene (the brilliance of the thunderbolt), here Apollonius underscores the aural quality (the message we seem to hear).

---

32. Apollonius alluded to this at 1.525–27; cf. Vian 74 n. 4.

In sum, through the progression of the scenes on Jason's cloak from imminent κῦδος to the auspicious parallel hinting at the successful completion of the expedition, Apollonius provides a symbolic representation of the expedition. This symbolic treatment reflects general features as well as particular details of the quest for the golden fleece by echoing some of the themes already explored in earlier episodes and by hinting at specific events that the Argonauts will encounter. To the reader, the scenes of the cloak unfold in a suggestive fashion. Jason is on the verge of discovering his great weapon, love (α), which will prove to be more powerful than brute force (β). On their way to Colchis, and once there, they will encounter armed Aphrodites in Hypsipyle and Medea (γ); at Colchis they will lay claim to the fleece and eventually leave a field soaked with the blood of the Earthborn (δ; cf. *Argo.* 3.1391–1404). Jason will take Medea aboard the *Argo* as they flee from the navy of Æëtes, against whose son a treacherous plot will be laid (γ). The small number of Argonauts will ultimately outmaneuver the many Colchians in pursuit (and, beyond the scope of the poem, Jason will gain the upper hand over the wicked Pelias) through Medea's cunning (β; cf. 4.339); and the talking *Argo* will then bring Jason, his Colchian bride, and the fleece safely back to Greece (α).

Before concluding this discussion of Jason's cloak, I return to the introductory verses (a). In his overall description of the cloak, Apollonius emphasizes its ruddy brilliance:

> Τῆς μὲν ῥηίτερόν κεν ἐς ἠέλιον ἀνιόντα
> ὄσσε βάλοις ἢ κεῖνο μεταβλέψειας ἔρευθος·
> δὴ γάρ τοι μέσση μὲν ἐρευθήεσσα τέτυκτο,
> ἄκρα δὲ πορφυρέη πάντῃ πέλεν.
>
> (725–28a)

> More easily would you cast your eyes into the rising
> sun than gaze upon the cloak's ruddy brilliance.
> For the central area was given a reddish hue
> and the border was purple.

The key words are ἔρευθος and ἐρευθήεσσα. At the beginning of the third and final section of the episode (*A*a), when Jason approaches Myrine, Apollonius compares him to a star that charms (θέλγει) both the eyes of the brides in their chambers and the maiden who waits for her groom by virtue of this same quality (καλὸν ἐρευθόμενος, 777–78). When Jason is seated across from Hypsipyle, she, like the person looking into the cloak (ὄσσε βάλοις, 726), averts her eyes and blushes: 'Ἡ δ' ἐγκλιδὸν ὄσσε βαλοῦσα / παρθενικὰς ἐρύθηνε παρηΐδας (790–91). The cloak will have the effect of charming Hypsipyle, and she manifests the effects by assuming the salient feature of the cloak, its color.[33] Not only does Jason have a charm, but he also carries a weapon, the spear that Atalanta gave to him.[34] These details play an important role in an allusion that informs our reading of the second half of the episode.

A. The Encounter and Departure (774–909)

This final section of the Lemnian sojourn possesses an extended ring structure much like that of the description of Jason's cloak. To summarize what was said above: it begins with Jason's approach to and arrival in Myrine (a, 774–90a) and ends with his departure from the city and the island (a, 910a). A conversation between Jason and Hypsipyle follows Jason's arrival (b, 790b–841) and precedes his departure (b, 886–909), and during both conversations Hypsipyle offers her kingdom to Jason. After the first conversation the Argonauts proceed to Myrine (c, 842–60) and before the last they leave the city (c, 875–85). In the middle stands the assembly of the Argonauts (d, 861–84), which corresponds to the assembly of the Lemnian women in the first half. The central positioning of a significant section once again proves to be instructive. For the Argonautic assembly not only contains a reference to an Odyssean episode that will emerge as an important subtext in this half of the Lemnian sojourn, but also herein Heracles makes an assertion that evinces his approach to the heroic ἄεθλος. As we shall observe in the final episode of the book, his approach proves to be inappropriate for the Argonautic ἄεθλος.

In her first speech to Jason, Hypsipyle gives her explanation for the absence of men on the island and invites the Argonauts to visit her city; she even goes so far as to offer Jason rule of

---

33. On the importance of ἔρευθος in the *Argonautica*, see A. Rose, "Clothing Imagery in Apollonius' *Argonautica*," *QUCC*, n.s., 21 (1985) 38–39; and Pavlock (supra n. 6) 29–34.

34. E. Phinney called to my attention that the spear also "hints at bad luck in love, as Atalanta attracted Meleager, only to set in force a chain of events that led to Meleager's death."

her kingdom. The men, with the exception of Heracles and a few others, accept the invitation to come into the city and go to the homes of the women. They stay for an unspecified time and give no indication of being about to leave until finally Heracles calls an assembly, reminding them of their need to fetch the golden fleece. Only then do the Argonauts leave the island. Hypsipyle and the women of Lemnos have thus become the first real threat to the expedition; for had Jason accepted Hypsipyle's offer, the mission would have come to a halt and failed. In this way, the Lemnian sojourn parallels Odysseus's encounters with Calypso, Nausicaa, and especially Circe, all of whom, like Hypsipyle, live on islands.

When Jason arrives within the city, the women rejoice at the sight of the first man they have seen in their midst in a year. In their eagerness to meet Jason, they almost attack him (ἐπεχλονέοντο, 783), and his embarassment shows as he proceeds with his eyes on the ground (784-85).³⁵ The behavior of the women, repeated as Jason leaves to summon his men (843-44), appears extraordinary, almost unnatural. Once we become aware that Apollonius has the Circe episode in mind in what follows (see immediately below), the behavior of the women can be appreciated for what it is, an adaptation of the unnatural behavior of the wild animals outside Circe's hut. In that episode the wolves and lions did not rush at Odysseus's men, but were unnaturally docile, fawning on them with their tails (*Od.* 10.212-19). The poet provides the first verbal clue that Circe is an important model for Hypsipyle in this scene when Jason arrives at the palace of the queen. After the servants open the door, Iphinoë leads the Iolcan stranger to a seat across from her mistress:

> Ἄνεσαν δὲ <u>θύρας</u> προφανέντι θεράπναι
> δικλίδας, εὐτύκτοισιν ἀρηρεμένας σανίδεσσιν·
> ἔνθα μιν Ἰφινόη κλισμῷ ἐνὶ παμφανόωντι
> ἐσσυμένως καλῆς διὰ παστάδος <u>εἷσεν ἄγουσα</u>
> ἀντία δεσποίνης.
>
> (786b-90)

---

35. Fränkel *ad* 1.769-73 has pointed out the irony in Jason's reception in Myrine: he had refused to take Atalante along because problems would have arisen with her, the only woman in the midst of unruly men; Jason now finds himself the only man among very aggressive women.

Upon seeing him, the servants opened the double
folding doors, fitted with elegantly made louvers.
Here Iphinoë escorted him eagerly through the beautiful
colonnade and sat him upon a radiant couch
opposite her mistress.

When Odysseus arrived at Circe's cottage, she herself opened the doors and led her guest to his seat:

ἡ δ' αἶψ' ἐξελθοῦσα θύρας ὤιξε φαεινὰς
καὶ κάλει· αὐτὰρ ἐγὼν ἑπόμην ἀκαχήμενος ἦτορ.
εἷσε δέ μ' εἰσαγαγοῦσα[36] ἐπὶ θρόνου ἀργυροήλου,
καλοῦ δαιδαλέου· ὑπὸ δὲ θρῆνυς ποσὶν ἦεν·
(Od. 10.312-15)

Immediately she [sc. Circe] came out and opened the bright doors
and invited me in; and I followed, distressed in my heart.
She escorted me to a beautifully made couch, with inlaid silver,
and had me sit down. There was a stool for my feet.

Jason, dressed in his splendid cloak, thoroughly captivates Hypsipyle, whose face now reflects the color of his cloak. His royal host proceeds to explain the absence of the men on Lemnos and then goes on to offer Jason the throne of the island (793ff.). Apollonius describes her account of the Lemnian crime as "wily": ἔμπα δὲ τόν γε / αἰδομένη μύθοισι προσέννεπεν αἱμυλίοισι· (791–92).[37] αἱμύλιοι occurs only once in the Homeric corpus, and there it is in reference to the wily words that Calypso, the daughter of Atlas, used in her attempt to keep Odysseus on her island:[38]

---

36. The phrase εἷσε(ν) + εἰσαγαγοῦσα + a prepositional phrase indicating the seat in the Homeric poems is unique to the Circe episode: cf. Od. 10.233 (εἷσεν δ' εἰσαγαγοῦσα κατὰ κλισμούς τε θρόνους τε), 314, 366 (εἷσε δέ μ' εἰσαγαγοῦσα ἐπὶ θρόνου ἀργυροήλου); Campbell ad 1.788–89 cites only Od. 10.233. Even Apollonius's purported earlier version of these lines in the proecdosis (cf. Σ ad 1.788-89a) looks to the same model: ἐσσυμένως καλῆς ἐπὶ δίφρακος εἷσεν ἄγουσα.
37. For an example of Hypsipyle's "scharf geschliffene Zunge," cf. Giangrande 4 on the contrast between ἀτιμάζοντο and ἀνέτελλε in lines 809–10.
38. Cf. Ardizzoni ad 790 and M. Fantuzzi, "Omero 'autore' di Apollonio Rodio: Le formule introduttive al discorso diretto," MD 13 (1986) 101.

τοῦ θυγάτηρ δύστηνον ὀδυρόμενον κατερύκει,
αἰεὶ δὲ μαλακοῖσι καὶ <u>αἱμυλίοισι λόγοισι</u>
θέλγει, ὅπως Ἰθάκης ἐπιλήσεται·

(*Od.* 1.55-57a)

His [*sc.* Atlas's] daughter keeps him a prisoner in his sorry, wretched state,
always beguiling him with deceitful and <u>wily words</u>
so that he might forget Ithaca.

Hypsipyle's intention, like Calypso's, is to get Jason and the Argonauts to stay; and just as Calypso (*Od.* 5.160-70) misled Odysseus by suggesting that she was letting him go of her own volition (she never mentions the command she received from Hermes [ibid. 97-115]), Hypsipyle misinforms Jason by averring that the Lemnian men are still alive and living with their Thracian captives and legitimate sons. If Jason is taken in by these wily words, he runs the same risk that Odysseus did, of forfeiting his νόστος.[39]

At the end of her account, Hypsipyle offers Jason the throne of Lemnos:

Τῷ ὑμεῖς στρωφᾶσθ' ἐπιδήμιοι. <u>Εἰ</u> δέ κεν <u>αὖθι
ναιετάειν</u> ἐθέλοις <u>καί τοι ἅδο</u>., ἥ τ' ἂν ἔπειτα
πατρὸς ἐμεῖο Θόαντος ἔχοις γέρας. Οὐδέ σ' ὀίω
γαῖαν ὀνόσσεσθαι· περὶ γὰρ βαθυλήιος ἄλλων
νήσων Αἰγαίῃ ὅσαι εἰν ἁλὶ ναιετάουσιν.

(827-31)

And so, move about among the people, and <u>if</u> you should
want <u>to live here</u> and this <u>pleases you</u>, by all means then
you may have the office of my father, Thoas. I do not think
you will fault our land, for it is fertile beyond the other
islands that lie in the Ægæan Sea.

After Odysseus's bath on Phæacia, Nausicaa marveled at his appearance, much as Hypsipyle does here upon Jason's arrival. The Phæacian princess then made a wish that Odysseus remain as

---

39. νόστος to Greece was an issue for the Argonauts from the very beginning of the mission: this is what Pelias wants to deprive the Argonauts of (1.17), and this Jason mentions as part of their communal goal (1.336); cf. Fränkel *ad* 1.336ff.

her husband, a prospect that Alcinous later invited Odysseus to consider:[40]

> δή ῥα τότ' ἀμφιπόλοισιν ἐϋπλοκάμοισι μετηύδα·
> 'Κλῦτέ μευ, ἀμφίπολοι λευκώλενοι, ὄφρα τι εἴπω.[41]
> οὐ πάντων ἀέκητι θεῶν, οἳ Ὄλυμπον ἔχουσι,
> Φαιήκεσσ' ὅδ' ἀνὴρ ἐπιμίσγεται ἀντιθέοισι·
> πρόσθεν μὲν γὰρ δή μοι ἀεικέλιος δέατ' εἶναι,
> νῦν δὲ θεοῖσιν ἔοικε, τοὶ οὐρανὸν εὐρὺν ἔχουσιν.
> <u>αἲ γὰρ</u> ἐμοὶ τοιόσδε πόσις κεκλημένος εἴη
> ἐνθάδε <u>ναιετάων</u>, <u>καί οἱ ἅδοι</u> αὐτόθι μίμνειν.'
> (Od. 6.238-45)

Then she spoke to her long-haired servants:
"Hear what I have to say, my fair-armed servants.
Through the will of all the gods who inhabit Olympus
this man mingles with the godlike Phæacians.
Before he appeared to me to be unseemly,
but now he seems like the gods who inhabit the wide vault of heaven.
<u>If only</u> such a man might be called my husband,
<u>living</u> here, <u>and</u> if only <u>it might please</u> him to remain <u>here</u>."

> ξεῖν', οὔ μοι τοιοῦτον ἐνὶ στήθεσσι φίλον κῆρ
> μαψιδίως κεχολῶσθαι· ἀμείνω δ' αἴσιμα πάντα.
> <u>αἲ γὰρ</u>, Ζεῦ τε πάτερ καὶ Ἀθηναίη καὶ Ἄπολλον,
> τοῖος ἐὼν οἷός ἐσσι, τά τε φρονέων ἅ τ' ἐγώ περ,
> παῖδά τ' ἐμὴν ἐχέμεν καὶ ἐμὸς γαμβρὸς καλέεσθαι
> <u>αὖθι</u> μένων· οἶκον δέ κ' ἐγὼ καὶ κτήματα δοίην,
> εἴ κ' ἐθέλων γε μένοις· ἀέκοντα δέ σ' οὔ τις ἐρύξει
> Φαιήκων· μὴ τοῦτο φίλον Διὶ πατρὶ γένοιτο.
> (Od. 7.309-16)

Stranger, I do not have such a mind as to be angry
without a good reason. It is better when things are as they should be.
<u>If only</u>, O Father Zeus, Athena, and Apollo,
being such a man as you [sc. Odysseus] are, of one mind with me,

---

40. Ardizzoni and Campbell ad 1.828 observed the allusion to Od. 6.238ff. A. W. Bulloch brought the relevance of Od. 7.309ff. to my attention.

41. Livrea apud Vian 82 n. 5 observed that Apollonius reproduced the repetition of ἀμφιπόλοισιν/ἀμφίπολοι in this episode at 702-3.

you might take my daughter and be called my son-in-law,
living here. I would give you a house and property,
if you would stay here. But no one of the Phæacians will keep
    you here
against your will. May such behavior not be pleasing to Zeus.

The similarity of the offers in language and context invites us to see Hypsipyle as something of a Nausicaa, an innocent princess whose hand in marriage will bring with it the island kingdom of Lemnos but also take away the eagerly desired νόστος.

Hypsipyle concludes her speech by bidding Jason to go to his ship and bring back his comrades:

’Αλλ’ ἄγε νῦν ἐπὶ νῆα κιὼν ἑτάροισιν ἐνίσπες
μύθους ἡμετέρους, μηδ’ ἔκτοθι μίμνε πόληος.
(832-33)

But go now to your ship and tell your comrades
of our offer, and do not remain outside the city.

Circe similarly invited Odysseus to bring his men to her house:

Διογενὲς Λαερτιάδη, πολυμήχαν’ Ὀδυσσεῦ,
ἔρχεο νῦν ἐπὶ νῆα[42] θοὴν καὶ θῖνα θαλάσσης.
νῆα μὲν ἂρ πάμπρωτον ἐρύσσατε ἠπειρόνδε,
κτήματα δ’ ἐν σπήεσσι πελάσσατε ὅπλα τε πάντα·
αὐτὸς δ’ ἂψ ἰέναι καὶ ἄγειν ἐρίηρας ἑταίρους.
(Od. 10.401-5)

Zeus-born son of Laërtes, devious Odysseus,
go now to your swift ship and to the seashore.
First of all, drag your ship to the shore;
then set all your possessions and ship cables within the caves.
You yourself then return and bring back your trusty companions.

Thus in her initial encounter with Jason, Hypsipyle attempts to do what the wily Calypso, the innocent Nausicaa, and the sorceress Circe all tried and failed to do with Odysseus: to keep Jason on her island, an eventuality that would also have kept him from fulfilling his mission. Jason, however, fully aware of what her invitation

---

42. The *iunctura* νῦν ἐπὶ νῆα (in the same metrical *sedes* in both archaic and Hellenistic passages) is unique in Homer.

entails, politely refuses: ἔγωγε μὲν οὐκ ἀθερίζων / χάζομαι, ἀλλά με λυγροὶ ἐπισπέρχουσιν ἄεθλοι (840–41).

Hypsipyle's seductive invitation thus fails to divert Jason from his ἄεθλοι and final νόστος. As I mentioned above, Jason's cloak, bearing a symbolic representation of the Argonautic expedition, made him irresistible to Hypsipyle, who assumed its reddish hue. He also came armed with a spear. Given the allusion to the Circe episode (more elements of which will be explored below), Jason's arming now takes on a new significance. On his way to Circe's cottage, Odysseus met Hermes, who gave him a charm (μῶλυ) against Circe's magic and told him to take a sword with which to threaten her lest she unman him (*Od.* 10.281–301). There is the hint of such a threat in Heracles' speech and in the Argonauts' reaction to it, as I shall point out below. Like Odysseus, Jason has his charm and weapon as he approaches his Circe. The Argonautic equivalent to μῶλυ is not a magical plant, but consists of the brilliance of the ἄεθλοι that the scenes on the cloak represent. It is the κλέος won for heroic action—to which Heracles refers in his speech in the assembly, which is promised by the fulfillment of these ἄεθλοι, and which Jason tells Hypsipyle is the reason why he cannot stay (840–41)—that ultimately frees the Argonauts from the threat of the Lemnian women. Jason's weapon, although different from Odysseus's in kind, is similar in what it suggests. Both weapons are surely phallic in nature; both heroes are armed for erotic battle against women who make threatening sexual advances.

Reference to the Circe episode continues. Upon returning to the ship Jason reported Hypsipyle's invitation to the men (847). Some time thereafter, the women came to the shore with gifts and escorted the men to their homes. This, as we learn, was encouraged by Aphrodite, who, as a favor to her husband, Hephæstus, took advantage of the Argonautic sojourn to repopulate the island with men (850–52). But not all the Argonauts went up to the city; Heracles and a few comrades remained behind:

οἱ δ' ἄλλοι, ὅπη καὶ ἔκυρσαν ἕκαστος,
Ἡρακλῆος ἄνευθεν· ὁ γὰρ <u>παρὰ νηὶ λέλειπτο</u>
αὐτὸς ἑκὼν παῦροί τε διακρινθέντες ἑταῖροι.

(854b–56)

And the others ended up where chance had led each,
except for Heracles. For he <u>had been left behind at the ship</u>
of his own accord, together with a few chosen comrades.

This minor detail also pertains to the Odyssean sojourn on Æaea. Thoroughly terrified by his previous encounter with Circe, Eurylochus criticized what he thought was Odysseus's reckless behavior in his desire to return to the cottage (*Od.* 10.431–37). Odysseus would have killed him were it not for the others who intervened:

'Διογενές, τοῦτον μὲν ἐάσομεν, εἰ σὺ κελεύεις,
αὐτοῦ πὰρ νηί τε μένειν καὶ νῆα ἔρυσθαι·
ἡμῖν δ' ἡγεμόνευ' ἱερὰ πρὸς δώματα Κίρκης.'
Ὣς φάμενοι παρὰ νηὸς ἀνήιον ἠδὲ θαλάσσης.
οὐδὲ μὲν Εὐρύλοχος κοίλῃ <u>παρὰ νηὶ λέλειπτο</u>,[43]
ἀλλ' ἕπετ'· ἔδεισεν γὰρ ἐμὴν ἔκπαγλον ἐνιπήν.
                                    (*Od.* 10.443–48)

"O Zeus-born, we shall leave him behind, if this is your command,
to remain here alongside the ship and to guard the vessel,
but lead us to the sacred home of Circe."
Thus speaking they left the ship and the sea.
And Eurylochus had not been <u>left behind along the ship</u>,
but followed us, for he feared my terrible reprimand.

Like Eurylochus, Heracles wants nothing to do with the female inhabitants of the island, and he will voice his hostility toward their stay at the assembly he calls. On the other hand, unlike Eurylochus, Heracles does not fear Jason and chooses to stay on the beach.

At the center of the second half stands the assembly of the Argonauts, which begins with another reference to the Circe episode. When day after day passes and the Argonauts still do not leave the island, Heracles finally calls together the group and reminds them of their mission:

Ἀμβολίη δ' εἰς ἦμαρ ἀεὶ ἐξ ἤματος ἦεν
ναυτιλίης· δηρὸν δ' ἂν ἐλίνυον αὖθι μένοντες,
εἰ μὴ ἀολλίσσας ἑτάρους ἀπάνευθε γυναικῶν

---

43. The *iunctura* παρὰ νηὶ λέλειπτο is a Homeric δὶς λεγόμενον (*Il.* 10.256, *Od.* 10.447), as Campbell *ad* 1.855 notes.

'Ἡρακλέης τοίοισιν ἐνιπτάζων μετέειπε·
'Δαιμόνιοι, πάτρης ἐμφύλιον αἷμ' ἀποέργει
ἡμέας; Ἦε γάμων ἐπιδευέες ἐνθάδ' ἔβημεν
κεῖθεν, ὀνοσσάμενοι πολιήτιδας; Αὖθι δ' ἕαδε
ναίοντας λιπαρὴν ἄροσιν Λήμνοιο ταμέσθαι;'
(861–68)

Day after day they kept putting off their
journey, and they would have stayed there inactive for a long time
unless Heracles had assembled the comrades apart from
the women and upbraided them in these words:
"Fools! Does the shedding of native blood restrict us
from our fatherland? Have we come from there in need of
marriages, because we despise the women of our cities? Have we decided
to live here and to plow the fertile land of Lemnos?"

Similarly, after a year on Circe's island the men assembled and reminded Odyseus of their goal, their νόστος:

ἀλλ' ὅτε δή ῥ' ἐνιαυτὸς ἔην, περὶ δ' ἔτραπον ὧραι,
μηνῶν φθινόντων, περὶ δ' ἤματα μακρὰ τελέσθη,
καὶ τότε μ' ἐκκαλέσαντες ἔφαν ἐρίηρες ἑταῖροι·
'Δαιμόνι', ἤδη νῦν μιμνήσκεο πατρίδος αἴης,
εἴ τοι θέσφατόν ἐστι σαωθῆναι καὶ ἱκέσθαι
οἶκον ἐυκτίμενον καὶ σὴν ἐς πατρίδα γαῖαν.'
(*Od.* 10.469–74)

But when a year had passed and the seasons had made their circuit
as the months receded and the long days were completed,
it was then that my faithful comrades summoned me and said:
"Fool, now is the time to remember your native land,
if indeed it is fated for you to be saved and to reach
your well-made home and the land of your fathers."

Jason, then, is no different from his Homeric model in temporarily forgetting his mission; the delay on Lemnos does not *per se* mark Jason off as nonheroic. Heracles' speech, however, goes on to underscore the essential difference between Jason and himself with regard to their attitude toward heroic action. Heracles, ironically recalling the words of Polyxo (870–71 ≈ 685–87), asserts that one does not earn κλέος or a μεγάλη βάξις from spending time with foreign women:

Οὐ μὰν εὐκλειεῖς γε σὺν ὀθνείῃσι γυναιξὶν
ἐσσόμεθ᾽ ὧδ᾽ ἐπὶ δηρὸν ἐελμένοι· οὐδέ τι κῶας
αὐτόματον δώσει τις ἑλὼν θεὸς εὐξαμένοισιν.
Ἴομεν αὖτις ἕκαστοι ἐπὶ σφέα· τὸν δ᾽ ἐνὶ λέκτροις
Ὑψιπύλης εἰᾶτε πανήμερον, εἰσόκε Λῆμνον
παισὶν ἐπανδρώσῃ μεγάλη τέ ἑ βάξις ἵκηται.

(869–74)

Certainly we shall not become famous by cooping ourselves up
here for a long time with foreign women. The fleece does not move
on its own, and a god will not seize it and hand it over to us if
we say
a prayer. Let us go back to our own homes; let him stay in bed
all day with Hypsipyle until he repopulates Lemnos
with male children and great renown comes his way.

Yet Heracles is absolutely wrong in this assertion; for Jason, making foreign women fall in love with him is one of his special skills through which the mission will ultimately succeed. In Heracles' view, the hero is a man of bold physical action. Jason, however, will complete his mission and thereby attain κλέος precisely because of his ability to charm foreign women. His arming scene, accordingly, was the prelude to the kind of battle that Jason will always win; his *aristeia* lies in bed (ἐνὶ λέκτροις, 872). Nonetheless, Heracles prods the group, including Jason, to leave Lemnos by reminding them of their goal, the acquisition of the golden fleece (870–71). The allurement of the expedition—so brilliantly hinted at in the description of Jason's cloak, which stands at the center of the Lemnian episode—has saved the Argonauts from staying with the Lemnian women and thereby giving up their acquisition of the fleece and νόστος to Greece. It is his ambition to succeed in the ἄεθλος that causes Jason to reject Hypsipyle's first (840–41) and second (903) offers to stay on Lemnos.

Apollonius not only reveals Heracles' attitude toward heroic action; he also subtly calls into question the hero's credibility by casting him in a role that, although sharply contrasting with it, nonetheless provocatively recalls that of the cowardly Eurylochus. Significantly, part of Heracles' speech recalls another Homeric coward, Thersites. At the beginning of his speech, Heracles asked if the Argonauts left Greece because there were no suitable women: Ἦε γάμων ἐπιδευέες ἐνθάδ᾽ ἔβημεν / κεῖθεν, ὀνοσσάμενοι πολιήτιδας;

("Did we come here from home in need of marriages, out of scorn for the women of our cities?" 866-67.) This sarcastic question echoes Thersites' taunts at the assembly of the Greeks in Book 2 of the *Iliad*:[44]

ἤ ἔτι καὶ χρυσοῦ ἐπιδεύεαι, ὅν κέ τις οἴσει
Τρώων ἱπποδάμων ἐξ Ἰλίου υἷος ἄποινα,
ὅν κεν ἐγὼ δήσας ἀγάγω ἢ ἄλλος Ἀχαιῶν,
ἠὲ γυναῖκα νέην, ἵνα μίσγεαι ἐν φιλότητι,
ἥν τ' αὐτὸς ἀπονόσφι κατίσχεαι;
(*Il.* 2.229-33a)

Do you still need gold, which one of the horse-taming
Trojans will bring you from Ilion as a ransom for his son,
someone whom I, or another of the Achæans, have bound and
    led away?
Or perhaps a new woman so that you might lie with her,
someone whom you will keep apart for yourself?

At the end of his speech, Heracles tells the others to let Jason spend all day in bed with Hypsipyle while they go home (872-74, quoted above). In addition to envisaging Agamemnon in bed with Briseïs, Thersites likewise goes on to suggest that they go home, leaving Agamemnon to enjoy his prizes:

ὦ πέπονες, κάκ' ἐλέγχε', Ἀχαιΐδες, οὐκέτ' Ἀχαιοί,
οἴκαδέ περ σὺν νηυσὶ νεώμεθα, τόνδε δ' ἐῶμεν
αὐτοῦ ἐνὶ Τροίῃ γέρα πεσσέμεν, ὄφρα ἴδηται
ἤ ῥά τί οἱ χἠμεῖς προσαμύνομεν, ἦε καὶ οὐκί·
(*Il.* 2.235-38)

Cowards, objects of base reproach, Achæan women, no longer
    men,
let's sail home in our ships and abandon this one [*sc*. Agamemnon]
here in Troy to enjoy his prize, so that he might know
whether we shall be of any help to him or not.

The image of a Heracles who talks like a hero, but in words that recall Homeric cowards, creates a striking dissonance. His decision to remain at the shore with the ship and his reminder to continue the mission have led some to think of Heracles as a kind of

44. Cf. Mooney *ad* 1.873, Vian 91 n. 2, Campbell *ad* 1.872ff.

Stoic saint.[45] On the contrary, Heracles' words and actions, when seen through the Homeric subtexts, lose their edge. Moreover, the shallowness of his heroic bluster becomes clear when, soon after they leave Lemnos, Heracles is completely undone at the loss of his boyfriend, Hylas; he will discover just how powerful love, or rather passion, can be. Jason, on the other hand, never loses control in love; in fact, he never loses lovers, but only discards—or tries to discard—them.[46]

The reminiscence of the assembly of the Greeks at Troy in *Iliad* 2 continues as the poet tells of the Argonauts' departure from Myrine. When the Lemnian women hear the news that the men are leaving, they rush out of the town in tears to greet the Argonauts for the last time. Apollonius compares them to bees pouring out of a hive gathering "fruit" from flowers:

Ὡς δ' ὅτε λείρια καλὰ περιβρομέουσι μέλισσαι
πέτρης ἐκχύμεναι σιμβληίδος, ἀμφὶ δὲ λειμὼν
ἐρσήεις γάνυται, ταὶ δὲ γλυκὺν ἄλλοτε ἄλλον
καρπὸν ἀμέργουσιν πεποτημέναι· ὣς ἄρα ταί γε
ἐνδυκὲς ἀνέρας ἀμφὶ κινυρόμεναι προχέοντο
χερσί τε καὶ μύθοισιν ἐδεικανόωντο ἕκαστον,
εὐχόμεναι μακάρεσσιν ἀπήμονα νόστον ὀπάσσαι.
(879-85)

When bees engage in noisy flight around beautiful lilies
after pouring out of their nest among the rocks, and the dewy
glen all about appears happy, they fly to one flower and then to another
gathering their sweet fruit. Just like this the women
ardently rushed out among the men in tears,
bidding each farewell in words and gestures,
and praying to the blessed gods to grant them a safe return.

The action of the women prompted by the departure of the Argonauts corresponds to that in the scene of their arrival, when the women rushed out fearing an invasion (in particular, cf. προχέοντο,

---

45. See A. Ardizzoni, *L'Eracle "semnós" nel poema di Apollonio* (Catania 1937), and Vian 259 *ad* 856; cf. G. Karl Galinsky, *The Herakles Theme* (Oxford 1972) 113.
46. On the contrast between Jason's and Heracles' attitudes toward love in this episode, see C. R. Beye, "Jason as Love-Hero" (supra n. 28) 31-55.

635 ≈ 883). The second rush is quite different. Earlier they were armed for battle and tried to ward off the Argonauts; here, more like devoted wives than threatening warriors, they bid them a tearful goodbye and pray for a safe νόστος (885). The image echoes a Homeric bee simile that was applied to the Greeks running from their ships and tents to the very assembly at which Thersites spoke:[47]

ἠΰτε ἔθνεα εἶσι μελισσάων ἀδινάων,
πέτρης ἐκ γλαφυρῆς αἰεὶ νέον ἐρχομενάων·
βοτρυδὸν δὲ πέτονται ἐπ' ἄνθεσιν εἰαρινοῖσιν·
αἱ μέν τ' ἔνθα ἅλις πεποτήαται, αἱ δέ τε ἔνθα·
ὣς τῶν ἔθνεα πολλὰ νεῶν ἄπο καὶ κλισιάων
ἠιόνος προπάροιθε βαθείης ἐστιχόωντο
ἰλαδὸν εἰς ἀγορήν·

(*Il.* 2.87–93a)

Just as the various hives of bees go forth in great number
from a hollow rock in continual motion
and fly in a swarm upon the vernal flowers,
going here and there in their flight;
so too the many nationalities of men, leaving their ships and tents,
fell into ranks along the wide beach,
entering the assembly by company.

Ancient critics were divided over the success of the Argonautic simile. The scholiast *ad* 1.879–83d believed that the simile failed because the joy of the image did not match the gloom of the occasion. On the other hand, the comment preserved *ad* 1.879–83e defended the simile, arguing that the point is "beauty alone and ecphrasis." No scholar, however, (ancient or modern) has observed that the comparison presupposes apicultural theory in vogue in the ancient world, in particular the belief that bees collected their young from the flowers upon which they lighted.[48] In

---

47. On the allusion, see Mooney *ad* 1.879, Ardizzoni *ad* 880, Vian 91 n. 3, Campbell *ad* 1.879ff. In addition to the points of contact seen thus far between the two assemblies on Lemnos, I would add that Apollonius informed both with Homeric models, and that both models come from assemblies found in the same books of their respective epics: *Od.* 2 ≈ *Il.* 2.

48. Cf. Aristotle, *HA* 2.51, *GA* 3.10; Vergil *G.* 4.200–202; Columella 9.2.4. See Olck, "Biene," *RE* 3.1.434. I would now point out that W. Kofler, "Bienen Männer und Lemnos: Beobachtungen zu einem epischen Gleichnis bei

the first assembly, Polyxo advised the Lemnian women to take advantage of the presence of the Argonauts to reestablish their society and to provide for future generations. Aphrodite aided this plan as a favor to her husband, since the Lemnian men had helped him when he was in need. In fact, Heracles calls attention to the plight of the Lemnian women in his accusation that Jason was trying to repopulate the male segment of Lemnos singlehandedly. Thus, the simile can be seen as hinting at a central issue of the Lemnian encounter, the acquiring of children—an issue with which the episode will conclude. Inasmuch as bees were thought to gather their offspring from flowers, the simile intimates the success that the Lemnian women have had in their plan; like the bees, they have found a source for rejuvenating their population.

As the Lemnian women bid the Argonauts farewell, Apollonius reports the final words exchanged by Jason and Hypsipyle as a counterbalance to their first conversation. Hypsipyle speaks first (888–98). She prays for the successful completion of their mission and reiterates her offer of the kingship of her island. Realizing that Jason will probably never return, she begs to be remembered and asks for instructions about children, if she should become pregnant. In his reply (900–909), Jason accepts her prayer and again refuses the kingship on the ground of his ἄεθλοι. In response to her question about children, he thinks about the possibility that he might not himself ever return to Greece. He thus asks that, if this should happen, Hypsipyle send any son born of their union to his own parents when the son grows to such an age that he can provide the γηροτροφία that he, Jason, would have provided. In this final conversation, Apollonius has again returned to the encounter that Odysseus had with Nausicaa, which both the offer of kingship and the request to be remembered recall:[49]

Apollonius Rhodius (*Arg.* 1.878–885)," *Hermes* 120 (1992) 310–19, has recently addressed this issue. It is nice to see that the following interpretation, first made in my 1983 doctoral dissertation, has received independent support from Kofler's more detailed argument.

49. The imitation of μνήσῃ (Od. 8.462) in Μνώεο (896) was noted by Stössl (supra n. 1) 46 n. 34; A. W. Bulloch pointed out to me the other corresponsions between Nausicaa and Hypsipyle in their speeches.

"'Αλλ' οὐ σύ γε τήνδε μενοινὴν
σχήσεις, οὔτ' αὐτὴ προτιόσσομαι ὧδε τελεῖσθαι.
<u>Μνώεο μήν, ἀπεών περ ὁμῶς καὶ νόστιμος ἤδη</u>,
'Ὑψιπύλης.'
(894b-97)

"Ὑψιπύλη, <u>τὰ μὲν οὕτω ἐναίσιμα πάντα</u> γένοιτο
ἐκ μακάρων· τύνη δ' ἐμέθεν πέρι θυμὸν ἀρείω
ἴσχαν', ἐπεὶ πάτρην μοι ἅλις Πελίαο ἕκητι
ναιετάειν· μοῦνόν με θεοὶ λύσειαν ἀέθλων.'
(900-903)

<u>Ἦ καὶ ἔβαιν' ἐπὶ</u> νῆα παροίτατος·
(910a)

"But you will have no desire
to do this; I can see that this will not turn out so.
<u>Remember</u>, then, both <u>while you are away from home and when
you return</u>,
Hypsipyle."

"Hypsipyle, <u>may all you have said turn out favorably</u>
through the will of the gods! But have a better opinion
regarding me, since it is enough for me to live in my fatherland
by the good graces of Pelias. May the gods only free me from
my labors!"

<u>He spoke</u>, <u>and</u> was the first to get <u>aboard</u> the ship.

'Χαῖρε, ξεῖν', ἵνα καί <u>ποτ' ἐὼν ἐν πατρίδι γαίῃ
μνήσῃ ἐμεῖ</u>', ὅτι μοι πρώτῃ ζωάγρι' ὀφέλλεις.'
Τὴν δ' ἀπαμειβόμενος προσέφη πολύμητις Ὀδυσσεύς·
'Ναυσικάα, θύγατερ μεγαλήτορος Ἀλκινόοιο
<u>οὕτω νῦν Ζεὺς θείη</u>, ἐρίγδουπος πόσις Ἥρης
<u>οἴκαδέ τ' ἐλθέμεναι καὶ νόστιμον ἦμαρ ἰδέσθαι</u>·
τῷ κέν τοι κεῖθι θεῷ ὣς εὐχετοῴμην
αἰεὶ ἤματα πάντα· σὺ γάρ μ' ἐβιώσαο, κούρη.'
<u>Ἦ</u> ῥα <u>καὶ ἐς</u> θρόνον ἷζε παρ' Ἀλκίνοον βασιλῆα.
(Od. 8.461-69)

"Farewell, stranger. When you are once again in your native land,
remember me, since you owe me first and foremost for saving your
life."
In response, wily Odysseus said to her:
"Nausicaa, daughter of great-souled Alcinous,
may Zeus, the thunderous husband of Hera, so grant
that I return home and see my day of arrival.
At that time I would pray to you as a god
forever; for you, young woman, have restored my life."
Thus he spoke, and sat upon the couch alongside King Alcinous.

As the episode comes to a close, the reader is left with the image of a Nausicaa-like Hypsipyle; as beautiful and innocent as she may seem, her invitation, like that of her model, nonetheless threatens the hero's ἄεθλοι and νόστος.

I would like to return briefly to a point that I suggested above; namely, that the Argonauts risked their masculinity in their contact with the women of Lemnos. In the first half, Apollonius concentrates on the Lemnian women, who take on male roles both at the textual and subtextual levels. In the second half, where the structural focus is on the Argonautic assembly, one discerns hints that the Argonauts might be acting in a less than manly fashion. Not only did the women assume a more aggressive role in establishing relationships with the Argonauts, but there is allusion to several passages that suggest that contact with the Lemnian women has threatened to unman those Argonauts who left the shore.

First, in having Jason bring a charm and weapon on his first visit with Hypsipyle—which, as I have shown, in several details recalls Odysseus's encounter with Circe—Apollonius would seem to suggest that the former risks becoming ἀνήνωρ if he should sleep with his "Circe" (cf. *Od.* 10.301); and, as we hear from Heracles, Jason has been spending all day in bed with Hypsipyle. Second, as seen above, Heracles' speech to the Argonauts recalled Thersites' rebuke to his fellow soldiers. In this speech Thersites accuses the Greeks of behaving like women in his acerbic taunt ὦ πέπονες, κάκ' ἐλέγχε', Ἀχαιΐδες, οὐκέτ' Ἀχαιοί (*Il.* 2.235). Recollection of Thersites' speech could well bring this particular taunt to mind in the present passage. A third suggestion that the Argonauts have risked becoming less than virile can be observed also in their response to Heracles' rebuke. Like Jason as he entered the city of Myrine (cf. 784), they too keep their eyes on the ground as they leave the assembly in silence:

Ὣς νείκεσσεν ὅμιλον· ἐναντία δ' οὔ νύ τις ἔτλη
ὄμματ' ἀνασχεθέειν οὐδὲ προτιμυθήσασθαι·
(875-76)

Thus he rebuked the group, <u>and not anyone dared
to lift up his eyes toward him, nor to say a word</u>.

This description recalls the condition of Anticleia, Odysseus's mother, when the hero met her in the underworld:[50]

ἡ δ' ἀκέουσ' ἧσται σχεδὸν αἵματος, <u>οὐδ' ἑὸν υἱὸν
ἔτλη ἐσάντα ἰδεῖν οὐδὲ προτιμυθήσασθαι</u>.
(Od. 11.142-43)

And she [sc. Anticleia] sits in silence near the blood <u>and does
not dare
to look up at her son, nor to say a word</u>.

Recalling that Heracles had just told the men that they would not become εὐκλειεῖς (869) by associating with the women of Lemnos, the reader is invited to conclude from this suggestive description of the Argonauts that they have indeed become Ἀντίκλειαι; that is, effeminate men opposed to κλέος.[51] The subtextual indicators conspire to suggest that a prolonged stay on Lemnos would emasculate the Argonauts and Jason himself, the same threat faced by Odysseus (literally with Circe, and in a more figurative sense with Calypso and Nausicaa). For if Odysseus agreed to stay with any of these tempting women, he would give up the idea of returning home, avoid the contest that awaited him there, and forego the κλέος that would come from his victory over the suitors.

In sum, like Odysseus, Jason choses ἄεθλοι and νόστος over the lover's νῆσος. But in his last speech to Hypsipyle, Jason reveals

---

50. Cf. Ardizzoni ad 876, Campbell ad 1.875-76. προτιμυθήσασθαι is a Homeric hapax legomenon.
51. On this sense of ἀντί as a prefix, see LSJ s.v. C2, and E. Schwyzer, Griechische Grammatik (Munich 1975) 2.1.442.

wherein he differs from his Homeric model. His request that Hypsipyle give up her son to take care of his own parents anticipates his future request of Medea that she too give up her sons.[52] In this request, Jason reveals the selfish side of his personality so unforgettably portrayed by Euripides in the *Medea*. The Argonautic hero may look and act like an Odysseus when confronted by the feminine threat to his mission, but, as in his departure from home, comparison with his Homeric model underscores the great difference: Odysseus gave up Circe, Calypso, and Nausicaa and the immortality or life of ease they offered so that he could return to his wife and child. Years later Jason will be willing to give up his wife and children and accept the offer of a foreign king to marry his daughter to provide himself with a life of security. Upon comparison with his Homeric models, we may find Heracles' heroic rhetoric empty, especially when we see how he behaves in Mysia; at least he comes across as honest. Jason, on the other hand, proves both here in his concluding speech to Hypsipyle and later in his marriage with Medea (outside the limits of the poem) to be far less committed to the preservation of a family than Odysseus, his primary model in this episode. Such an unhappy contrast between Jason and his Homeric model recalls the unfavorable comparison with Hector in his departure from home.

THE encounter with the masculine and aggressive women of Lemnos has indeed threatened to unman the crew of the *Argo* and thus prevent the expedition from continuing. The Argonauts in the company of the Lemnian women temporarily lost sight of their goal until Heracles got them back on course by appealing to the κλέος that comes from the ἄεθλοι of which Jason's cloak stands as a mythological icon. Yet Apollonius calls Heracles' heroic status into question through comparison with Thersites, and in the last episode of the book he will have him become the victim of

---

52. This, I argued in Chapter 5, was the point behind the wrath of Thetis, which provided the Argonauts with the "Aulis" suited to their leader. For specific points of comparison between Jason's encounters with Hypsipyle and Medea, see Hunter *ad* 3.956–61, 975, 1008. To these I would add that the association of Hypsipyle with Circe, Medea's aunt, in the Lemnian episode, is yet another link between the two women.

his own violent "heroism." While it took Heracles, the more traditional type of hero, to remind the Argonauts of their goal, it is the longing to complete their ἄεθλοι that is Jason's μῶλυ and that prevents him from committing himself to Hypsipyle or even later to Medea (cf. 4.338–54)—until, that is, she frightens him into making a commitment. In the final episode, we shall find the situation on Lemnos reversed. Heracles will abandon the expedition in search of the one he loves so desperately, while Jason will finesse a crucial restoration of the group's harmony, momentarily lost following the accidental loss of Heracles, and, as Heracles does here on Lemnos, get the expedition back on track. It is Jason after all who, ambitious to retain the κῦδος of leading the expedition (cf. 351) and to win the κλέος that comes from its successful completion, never loses sight of the ἄεθλοι.

7

Initiation and Lustration
Sojourn on Oros Arkton (*Argo.* 1.910–1152)

THE EPISODE of the sojourn on the island of Oros Arkton (cf. 1.941), later to be named Cyzicus after the king whom the Argonauts encounter there, is, simply put, a brilliant *tour de force*. Contrary to the judgments of some earlier scholars, this episode does not constitute a loosely knit string of etiological tales devoid of poetic value.[1] Rather, Apollonius has successfully interwoven several different, and in some respects contradictory, traditions involving the etiological legend of King Cyzicus and has created a meticulously balanced and strikingly original version of the tale. Once again, the poet has availed himself of the ring format, and, not surprisingly, an important Homeric reference lies at the structural center of the narrative.

A brief account of Apollonius's use of his sources will demonstrate the extent and the originality of the *contaminatio* in this episode.[2] The scholia, though obscure through apparent abbreviation,[3] have nonetheless preserved important information concerning earlier accounts of this eventful stop on the Argonauts' journey to Colchis. Most would agree that Apollonius used Deiochus's account of the story as his main source but that he had a free hand in

---

1. See, for example, E. Fitch, "Apollonius Rhodius and Cyzicus," *AJP* 33 (1912) 43–56, who concluded that Apollonius's only interests in this episode were topographical and antiquarian; cf. also F. Stössl, *Apollonios Rhodios: Interpretationen zur Erzählungskunst und Quellenverwertung* (Bern 1941) 25, and Händel 50.
2. On Apollonius's sources for this episode, see Knorr 17–33, Vian 28–38, and P. M. Fraser, *Ptolemaic Alexandria* (Oxford 1972) 1.627–30.
3. See Fitch (supra n. 1) 53, and Jacoby *ad* Deiochus *FGrHist* 471 F 4–10.

adapting and introducing other versions that he found elsewhere. According to Deiochus, a fifth-century-B.C. chronicler, the Argonauts fought neither the Gegeneis nor the Doliones (as in Apollonius's creative adaptation), but the Pelasgi, who had previously been driven out of Thessaly. Learning that many of the Argonauts were from Thessaly, the vengeful Pelasgi attacked Jason and his men at night, even trying to block the *Argo* within the harbor. Cyzicus was killed when he intervened and tried to stop the battle. He was buried on the Leimonian Plain, and his wife, Cleite, the daughter of Merops, died thereafter of grief. At some point the Argonauts constructed and dedicated an altar to Jasonian Apollo.[4] The Doliones may not have played a role in Deiochus's version,[5] but they do seem to have been identified with the Pelasgians in the versions of Conon and Ephorus.[6] Possibly Apollonius borrowed the Doliones from this tradition. At any rate, Apollonius completely changed the nature of the conflict. The battle between the Argonauts and the people of Oros Arkton does not arise out of hatred for the Thessalian Argonauts as in Deiochus, but through a case of mistaken identity: strong headwinds blow the Argonauts back to the island during the night, and the Doliones believe that the returning Argonauts are their enemies, the Pelasgian Macries.[7] As will be seen below, a famous passage in the *Odyssey* was the inspiration for the detail of the wind, which the poet has set conspicuously at the center of the episode.[8] This is the means through which the oracle regarding Cyzicus—that he would fall at the hands of a θεῖος στόλος (970), another invention on the part of the poet—is fulfilled.

In a completely unrelated story, Herodorus in his *Argonautica* wrote that Heracles fought with the monstrous Gegeneis in this

---

4. This much has been preserved by Σ *ad* 1.961–63, 966, 974–76a, 987a, 989–91, 1037–38b, 1061, 1063; cf. Deiochus *FGrHist* 471 F 7–8.

5. So Σ *ad* 1.961–63. Vian 32, however, suggests that in Deiochus's account, the Pelasgians "devaient être considérés comme une population asservie aux Dolions."

6. See Conon *FGrHist* 26 F 1, Ephorus *FGrHist* 70 F 61 (= Σ *ad* 1.1037–38b).

7. The nationality of the Macries is a nod to the Deiochan tradition.

8. Cf. M. Dufner, "The *Odyssey* in the *Argonautica*: Reminiscences, Revision, Reconstruction" (diss. Princeton 1988) 245–61, offers a fine analysis of the Odyssean elements of this episode.

region.⁹ Since in his account of the Argonautic expedition Heracles was not a participant,¹⁰ this incident could not have been associated with the Argonauts' experiences on Cyzicus. Apollonius then grafted this story onto his Cyzicene narrative by having the Gegeneis attack Heracles, separated from the rest of the Argonauts with only a few men, when Jason makes his first attempt to climb Mount Dindymon.

To Deiochus's account Apollonius subjoined yet another local legend. According to Neanthes, a local chronicler, the Argonauts founded the cult of the Idæan Mother near Cyzicus.¹¹ Apollonius makes the inauguration of this cult the climax of the episode, and, as I will explain below, it corresponds structurally with the initiation of the Argonauts into the Samothracian rites with which the episode begins.¹² The connection between the cult of Meter on Mount Dindymon, apparently not a part of Deiochus's account, and the story proper was effected through another learned borrowing. The scholiast ad 1.1085–87b attributed the story of the halcyon, which announced the cessation of the bad weather keeping the Argonauts from leaving Oros Arkton, to a *Pæan* of Pindar (fr. 62 Snell). According to the scholiast, Hera sent the halcyon in the Pindaric poem; for Apollonius, the θεός mentioned at 1088 is Rhea, whose cult the Argonauts would immediately found.¹³ Much of the success of Apollonius's *contaminatio* lies in the felicitous combination of so many diverse traditions into a smooth, unified, and convincing story.

---

9. See Σ *ad* 1.936–490; cf. Herodorus *FGrHist* 31 F 7 and 41. Knorr 28ff. believes that the scholiast was incorrect in identifying the *Argonautica* as the source of this tale, and attributes it instead to Herodorus's *Heracleia*.
10. See Σ *ad* 1.1289–91a; Herodorus *FGrHist* 31 F 7, 41.
11. See Neanthes *FGrHist* 84 F 11–12 (= Σ *ad* 1.1063, 1065–66). Herodotus refers to this cult at 4.76.
12. Cf. Hurst 62ff., who observed the relevance of the Samothracian Mysteries to the structure of the whole episode, *pace* Levin 87.
13. See Vian 37, Levin 105 n. 5. Fränkel *ad* 1.1088, however, maintains that Hera is the θεός. D. C. Feeney, *The Gods in Epic* (Oxford 1991) 88–89, observes that Apollonius's vagueness in this instance is purposeful and fits into a larger pattern, in which "the difficulties of understanding which god is acting, or how the gods act, and the difficulties of understanding human motivations all run together."

STRUCTURE

Discernible corresponsions on either side of a self-contained central section reveal the same basic tripartite structure seen in the last episode. After departing from Lemnos the Argo sails to Samothrace, where Orpheus initiates the Argonauts in the rites of the Cabiri (915–21); the episode will conclude with the inauguration of a cult of Meter on Mount Dindymon for which Orpheus will provide the music (1117–52). Moreover, as the Argonauts reach Samothrace by rowing (911–14), they will eventually row away from Oros Arkton to their next destination, Mysia (1151–52). In addition to this, details mentioned in the second initiation on Mount Dindymon recall points in the narrative describing the journey from Samothrace to Oros Arkton: the Argonauts pass by Mount Ida (930) ≈ they will later set up a cult to the Idæan Meter, with whom the Idæan Dactyls are associated (1128–29); the phrase ἔστι δέ τις (936) introducing the description of Ὄρος Ἄρκτων (941) ≈ the phrase ἔσκε δέ τι (1117) introducing the description of the cult statue of Meter on Οὔρεα Ἄρκτων (1150); the description of the Gegeneis (942–46) ≈ the description of the birth of the Dactyls (1127–31; both are, significantly, offspring of the earth); finally, the dedication of the original anchor stone at the Artacië Fountain, later to be moved to the shrine of Jasonian Athena founded (ἱδρύσαντο) by the Ionians (955–60) ≈ the miraculous appearance of the Jasonian Fountain near the shrine to Rhea that the Argonauts found (ἴδρυσαν, 1117–49). These corresponsions make of the first (A) and third (A) sections a suitable frame for the two ascents of Mount Dindymon and the two battles in which the Argonauts successively engage the Gegeneis and the Doliones (B).

The central section itself (B) unfolds in an extended ring: the two ascents of the mountain (a–a) enclose the two battles (b–b), while at the center of the two battles there lies the incident that brings about the second and tragic battle with Cyzicus: namely, the shift in the winds (c). In addition to this, elements in the second ascent of the mountain (a) clearly echo by way of similarity and contrast details in the first (a): the provision of food and wine for the Argonautic sacrifice and the subsequent feast (965–84) ≈ the fast after the deaths of Cyzicus and Cleite (1070–77);

the omen stating that Cyzicus will die at the hands of a θεῖος στόλος (969–71) ≈ the appearance of the halcyon over Jason's head signaling the end of the bad weather and the need to propitiate Rhea (1084–1102); the Argonauts' move from City Harbor to Chytus Harbor (964–65) immediately before the first attempt to climb Mount Dindymon for a view of the surrounding area ≈ the Argonauts' move from Hiere Petre to Thracian Harbor just before their second ascent of Mount Dindymon, where they succeed in attaining the desired view (1109–16); several men are left behind for both climbs of Mount Dindymon (992–94 ≈ 1110–11). Finally, the battles with the Gegeneis (b) and the Dolonies (b) are each qualified by two similes (991, 1003–5 ≈ 1027–28, 1049–50) that frame the description of the battle. The following, then, represents the overall scheme of the episode:[14]

Sojourn on Oros Arkton, 910–1152

A. The Samothracian Mysteries and
   Passage to Oros Arkton   (910–60)
    Rowing from Lemnos to Samothrace
    Rites Officiated by Orpheus
    Mention of Mount Ida
    Ἔστι δέ τις
    Ὄρος Ἄρκτων
    Γεγενέες (Earthborn Dæmons)
    Artacië Fountain and Temple of
       Jasonian Athena

B. The Two Ascents of Mount Dindymon:
   The Deaths of the Gegeneis and Cyzicus   (961–1116)
   a. The First Ascent   (961–88)
     Feasting; Omen Involving Cyzicus
     Move to Chytus Harbor Prior to
       First Ascent of Mount Dindymon

---

14. Since the corresponding elements in sections A and A do not occur in exactly the same or in an inverted order, I have listed them in their order of occurrence without reference to subsections.

The First Ascent of Mount Dindymon
   Made along the Jasonian Path After Men
   Have Been Left Behind
 b. Battle with the Gegeneis: Two Similes   (989–1011)
 c. Wind Blows the Argonauts Back   (1012–25)
 b. Battle with the Doliones: Two Similes   (1026–52)
 a. The Second Ascent   (1053–1116)
   Recognition of the Error; Funeral of Cyzicus;
      Cleite Fountain
   Fasting; Omen Involving Jason
   Move to Thracian Harbor Prior to Second
      Ascent of Mount Dindymon
   The Second Ascent of Mount Dindymon Made
      After Men Have Been Left Behind
A. The Mysteries of Rhea on Mount Dindymon
   and Departure from Oros Arkton   (1117–52)
   Ἔσκε δέ τις
   Rites of Meter Assisted by Orpheus
   Ἰδαῖοι Δάκτυλοι (Earthborn Dæmons)
   Οὔρεα Ἄρκτων
   Jasonian Fountain
   Rowing from Cyzicus

A. The Samothracian Mysteries and Passage to Oros Arkton (910–60)

Apollonius did not invent the detail regarding the Argonauts' stop at Samothrace. In his satyr play *The Cabiri* (cf. Athenæus 10.428f [= 95–97a Radt]), Æschylus portrays the Argonauts in a drunken celebration on the island. Moreover, Diodorus (4.43.1–2) recorded a tradition wherein the Argonauts were saved in a storm as a result of Orpheus's initiation into these rites. Apollonius's innovation would appear to be his integration of this detail of the Argonautic tradition in the episode involving Oros Arkton. Of particular note is the fact that the poet has so neatly associated the rites on Samothrace with those on Mount Dindymon through the structure of the episode and the several verbal correspondences noted above. In addition to this, one can observe that certain mythological and legendary details regarding the Samothracian Mysteries parallel the events on Oros Arkton, which I shall examine below. I shall point out here instead that the manner in which Apollonius presents the two corresponding rites parallels the embassies of Æthalides and Iphinoë in the previous episode. There, Apollonius explicitly refused to mention Æthalides' μῦθοι (648–49) while he reported Iphinoë's speech in full (710–16).[15] In the present episode, Apollonius similarly does not divulge the Mysteries of Samothrace (τῶν μὲν ἔτ' οὐ προτέρω μυθήσομαι, 919), but in the corresponding section gives a full account of the rites on Mount Dindymon (1117–52).

The rest of the first section contains an account of the journey from Samothrace to Oros Arkton and a brief description of the island-peninsula and its people. In describing the passage through the Hellespont, Apollonius has his eye on Homer's brief description of the area in the Iliadic Catalogue; in particular, for lines 928–35 the poet is indebted to *Il.* 2.819–43, about which Delage stated: "L'ordre suivi par Apollonius est à remarquer; il a énuméré toutes ces villes à leur place exacte, dans l'ordre où on les trouve en remontant l'Helléspont comme s'il avait eu sous les yeux une carte ou un périple. Il a donc complété en les précisant les renseignements que lui fournissait Homère."[16] In his adaptation of these Homeric verses the poet would appear to have gone beyond a mere updating of geographical details. We learn in the second and central section of the episode (B) that Cleite, the wife of Cyzicus, who will commit suicide after her husband's death, is the daughter of Merops of Percote:

> ἀλλ' ἔτι οἱ κατὰ δώματ' ἀκήρατος ἦεν ἄκοιτις
> ὠδίνων, Μέροπος Περκωσίου ἐκγεγαυῖα
> Κλείτη ἐυπλόκαμος.
>
> (974–76a)

But still at home his wife, fair-haired Cleite,
offspring of Percosian Merops, had no experience
of the pains of labor.

---

15. See Chapter 6, pp. 114–16.
16. Delage 93.

Homer mentioned this same Percosian prince within the Iliadic passage that inspired Apollonius's description of the journey to Oros Arkton:[17]

τῶν ἦρχ' Ἄδρηστός τε καὶ Ἄμφιος λινοθώρηξ
υἷε δύω Μέροπος Περκωσίου, ὃς περὶ πάντων
ᾔδεε μαντοσύνας, οὐδὲ οὓς παῖδας ἔασκε
στείχειν ἐς πόλεμον φθισήνορα· τὼ δέ οἱ οὔ τι
πειθέσθην· κῆρες γὰρ ἄγον μέλανος θανάτοιο.
(Il. 2.830–34)

These men were in the charge of Adrastus and Amphius of the
  linen cuirass,
the two sons of Percosian Merops, a man who excelled all others
in the knowledge of prophecies and thus did not allow his sons
to go to war, the destroyer of men. Yet the two sons
did not obey, for the fates were leading them on toward black
  death.

As we observe, Merops was the father of two other children in addition to Cleite, sons whose premature deaths in the Trojan War he had foreseen and in vain tried to prevent. Quite appropriately, then, he is also the father of Cleite, who married a man whose death in battle has been foreseen and who will herself die young. From this Iliadic model, Apollonius may well have conceived the idea of using a prophecy to motivate Cyzicus's welcome of the Argonauts, which tragically leads to his death.

Homeric references in the brief description of Oros Arkton in section A, which immediately follows the account of their journey there, similarly look forward to certain details of the narrative in section B. The first occurs in the identification of the island:

Ἔστι δέ τις αἰπεῖα Προποντίδος ἔνδοθι νῆσος,
τυτθὸν ἀπὸ Φρυγίης πολυληίου ἠπείροιο
εἰς ἅλα κεκλιμένη ὅσσον τ' ἐπιμύρεται ἰσθμός,

---

17. Σ ad 1.977, Mooney, Ardizzoni, and Campbell ad 1.975, and Vian 96 n. 3 have all noticed this borrowing. In particular, one notes that the phrase Μέροπος Περκωσίου is in the same metrical sedes in each passage. Moreover, Cleite's Homeric epithet, ἐυπλόκαμος, strengthens the association with this Iliadic passage.

χέρσῳ ἔπι πρηνὴς καταειμένη· ἐν δέ οἱ ἀκταὶ
ἀμφίδυμοι· κεῖται δ' ὑπὲρ ὕδατος Αἰσήποιο·
(936–40)

There is a steep island within the Propontis,
not far from the fertile mainland of Phrygia.
It lies out in the sea as far as its flooded isthmus stretches,
sloping toward the continent. On it are twin
headlands, and it lies beyond the Æsepus River.

In this description, Apollonius has the following Odyssean passage in mind:[18]

ἔστι δέ τις νῆσος μέσσῃ ἁλὶ πετρήεσσα,
μεσσηγὺς Ἰθάκης τε Σάμοιό τε παιπαλοέσσης,
Ἀστερίς, οὐ μεγάλη· λιμένες δ' ἔνι ναύλοχοι αὐτῇ
ἀμφίδυμοι· τῇ τόν γε μένον λοχόωντες Ἀχαιοί.
(Od. 4.844–47)

There is a rocky island in the middle of the sea,
in between Ithaca and rugged Samos,
Asteris, not very large in size. On it are twin
harbors for ships. There the Achæans lay in wait for him
    [sc. Telemachus].

Although the phrase ἔστι δέ τις does not call attention to itself *per se*, several other points of contact argue that Apollonius is imitating this specific Homeric passage. First, *Od.* 4.847 is the only instance in Homer where the ἔστι δέ τις formula pertains to an island (cf. *Il.* 2.811; 11.711, 722; 13.32; *Od.* 3.293); second, ἀμφίδυμοι is a Homeric *hapax legomenon*; and third, the island of Asteris shared a peculiar feature with the island of Cyzicus to which Apollonius's ambiguous account, I suggest, makes a subtle reference. After stating that Oros Arkton was an island, Apollonius adds that it had an isthmus (εἰς ἅλα κεκλιμένη ὅσσον τ' ἐπιμύρεται ἰσθμός).[19] Demetrius of Scepsis (cf. Strabo 10.456, 1.59) reported that the island of Asteris was becoming connected to the mainland as a result of constant silting; Asteris, then, was an island with an

---

18. Cf. Ardizzoni *ad* 936, Campbell *ad* 1.936ff.
19. For an important discussion of the status of Cyzicus, see F. Vian, "L'isthme de Cyzique d'après Apollonios de Rhodes (1.936–941)," *REG* 91 (1978) 96–106.

isthmus. Silting was also responsible for connecting Cyzicus to the mainland in historical times.[20] In fact, there was a geographical controversy regarding the status of Cyzicus that went back at least to the fourth century B.C.: some held that Cyzicus was an island (Anaximenes of Lampsacus; cf. Strabo 14.635); others, that it was a peninsula with an isthmus (Scylax 94 *GGM*).[21] Apollonius in typically Hellenistic fashion would seem to be responding to the disputed question by alluding to an answer; the imitation is Apollonius's erudite way of saying, "Cf. Asteris." And yet the reference is not purely academic. The context of the passage is germane to an important element of the Cyzicene episode: Asteris was also the place where the suitors set an ambush (λοχόωντες, 847) for Telemachus on his return to Ithaca. The allusive description thus strikes an ominous chord: someone may be lying in wait for the Argonauts. In fact, in section B we learn that the Gegeneis are lying in ambush (cf. λοχώμενοι, 991) for Heracles; moreover, the Cyzicene army will ultimately launch a nocturnal attack against the returning Argonauts.

In the course of the episode, the Argonauts encounter both a hospitable and a hostile reception from the Doliones.[22] At first, when Cyzicus learns the identity of the Argonauts, he entertains them graciously. Later, however, when the wind blows them back during the night in their first attempt to leave the island, the young king leads an attack against the returning guests in the mistaken belief that they are enemies, the Pelasgian Macries. Apollonius sets the scene for this double reception with a subtle *contaminatio* of two Odyssean passages in the concluding lines of section

---

20. See A. Philippson, "Reisen und Forschungen im westlichen Kleinasien," *Petermanns Mitteilungen* 167 (1910) 50ff., cited by Delage 97–98.
21. For other ancient opinions that likewise were split over this issue, cf. Ruge, "Kyzikos," *RE* 12.1.295, who provides an intelligent discussion of the issue.
22. A. R. Rose, "Three Narrative Themes in Apollonios' Bebrykian Episode (*Argonautica* 2.1–163)," *WS* 18 (1984) 117–18 (cf. Lawall 152, whom she cites in note 7), points out that in this respect, the present episode represents an inversion of the previous: the Lemnian women at first armed themselves for combat against the Argonauts and then, after receiving their embassy and after Hypsipyle spoke with Jason, welcomed them into their city; on Oros Arkton, the Doliones at first welcome the Argonauts and later, on their unexpected return, go to meet them in battle.

A that anticipate both hospitable and inhospitable receptions in Section B.

The first place where the Argonauts land is the port of Kalos Limen,[23] near which lies the Artacië Fountain, where the Argonauts will leave their anchor.[24] The phrase referring to this harbor recalls an Odyssean passage where the phrase καλὸς δὲ λιμήν is found in the same metrical position:[25]

Καλὸς δὲ Λιμὴν ὑπέδεχτο θέουσαν.
Κεῖσε καὶ εὐναίης ὀλίγον λίθον ἐκλύσαντες
Τίφυος ἐννεσίῃσιν ὑπὸ κρήνῃ ἐλίποντο,
κρήνῃ ὑπ' Ἀρταχίῃ· ἕτερον δ' ἕλον, ὅς τις ἀρήρει,
βριθύν· ἀτὰρ κεῖνόν γε θεοπροπίαις Ἑκάτοιο
Νηλεῖδαι μετόπισθεν Ἰάονες ἱδρύσαντο
ἱερόν, ἧ θέμις ἦεν, Ἰησονίης ἐν Ἀθήνης.
(954b-60)

The port of Fair Harbor received the ship in its course.
There they removed the small stone they were using as an anchor,
and, on the advice of Tiphys, they left it under a fountain,
the Artacië Fountain. They took another, heavy one
that suited their needs. The Ionian Neleids years later,
in obedience to the oracle of Apollo, duly set up the first anchor
as a sacred offering in the sanctuary of Jasonian Athena.

καλὸς δὲ λιμὴν ἑκάτερθε πόληος,
λεπτὴ δ' εἰσίθμη· νῆες δ' ὁδὸν ἀμφιέλισσαι
εἰρύαται· πᾶσιν γὰρ ἐπίστιόν ἐστιν ἑκάστῳ.
ἔνθα δέ τέ σφ' ἀγορή, καλὸν Ποσιδήιον ἀμφίς,
ῥυτοῖσιν λάεσσι κατωρυχέεσσ' ἀραρυῖα.
(Od. 6.263b-67)

23. There is a question as to whether Καλὸς Λιμήν (954) was a proper name (as printed by Merkel originally and followed by Mooney, Fränkel, and Vian) or simply a descriptive phrase (as Ardizzoni ad 954, and Delage 99). The use of place names for the other points of disembarkation (986, 1019, 1110) would, to my mind, argue for the former, but it is far from certain.

24. The place where the Argonauts left their first anchor varies in some accounts: Callimachus locates it in Panormus, on the eastern side of the isthmus connecting Oros Arkton to the mainland (Ætia fr. 108 Pf.); Dionysius of Byzantium (87) set it at Ankyraion near the exit of the Bosporus, and Arrian (Periplus 9.2) at the mouth of the Phasis.

25. Noted by Mooney, Ardizzoni, and Campbell ad 1.954, and Vian 261 ad 954.

A fair harbor lies on either side of the city
with a narrow entrance where curved ships
are docked; for there is a ship shed for all vessels.
Here there is also an agora near the beautiful sanctuary of
  Poseidon,
an area marked off by deep-set rocks hauled there for this purpose.

Apollonius not only borrows the phrase but appears also to have adapted an important detail of the Phæacian harbor, near which lay a sanctuary of Poseidon. For near the Cyzicene harbor the Ionians will build in time to come a sanctuary in honor of Jasonian Athena. We should also note a minor detail in which Apollonius seems to have inverted his model. The Phæacian sanctuary was located in the vicinity of the agora, where *large* quarried stones were sunk into the ground; conversely, the Argonauts leave their *small* anchor stone, which will eventually be dedicated in the sanctuary of Athena, at the Artacië Fountain.

This Odyssean passage comes from a speech of Nausicaa (ibid., 255-315) in which she offers to lead Odysseus to the house of Alcinous, her father. There he will eventually be welcomed and entertained. On the other hand, mention of the Artacië Fountain calls to mind another passage in the *Odyssey* where the exact opposite occurred:[26]

οἱ δ' ἴσαν ἐκβάντες λείην ὁδόν, ᾗ περ ἄμαξαι
ἄστυδ' ἀφ' ὑψηλῶν ὀρέων καταγίνεον ὕλην,
κούρῃ δὲ ξύμβληντο πρὸ ἄστεος ὑδρευούσῃ,
θυγατέρ' ἰφθίμη Λαιστρυγόνος Ἀντιφάταο.
ἡ μὲν ἄρ' ἐς κρήνην κατεβήσετο καλλιρέεθρον
Ἀρταχίην· ἔνθεν γὰρ ὕδωρ προτὶ ἄστυ φέρεσκον.

(*Od.* 10.103-8)

After disembarking, they [*sc.* Odysseus's men] went on a level
  road, along which wagons
brought wood down from the lofty mountains to the city.
There before reaching the town they met a young girl fetching
  water—
the virtuous daughter of the Læstrygonian Antiphates.

---

26. Mooney, Ardizzoni, and Campbell *ad* 1.957 refer to this passage without comment on the possible relevance of the Homeric context to the Argonautic.

She had come down to the crystal-clear fountain,
<u>Artacië</u>, from which spring the people were wont to get their water.

In this passage, Odysseus's men meet the daughter of Antiphates, king of the Læstrygonians, also at an Artacië Fountain; like Nausicaa, the princess will lead them to her father's home. But rather than being welcomed and entertained, they are savagely killed and eaten by the cannibalistic Læstrygonians, who according to Homer resembled giants: οὐκ ἄνδρεσσιν ἐοικότες, ἀλλὰ Γίγασιν (ibid. 120). As Delage observed, mention of Artacië anticipates the attack of the gigantic Gegeneis, whom Apollonius had just described several lines earlier.[27] Moreover, in his description of the Læstrygonian onslaught, Homer says that the giants were spearing Odysseus's men like fish: ἰχθῦς δ' ὣς πείροντες ἀτερπέα δαῖτα φέροντο (*Od.* 10.124); Apollonius, I suspect, had this incident in mind in his simile describing the attack of the Gegeneis: πόντιον οἷά τε θῆρα λοχώμενοι ἔνδον ἐόντα (991). The point of contact between the two passages to which Apollonius alludes (the daughters of the local kings lead the strangers to their respective homes with opposite results) thus parallels and to a certain extent foreshadows the two very different receptions that the Argonauts will encounter on Oros Arkton.

B. The Two Ascents of Mount Dindymon: The Deaths of the Gegeneis and Cyzicus (961–1117)

Once the Argonauts make contact with the inhabitants of Oros Arkton, Cyzicus first inquires who they are;[28] for, as Apollonius tells us, he received a prophecy warning him not to engage in combat with a group characterized as an ἀνδρῶν ἡρώων θεῖος στόλος (970). After discovering that the Argonauts comprised such a group, Cyzicus graciously receives them and invites them to row into City Harbor.[29] At a banquet in their honor, the king

---

27. Delage 100–101. On the connection between the Læstrygonians and the Gegeneis, see also F. Vian, "Les ΓΗΓΕΝΕΙΣ de Cyzique et la Grande Mère des Dieux," *RA* 37 (1951) 19–20 n. 6.
28. Levin 92 believes that Cyzicus was going against Homeric etiquette by asking questions first and feeding afterwards. F. Vian in his review of Levin's book, *Gnomon* 46 (1974) 350, shows, however, that this is actually the regular practice in the *Argonautica*.
29. On the plausibility of this scenario, cf. Delage 100.

learns of their mission, and the Argonauts in turn seek information regarding the journey ahead of them. Since Cyzicus does not know what lies beyond the Propontis, the Argonauts decide to climb Mount Dindymon the next day to get more information than the king could offer about what lies before them.[30]

At dawn, Heracles and the younger men move the *Argo* into Chytus Harbor while Jason and the others head to the top of Mount Dindymon along what in the future will be called the Jasonian Path (a). Suddenly the Gegeneis, finding Heracles isolated from the others with only a small group of the younger Argonauts, attack from their place of ambush. In their attempt to trap the men and the ship, they throw boulders down from above. The result is the creation of Chytus—or "Heaped Up"—Harbor. Allusion to the Læstrygonians and the suitors in the previous section looked forward to such an attack. The ensuing battle, a parergon concocted for Heracles by Hera, draws the other Argonauts back from the mountain, and in the end the heroes kill all the Gegeneis (b). The Argonauts then decide to give up the idea of reclimbing Mount Dindymon and to move on instead, without a clear idea of what to expect.

The heroes leave under sail and continue until night, when suddenly the wind shifts and they are blown back to the island. Here, at the center of the central section of the episode (c), Apollonius has indicated that his model for this incident is another well-known Odyssean episode. When Odysseus visited Æolus on his island, he and his men were entertained by the king, who inquired about their experiences; Odysseus, like the Argonauts, also asked information regarding the continuation of his journey home:

μῆνα δὲ πάντα φίλει με καὶ ἐξερέεινεν ἕκαστα,
Ἴλιον Ἀργείων τε νέας καὶ νόστον Ἀχαιῶν·

---

30. This ignorance contrasts with the extensive knowledge of the seas of the inhabitants of the other καλὸς λιμήν, the Phæacians. Cyzicus's ignorance of geography outside the Propontis—whether a result of his ἀπραγμοσύνη (Σ ad 1.979) or of his fear of strangers (Levin 97)—serves two dramatic functions: the realistic need to know where they were going prompts the Argonauts to climb Mount Dindymon, bringing them into contact with the Gegeneis (cf. Fränkel *ad* 1.982–86); and the inability to acquire information about their journey beyond the Propontis makes their inquiry of Phineus all the more necessary (cf. Vian [supra n. 27] 348).

καὶ μὲν ἐγὼ τῷ πάντα κατὰ μοῖραν <u>κατέλεξα</u>.
ἀλλ' ὅτε δὴ καὶ ἐγὼ ὁδὸν ᾔτεον ἠδ' ἐκέλευον
πεμπέμεν, οὐδέ τι κεῖνος ἀνήνατο, τεῦχε δὲ πομπήν.
(*Od.* 10.14–18)

> For a whole month he entertained me and <u>asked</u> me all sorts of questions,
> about Ilion, the ships of the Argives, and the return of the Achæans.
> And I <u>told</u> him exactly how everything happened.
> Then when I asked him for permission to leave and insisted
> that he let me go, he did not refuse, but even assisted my departure.

This incident parallels Jason's experience on Oros Arkton at the home of Cyzicus, where host and guest likewise question each other:[31]

Ἀλλήλους δ' <u>ἐρέεινον</u> ἀμοιβαδίς· ἤτοι ὁ μέν σφεων
πεύθετο ναυτιλίης ἄνυσιν Πελίαό τ' ἐφετμάς·
οἱ δὲ περικτιόνων πόλιας καὶ κόλπον ἅπαντα
εὐρείης πεύθοντο Προποντίδος· οὐ μὲν ἐπιπρὸ
ἠείδει <u>καταλέξαι</u> ἐελδομένοισι δαῆναι.
(980–84)

> They <u>asked</u> each other questions in turn. The king learned about
> the goal of their expedition and about the commands of Pelias;
> the men learned about the cities of the neighboring peoples and the
> entire gulf of the wide Propontis. But he was not able to <u>tell</u> them
> about the areas beyond the gulf, despite their desire to learn.

More significant, after a friendly reception and exchange of information, the wind blows the Argonauts back to a hostile reception on Oros Arkton:

Ἡ δ' ἔθεεν λαίφεσσι πανήμερος· οὐ μὲν ἰούσης
νυκτὸς ἔτι ῥιπὴ μένεν ἔμπεδον, <u>ἀλλὰ θύελλαι
ἀντίαι ἁρπάγδην ὀπίσω φέρον</u>, ὄφρ' ἐπέλασσαν
αὖτις ἐϋξείνοισι Δολίοσιν.
(1015–18a)

---

31. Cyzicus's ignorance significantly contrasts with the knowledge of his model, Æolus.

The ship ran all day under sail. As night fell,
the current of the wind no longer remained steady, <u>but squalls
coming from the opposite direction carried the ship by force
backwards</u>
until they approached once again the hospitable Doliones.

This is precisely what happened to Odysseus, who also experienced an unfriendly welcome upon his return to Æolus's island home because of an unexpected blast of wind:[32]

τοὺς δ' αἶψ' ἁρπάξασα φέρεν πόντονδε θύελλα
κλαίοντας, γαίης ἄπο πατρίδος.
                                    (Od.10.48-49)

Immediately <u>a squall seized them and carried them out to sea</u>
weeping, far away from their homeland.

When Odysseus returned to Æolus's island, his former host, now no longer hospitable, required him to leave at once because, in his (Æolus's) eyes, Odysseus was hated by the gods (ibid. 72-75, quoted below); when the Argonauts return, their former host, Cyzicus, unwittingly leads his army against them and tragically dies in the fray (b). The poet, as we have seen him do so frequently, highlights an important Homeric imitation by placing it at the center of its section, and, as in this case, also at the center of the episode. The imitation of the Æolus episode not only is a subtextual reflection of the friendly and unfriendly receptions that the Argonauts encounter on Oros Arkton, but also provides the link between two unrelated stories, one about the deaths of the Gegeneis and the other about the death of Cyzicus, brought together by Apollonius almost certainly for the first time.

In the wider context of the borrowed verse in question, Æolus refused to entertain Odysseus when he showed up for a second time on his island, because in his eyes Odysseus's return was an indication that he was hated by the gods:

---

32. Mooney *ad* 1.1017, and Campbell *ad* 1.1016–17 both observed the verbal echo. Apollonius will look to this Odyssean episode once again in Book 3; there Jason's interview with Æëtes recalls Odysseus's unfriendly second reception by Æolus; cf. Hunter *ad* 299–438.

Ἔρρ' ἐκ νήσου θᾶσσον, ἐλέγχιστε ζωόντων·
οὐ γάρ μοι θέμις ἐστὶ κομιζέμεν οὐδ' ἀποπέμπειν
ἄνδρα τὸν ὅς κε θεοῖσιν ἀπέχθηται μακάρεσσιν.
ἔρρ', ἐπεὶ ἀθανάτοισιν ἀπεχθόμενος τόδ' ἱκάνεις.
(*Od.* 10.72-75)

Depart from this island quickly, most hated of all people alive.
It is not right for me to assist or send off
a man who is hated by the blessed gods.
Depart, since you have come here hated by the immortals.

Comparison between the Odyssean and Argonautic situations suggests that in their return to Oros Arkton, the Argonauts too have somehow angered the gods. In fact, the men soon learn from the seer Mopsus that they must propitiate the mother of all the gods (Μητέρα συμπάντων μακάρων, 1094), identified as Rhea at 1139. The divine wrath, implicit in the need for propitiation and suggested by the Odyssean model, must result at least in part from the killing of the stone-throwing Gegeneis (cf. 994–95), who, as their name implies, are the sons of Ge, or Earth, with whom Rhea is identified.[33] It is therefore significant that when Apollonius first described the Gegeneis, he used phraseology recalling Hesiod's description of the Hecatonchires, who are likewise stone-throwing sons of Earth, in the *Theogony*:[34]

ἐξ γὰρ ἑκάστῳ χεῖρες ὑπέρβιοι ἠερέθοντο,
αἱ μὲν ἀπὸ στιβαρῶν ὤμων δύο, ταὶ δ' ὑπένερθεν
τέσσαρες αἰνοτάτῃσιν ἐπὶ πλευρῇς ἀραρυῖαι.
(944–46)

For they each had six enormous arms above their waists:
two emanating from their powerful shoulders, four
attached to their gruesome sides below.

Ἄλλοι δ' αὖ Γαίης τε καὶ Οὐρανοῦ ἐξεγένοντο
τρεῖς παῖδες μεγάλοι <τε> καὶ ὄβριμοι, οὐκ ὀνομαστοί,
Κόττος τε Βριάρεώς τε Γύγης θ', ὑπερήφανα τέκνα.
τῶν ἑκατὸν μὲν χεῖρες ἀπ' ὤμων ἀΐσσοντο

---

33. E.g., Æschylus *Supp.* 892, Sophocles *Ph.* 391; see Rapp, "Rhea," Roscher 4.92–93.
34. Vian 95 n. 1 and Campbell *ad* 1.944–45 observed the borrowing; N.B. *Th.* 150–53 are repeated once again at lines 671–73 in the Hesiodic poem.

ἄπλαστοι, κεφαλαὶ δὲ ἑκάστῳ πεντήκοντα
ἐξ ὤμων ἐπέφυκον ἐπὶ στιβαροῖσι μέλεσσιν,
ἰσχὺς δ' ἄπλητος κρατερὴ μεγάλῳ ἐπὶ εἴδει.
(*Th.* 147–53)

Three other sons were born from Gaia and Uranus,
huge, powerful, and indescribable:
Cottus, Briareus, and Gyes, hybristic offspring.
One hundred arms sprang from their shoulders,
unapproachable, and they each had fifty heads
growing from their shoulders upon their strong limbs;
the enormous strength in their awesome presence was terrifying.

Although Apollonius nowhere says so, Rhea would seem to have been responsible for sending the winds that drove the Argonauts back to Oros Arkton, and the only apparent reason suggested by the text is the death of the Gegeneis. In turn, the Argonauts, forced to go back to Oros Arkton as a result of the first battle, must then face the second, in which Cyzicus dies. In this way the young king fulfills his destiny by dying at the hands of a θεῖος στόλος.[35] Accordingly, Apollonius's association of these two battles through the Homeric imitation suggests to the reader a fact that Mopsus will only later recognize through the omen: the Argonauts have angered the gods.

After the battle, dawn appears—it was also at dawn that the Argonauts began their ascent of Mount Dindymon, which led to their fight with the Gegeneis—and reveals the disaster (*a*). There follow three days of lamentation, with a funeral that consists of a triple procession around the body of the king, and then the solemn burial in the Leimonian Plain (1057–62). Thereafter, the king's wife, Cleite, commits suicide out of grief, and the nymphs of the region cry so profusely that their tears become an everlasting fountain, which they call Cleite after Cyzicus's hapless bride (1063–69).[36] The double tragedy instigates a fast. This ritual

---

35. In addition to generating sympathy by emphasizing Cyzicus's youthfulness (cf. Fränkel *ad* 1.972c), Apollonius also casts him in the role of the young vegetation god who, like Atys and Adonis, favorites of the earth goddess, dies in his prime; cf. Vian (supra n. 27) 20–21.

36. Cf. A. Ardizzoni, "Cleite, ovvero la fonte delle lacrime," *Mythos: Scripta in honorem M. Untersteiner* (Genoa 1970) 37–42, who has argued quite

fasting corresponds structurally with the banquet at the beginning of this section. The Doliones not only abstain from food; they even stop milling grain for a long time, and afterwards, when they break their fast, they eat only uncooked meals. This practice, we are told, will evolve into the annual custom of milling the grain for sacrificial cakes at public mills among the future Ionian inhabitants of Cyzicus (cf. 1071–77).[37]

Despite the apparent reconciliation with the Doliones, however, the Argonauts are not yet in the clear; they face further problems with the winds. Harsh storms keep them from leaving for twelve days. The number, I believe, is significant. Since twelve Doliones perished along with Cyzicus during the battle (cf. 1040–47), it would appear that the Argonauts must stay on the island one day for each of the warriors they killed.[38] From this, one would conclude that Rhea's anger springs from the deaths of Cyzicus and

---

persuasively that the fountain was formed not from the tears of Cleite, but from those of the local nymphs. As he points out (42), Apollonius's account, unlike his models' (Deiochus and Neanthes), does not emphasize the wonder of the metamorphosis, but the sympathy that nature reveals at the passing of the young bride. Cf. Giangrande 5–6.

37. On these lines, cf. B. A. van Groningen, "Un passage difficile d'Apollonios de Rhodes (*Argonautiques* 1.1071–1077)," *Mnemosyne* 15 (1962) 268–70, who argues that οὐδὲ γὰρ αὐτῶν / ἔτλη τις πάσσασθαι ἐδητύος (1071b–72a) was an earlier version that crept into the text from the margin and should be excised, and accordingly that Apollonius changed his account from one dealing with a communal fast in response to Cyzicus's death to an etiological story explaining the later Ionian custom of the ritual use of public mills. Van Groningen also suggests changing ἄφλεκτα (1074) to the unattested ἄφλαστα (i.e., "unmilled") to bring this line as well into conformity with the ætion. I find no problem with the transmitted text, however; the transition from a fast to the breaking of that fast with a special concoction, in this case unmilled and uncooked food, seems quite normal (one thinks of the drinking of kykeon in the Eleusinian Mysteries).

38. There was a controversy among early Apollonian commentators as to whether or not the poet invented the names of the Cyzicene warriors who died in the battle with the Argonauts. Sophocleius (cf. Σ *ad* 1.1039) stated that the names came from Deiochus. Commenting on Τηλεκλῆα ἠδὲ Μεγαβρόντην, Σ *ad* 1.1040–41 reported the opinion of Lucillus Tarrhæus, that Apollonius invented these names and did not get them from a historical account. F. Hasluck, *Cyzicus* (Cambridge 1910) 240 n. 2, has, to my mind, pointed the way to the best solution to the apparent discrepancy: Apollonius took ten names from Deiochus and invented only these two cited by the scholiast. If this is so, the addition of the two warriors suggests that the number twelve was significant for the poet.

the Doliones in addition to those of the Gegeneis.[39] Afterwards, on the thirteenth night, a halcyon, sent by the goddess Rhea, appears over Jason's head—a detail, as the scholiast *ad* 1.1085–87b reports (noted above), that Apollonius borrowed from a *Pæan* of Pindar (fr. 62 Snell). Mopsus, who is on guard duty, observes the bird and interprets its cries as a signal that the end of the storm is near. He arouses Jason from sleep and informs him both of this sign and of the need to propitiate Rhea. Mention of Rhea may at first appear surprising, even intrusive; but, as we have seen above, details in the narrative show how fitting the earth goddess's interest in the battles on Oros Arkton is. The slaughter of the Gegeneis, who are children of Earth (Ge), points to such an interpretation, as does the premature death of Cyzicus, which is reminiscent of the death of the young male associate of the earth goddess. The description of the Argonauts' celebration of Rhea, which follows in the third and final section of the episode, will thus prove to be a fitting conclusion to the events on Oros Arkton.

In response to Mopsus's interpretation of the halcyon's message, the Argonauts make a second ascent of Mount Dindymon, this time without incident. Just as in their first attempt, they move their ship to a different harbor before the climb and leave several men behind (1109–11). At this point, the Argonauts view the area that prompted their first attempt to scale the mountain. The sojourn on Oros Arkton offered the Argonauts the possibility of securing both provisions and information about the voyage ahead of them. Both needs initiate a series of violent events, including the destruction of the Gegeneis and the death of Cyzicus, which result in the foundation of the cult of Rhea on Mount Dindymon.

A. The Mysteries of Rhea on Mount Dindymon and Departure from Oros Arkton (1117–52)

The initiation of the rites in honor of Rhea (*A*) structurally balances the Argonauts' initiation into the Samothracian rites on their way to Cyzicus (A).[40] I have already mentioned several

---

39. Such a conclusion is also tempting given the similarity between Cyzicus and the young male associate of the earth goddess, as Vian pointed out (cf. supra n. 35).
40. D. A. van Krevelen, "Der Kybelekult in den *Argonautika* des Apollonios von Rhodos 1.1078–1153," *RhM* 97 (1954) 75–82, stated that Apollonius's

verbal and thematic details shared by the two sections that underscore the corresponsion. In addition to these explicit points of contact, certain ritual and legendary elements of the Samothracian Mysteries that Apollonius does not describe, but that we know from other sources, resemble salient features of the Argonauts' sojourn on Oros Arkton and their celebration of Rhea on Mount Dindymon:[41] the inhabitants of Samothrace were called Pelasgians (cf. Herodotus 2.51) ≈ the inhabitants of Oros Arkton, whom the Argonauts meet in Deiochus's account (cf. Σ *ad* 1.987a), and the enemies of the Doliones in Apollonius's version are likewise Pelasgians (1024); the Dactyls were associated both with the Samothracian (cf. Ephorus *FGrHist* 70 F 104) and the Cyzicene (1126–30) Mysteries; the Samothracian initiation took place at night (cf. Val. Flacc. *Arg.* 2.439–42) ≈ the Argonauts likewise celebrate a pannychis (1150–52); in both the Samothracian (cf. Nonn. *D.* 3.61–78) and the Cyzicene (1134–38) rites the celebrants perform an armed dance.[42] Moreover, in Samothracian legend Dardanus, the son of Zeus and the Atlantid Electra, left the island because, in some accounts, he killed his brother Eëtion (cf. Servius *ad Æn.* 3.167); from there he sailed on a raft to Phrygia and established on Mount Ida a cult to Meter (cf. Diod. 5.49). This feature of Samothracian mythology might well explain the poet's association of the two cults. For as it turns out, the Argonauts' journey to Oros Arkton closely parallels that of Dardanus in that, like Dardanus, they sail from Samothrace to the region of Phrygia (cf. 937, 1139), establish a cult to Meter, identified as Rhea, and, as he is, they are held accountable for killing a young man.

Apollonius begins his account of the Argonauts' cult in honor of Meter/Rhea with mention of the cult statue that Argus makes

---

interest in this cult was propagandistic: the Ptolemies promoted the development of the cult of Cybele. Although this may be so, the episode gives no explicit or implicit indications that this is the case. Van Krevelen's argument that the cult stands apart from the rest of the action is incorrect, as I hope my analysis shows.

41. On the Samothracian Mysteries, see, for example, W. Burkert, *Greek Religion,* trans. J. Raffan (Cambridge, Mass., 1985) 281–85; and S. G. Cole, *Theoi Megaloi: The Cult of the Great Gods at Samothrace* (Leiden 1984).

42. See Cole (supra n. 41) 29.

from a vine stump (1117). There follows a description of the sanctuary that they construct (1120–24). The men then call upon Meter Dindymië and her assistants, Titias and Cyllenus, two of the Idæan Dactyls, who were born in a cave on Mount Dicte in Crete (1125–31). Jason offers prayers and libations to the goddess while Orpheus leads an armed dance to drown out the cries of the Doliones, who are lamenting their king. This scene recalls a practice that continued among the Phrygians, who used the rhombus and tambourine instead of weapons and armor to honor Rhea (1132–39). There appear thereafter miraculous signs indicating the goddess's acceptance of the ritual: the vegetation blooms, wild animals leave their lairs and rub up tamely against the Argonauts, and a fountain suddenly appears in a place that up to that moment was dry; in the future, people will call this the Jasonian Fountain (1140–50). Finally, the men celebrate an all-night banquet and leave at dawn after the winds have died down (1151–52).

Apollonius's description of the Argonautic rite contains many striking points of contact with Callimachus's *Hymn to Zeus*.[43] I summarize the relevant section of the hymn: following a humorous introductory section in which he establishes Zeus's place of birth (*H*. 1.1–9), Callimachus briefly describes the god's birth to Rhea and the goddess's subsequent quandary: there is no water for cleansing the blood of childbirth (ibid. 10–17). Rhea then strikes the earth, which produces the waters of Arcadia, a place that up to that time lacked water (ibid. 18–32). The nymph Neda, who will give her name to the largest river of Arcadia, carries Zeus from Arcadia to Thenae and from there to Cnossus, where he will live in a cave. He will be attended by the Dictæan Meliae and Adrasteia, suckled by Amaltheia, and protected by the war dance of the Curetes from exposing his existence to Cronus through his cries (ibid. 33–54). Accordingly, the following explicit correspondences exist between the two poems:

- Rhea is the goddess featured in both accounts.
- Rhea produces water in Arcadia and on top of Mount Dindymon, both of which up to that time lacked water.

---

43. Fraser (supra n. 2) 1.635–36, although acknowledging Apollonius's debt to Callimachus and referring specifically to his hymns, does not list the *Hymn to Zeus* among the examples cited (cf. ibid. 2.897 *ad* n. 162).

- Both the Curetes and the Argonauts perform a war dance to drown out crying.

In addition to these, there are other, more subtle points of contact between the two poems. A. H. Griffiths observed a neat geographical trick that Callimachus played in the *Hymn to Zeus*.[44] At line 42, we learn that Neda left Thenae, and in the next line the poet notes parenthetically that Thenae was near Cnossus. The location of Thenae was a matter of dispute: some placed it in Arcadia, and others on Crete. Since Neda begins her journey in Arcadia, one naturally believes that the poet locates Thenae in Arcadia. But in line 43, we are disabused of this notion with the statement Θεναὶ δ' ἔσαν ἐγγύθι Κνωσοῦ. In a similar fashion, in the Argonautic passage under consideration, Titias and Cyllenus are called in line 1128 the assistants of Μήτηρ Ἰδαίη, and since the Argonauts are near Phrygia, one thinks that the poet is referring to the Phrygian Mount Ida. In the very next line, however, Apollonius identifies these assistants as the Δάκτυλοι Ἰδαῖοι Κρηταέες, and so he has the Cretan and not the Phrygian Ida in mind.

Other points are to be noted: the Διχταῖαι Μελίαι and Ἀδρήστεια attend the infant Zeus on Crete (*H.* 1.47) ≈ the Δάκτυλοι Ἰδαῖοι attend Rhea on Mount Dindymon (*Argo.* 1.1129), and from the top of the mountain the Argonauts can see the πεδίον Νηπήιον Ἀδρηστείης (ibid. 1116);[45] Zeus was reared in a cave on Mount Dicte (cf. *H.* 1.34, 47) ≈ the Dactyls were born in a cave on Mount Dicte (*Argo.* 1.1130); finally, Callimachus calls the Arcadians the grandsons of the Lycaonian Bear (Λυκαονίης ἄρκτοιο, 41) ≈ the Argonauts initiate the rites in honor of Rhea on Bear Mountain (Οὔρεσιν Ἄρκτων, 1150).

Although the dating of these two poems is by no means secure, few would deny that the *Hymn to Zeus* is one of Callimachus's earliest extant poems.[46] If, as seems most likely, this hymn antedates

---

44. "Six Passages in Callimachus and the Anthology," *BICS* 17 (1970) 32–33; cf. G. R. McLennan, *Callimachus: Hymn to Zeus* (Rome 1977) *ad* 42.

45. Callimachus mentions Ἀδρήστεια in conjunction with the πεδίον Νηπήιον and also the river Αἴσηπος (cf. *Argo.* 1.1116) at *Hecala* fr. 299 Pf. (= Hollis fr. 116); the connection of Adrasteia and the Nepeian Plain with the Æsepus, however, is far from certain; cf. Pfeiffer *ad loc.*

46. I have discussed this issue elsewhere: cf. "Lies and Allusions: The Addressee and Date of Callimachus' *Hymn to Zeus*," *ClAnt* 5 (1986) 155–70,

the *Argonautica*,[47] and if Apollonius had this piece in mind when he wrote the Cyzicus episode (as the many points of contact lead one to believe), the question arises: Does recognition of the imitation affect or enhance in any way our understanding of the Argonautic passage?

As we have seen above, Apollonius never explicitly tells his reader why the Argonauts return to Oros Arkton or why Rhea needs to be propitiated. Rather, the reader is asked to draw implications from elements in both the text and subtext. One of these lies at the center of the episode, where the poet highlights a Homeric imitation that appears to confirm what one infers from the connection between the Gegeneis, the sons of Earth killed by the Argonauts, and Rhea, the earth goddess, who Mopsus later states requires propitiation: the Argonauts, like Odysseus, have offended a divinity who is to be seen as responsible for having them blown back to Oros Arkton. The structural connection with the Samothracian Mysteries, as I suggested above, sheds further light on the significance of the rites on Mount Dindymon. Like Dardanus, Jason and the Argonauts must atone for bloodshed by instituting a cult. Reference to the *Hymn to Zeus*, I posit, exerts a similar effect on our understanding of the events atop Mount Dindymon. In the Callimachean poem, Rhea needed water to cleanse the blood of childbirth, and so she caused the earth to bring forth water in Arcadia for the first time. Observing this similarity, one might well conclude that the purpose for the water is related. The Argonauts, like Rhea, can now cleanse themselves of the blood both of Cyzicus and of the Gegeneis, the latter being, like Zeus, children of the same divinity.

At the beginning of the episode, the Argonauts were initiated into the Samothracian Mysteries; and at the conclusion, following the first blood that they will shed on their mission, they are initiated into the Mysteries of Rhea on Mount Dindymon. It would appear that the experience on Oros Arkton marks an important,

---

in particular 156–57 n. 5 for citations of earlier opinions regarding the date of the hymn. Vian 230 n. 3 too believes that the Callimachean hymn was the earlier piece and that Apollonius had it in mind at 2.1123–24 and 1179–80.

47. This would be the case even if one places the writing of Book 1 as early as the mid- to late 270s; cf. Vian x, and T. B. L. Webster, "Chronological Problems in Early Alexandrian Poetry," *WS* 76 (1963) 68–78.

almost liminal, stage in the Argonautic expedition. Before they go on to the next phase of their journey, they encounter death, and then, like Rhea in Callimachus's hymn, they undergo purification for the blood they have spilled.[48] For the Argonauts, and for Jason in particular, Oros Arkton proves to be a crucial phase in the expedition to Colchis. They have already affirmed their commitment to the mission by refusing the tempting offer of the Lemnian women. Now they must overcome further obstacles to their advance: monsters sent by an angry stepmother and, oddly enough, a timorous young man who lives in fear of his fate. The first obstacle was sent specifically against Heracles; Jason forms a close bond with the second, both being the youthful leaders of their groups. The identification of Heracles and Jason with their victims once again sets the two heroes in vivid contrast. Moreover, as becomes clear through the structural parallelism of the two battles on Oros Arkton, their involvement in the killings parallels their divergent approaches to heroic action.

When Heracles and several of the younger men had moved the *Argo* into Chytus Harbor, the Gegeneis attacked, and a battle ensued (Bb). Two similes frame the battle. In the first, Apollonius compares the attempt to trap Heracles and the others within the harbor to fishermen trying to catch a sea creature (991). The incident concludes with the laying-out of the bodies of the dead monsters on the shore. Some of the monsters have their heads and chests in the water; others, their legs. The Argonauts are likened to lumberjacks who set out logs on the beach for soaking (1003–5). Each simile features the occupation of people who control some facet of nature in their profession. The similes, then, furnish apt comparisons for an armed encounter arranged by Hera against Heracles, the great monster killer and, as Burkert calls him, "Master of Animals."[49]

In the corresponding battle with the Doliones (B*b*), once again two similes frame the conflict. In the first, the vehement attack of the combatants is likened to a swift fire that falls on dry brush

---

48. This episode would seem to be balanced by the purification Jason and Medea undergo in Book 4 (659–752) for the murder of Apsyrtus.

49. W. Burkert, *Structure and History in Greek Mythology and Ritual* (Berkeley and Los Angeles 1979) 78ff.

(1027–28). It is during this battle that Jason unwittingly kills Cyzicus, who thus fulfills his destiny, and that twelve other Dolionian soldiers fall at the hands of the Argonauts. Apollonius compares the surviving Doliones in their flight to doves who flee before swift hawks (1049–50). In this second battle, it was the wind, a force that can fan a fire out of control, that drove the helpless Argonauts back to Oros Arkton; and in the bloody battle that ensued the helpless Doliones, attempting a vain defense against their recently departed guest-friends, fled like doves back to the protection of their walls. Like the fire and hawks that characterize the victors, their leader can be seen as the instantiation of an uncontrollable force of destruction, lacking any feeling or rational planning for his actions because of his ignorance of the enemy he faces in an unexpected battle.

The differences between the two battles and the Argonauts associated with each are telling. When it comes to heroic feats, Heracles, like the fishermen and lumberjacks, is in complete control. It is only in matters of love and passion that he is outmatched, as will be seen in the very next episode. Moreover, in his overbearing self-confidence, Heracles will even choose to act contrary to μοῖρα (1317) in the pursuit of a heroic adventure (cf. 1.122–31). Jason is quite the opposite. Although he will prove to be just as efficient in achieving his goal as Heracles, he nonetheless gives no evidence of controlling the avenues to his success. Like the fire and hawks, he turns out to be a consuming and uncaring agent of destruction, leaving in his wake the lifeless body, not of a monster, but of a newly married and childless young man. And unlike Heracles, who is forced to leave the expedition and thus to conform to μοῖρα, as Glaucus will announce near the end of the book (1315–25), Jason is ever the unwitting agent of fate. On Oros Arkton, he brings about Cyzicus's μοῖρα (1035), just as on Lemnos he and the Argonauts restored the male population of the island for Aphrodite, and just as ultimately he will bring about the fated death of Pelias through the agency of Medea for Hera. Of particular note in this comparison are the victims of the two battles. Since Heracles, the man of strength, is associated with violent and awesome creatures like himself, I think it fair to say that Jason is to be linked with the young man he slew on the battlefield not only in their ages and roles of leadership but also in their unfortunate marriages, from which neither will be survived by children (on Cyzicus, cf. 973-75).

If this identification of victor and vanquished is valid, a more speculative implication of the killings on Oros Arkton suggests itself. In an episode framed with scenes of initiation and lustration, Heracles and Jason might be thought of as immolating virtual representatives of themselves. Since in Mystery religions—the cults at Samothrace and on Mount Dindymon are μυστήρια—the death and rebirth of the celebrants are ritually enacted or vicariously experienced in the sacrifice as an anticipation of their future death and rebirth into a new life, it would appear that the killing of the Gegeneis and Cyzicus in some sense sanctifies Heracles and Jason, the two heroic prototypes, for their respective heroic careers, which will diverge in the next episode.[50] Both men will go on to achieve their goals within the temporal confines of the poem: Heracles crushing Ladon and seizing the golden apples of the Hesperides through his irresistible strength, and Jason plowing the field with fire-breathing bulls, killing the offspring of the sown dragon's teeth, and taking the golden fleece from the drugged serpent through the magic of Medea, the young and unfortunate victim of Jason's irresistible charm.

THE episode of the sojourn on Oros Arkton is striking indeed. Apollonius has succeeded in creating a unified and convincing story out of many heterogeneous elements, interweaving at the same time many academic points of interest (e.g., topographical, cultural, and historical) into the fabric of the narrative. In this daring version of the Cyzicus tale, one can observe the felicitous marriage of Alexandrian scholarship and the kind of tragedy one

---

50. Cf. W. Burkert, *Homo Necans*, trans. P. Bing (Berkeley and Los Angeles 1983) 296, who states: "In order to reach a new plane of existence in the initiation ritual, one must normally undergo 'sufferings,' an encounter with death, through which death is overcome: in sacrifice, in the act of killing, the will to live rises triumphant over the fallen victim." If I am correct in this interpretation, I would add that such symbolic death and rebirth of the hero is encountered by both Achilles and Odysseus in their respective epics: Achilles "dies" in the person of Patroclus, whom Hector slays dressed in Achilles' armor, and Odysseus goes to and returns from the underworld, both prior to committing themselves to their climactic ἄεθλος.

associates with the classical era,⁵¹ and in the course of this Cyzicene tragedy, Apollonius affords us another glimpse of the stark contrast between Jason and Heracles. Both are dangerous men, but for dissimilar reasons and with distinctive results.

51. Levin 96 appropriately makes the comparison between Apollonius's Cyzicus and Sophocles' Œdipus; cf. Stössl (supra n. 1) 13 n. 14 and 19 n. 27, who, despite his overall negative view of this episode, calls attention to the Herodotean manner in which the oracle has been fulfilled.

8

The Best of the Argonauts
Heracles Abandoned (*Argo.* 1.1153–1362)

HERACLES' abandonment of the Argonauts before their arrival in Colchis comes as no surprise. In most versions of the story, the great hero never faced Æëtes.[1] Dramatic reasons, and not tradition alone, preclude his participation in the taking of the fleece. To rephrase what one of the Argonauts said after they defeated the Bebrycians in battle (*Argo.* 2.145–50): What would Æëtes have done if some god had brought Heracles to Colchis? One might better ask, What would Jason have done? Apollonius makes it apparent that Heracles could have managed the expedition completely on his own; not only can he row the *Argo* by himself, as he does when the others give up from exhaustion in the rowing contest that takes place in the present episode (cf. 1161–62), but he would not have needed or even, like Idas (cf. *Argo.* 3.556–63), have accepted the help of Medea (Heracles made his negative attitude toward dalliance with women quite clear on Lemnos). Moreover, Apollonius gives a vivid illustration of Heracles' heroic self-sufficiency in Book 4: just before the Argonauts come close to meeting up with Heracles in North Africa, he has

---

1. In one account, Heracles never sailed with the Argonauts, but at the time of the expedition was a slave to Omphale (Herodorus *FGrHist* 31 F 41); in others, he was abandoned either at Aphetae (Hesiod *Ceycos Gamos* 263 M&W, Herodotus 7.193) because he was too heavy (Pherecydes *FGrHist* 3 F 111) or in Mysia while looking for Hylas (as in Apollonius and Theocritus *Id.* 13 in part). In a few versions, however, Heracles does make the journey all the way to Colchis, either together with the Argonauts (Dionysius of Mytilene [Scytobrachion] *FGrHist* 32 F 6b, Demaratus *FGrHist* 42 F 2b) or on foot after the Argonauts arrive (Theocritus *Id.* 13.73–75). Σ *ad* 1.1289–91a provides a useful summary of several different versions; see Knorr 33–43.

slain the dragon, Ladon, who guarded the golden apples of the Hesperides (4.1393–1405).[2] Certainly Ladon plays a role comparable to that of Æëtes' dragon, who guarded the golden fleece. Had Heracles reached Colchis, Medea's aid would have been superfluous; he could have faced Æëtes (cf. *Argo.* 3.1232–34) and taken the fleece by himself.[3] On the other hand, no one among the rest of the Argonauts, including Jason, could possibly achieve the goal of the quest by himself. Without Heracles, the Argonauts must rely upon themselves and the timely aid of others.

Up to the present episode, Apollonius presented sharply divergent pictures of Jason and Heracles. On the beach at Pagasae, Jason broods over the many details involved in organizing the expedition; Heracles fells an ox with a blow from his club. On Lemnos, Jason prefers to stay in bed with Hypsipyle while Heracles impatiently waits, and finally issues a caustic call for action. On Oros Arkton, the similes that characterize the two battles featuring Heracles and Jason, respectively, underscore Heracles' dynamic control of, and Jason's passive surrender to, the power of nature. In Mysia we shall encounter yet another view of this heroic antithesis, but from a slightly different angle. For while in the previous two episodes on Lemnos and Oros Arkton Jason's passivity looks bad alongside Heracles' impressive dynamism, in Mysia the latter's impulsiveness leads to his suffering and abandonment, while the former's inactivity, born of ἀμηχανίη, and his ability to handle νείκεα lead ultimately to an even stronger bond among the men and thereby establish him as the best of the Argonauts.

STRUCTURE

Once again Apollonius takes advantage of the ring structure to accentuate contrasting portraits of Heracles and Jason.[4] Two

---

2. Cf. D. C. Feeney, "Following after Hercules in Virgil and Apollonius," *PVS* 18 (1986) 62–66 (cf. *The Gods in Epic* [Oxford 1991] 94–98); J. S. Rusten, *Dionysius Scytobrachion* (Opladen 1982) 1–18, 65–76.

3. Lawall 130 observed that Heracles in Colchis would have been an embarrassment to the poet; cf. M. G. Palombi, "Eracle e Ila nelle *Argonautiche* di Apollonio Rodio," *SCO* 35 (1985) 85.

4. For this section, besides Hurst 64–66 and 129–33, cf. also P. Thierstein, *Bau der Szenen in den Argonautika des Apollonios Rhodios* (Bern 1971)

corresponding sections, one focusing on Heracles (A) and the other on Jason (A), fall on either side of a brief central scene, in which the poet sets the moment when the Argonauts sail from Mysia, accidentally leaving Heracles, Hylas, and Polyphemus behind (B). In section A, the circumstances that lead up to Heracles' abandonment unfold in two internally balanced subsections. In the first (Aa), during the rowing contest that ensues as a result of the absence of wind, Heracles loses his oar, which breaks while he singlehandedly rows the *Argo*; after this, they pull into Mysia late in the day—the time, Apollonius says, when a plowman curses his stomach because of his hunger (α). Then, Heracles goes off in search of a tree out of which he can make an oar (β). It is while doing this that he loses Hylas, whom a nymph spies and draws into her pool.[5] A brief digression about how Heracles acquired control of Hylas precedes the poet's account of the rape of the youth: a hungry Heracles took him as his servant after first killing the youth's father over a draft animal that he refused to give him to eat; this, we are told, is the way Heracles initiated a war against the Dryopians (α). As can be seen from this summary, the plowman Theiodamas attacked by the hungry Heracles in subsection α recalls the simile of the hungry plowman in α, thus enclosing this portion of the episode. As I shall argue below, hunger will prove to be an important element in Heracles' abandonment. In the second half of the first section of the episode (Ab), Apollonius contrasts two reactions to the loss of Hylas—those of Polyphemus (α) and Heracles (α)—and qualifies each with an animal simile. The bridge between the two portraits is Polyphemus's brief speech informing Heracles of the disappearance of Hylas (β). Thus, in section A, we see two sides of Heracles: he is the powerful hero who can row the *Argo* by himself, uproot a tree for his new oar, and conquer the Dryopians (Aa), and he is the frantic lover who loses complete control of himself when his young boyfriend, Hylas, disappears (Ab).

48–57; and A. Köhnken, *Apollonios Rhodios und Theokrit. Die Hylas- und die Amykosgeschichten beider Dichter und die Frage der Priorität*, Hypomnemata 12 (Gottingen 1965) 17–25.

5. On the parallelism and simultaneity of the actions of Heracles and Hylas, cf. Palombi (supra n. 3) 72.

In the corresponding section of the episode (*A*), the structure of which section is an extended ring, Apollonius focuses upon Jason. When dawn reveals that Heracles, together with Polyphemus and Hylas, has been left behind, the second νεῖκος of the book ensues, in which Telamon accuses Jason of abandoning Heracles (*a*). The initiation of the νεῖκος corresponds to its resolution in an amicable reconciliation after the men learn that Zeus ordained Heracles' departure from the group (*a*). In between, the crisis initiated by the loss of Heracles is worked out. As the men are about to go back to Mysia to search for Heracles upon Telamon's insistence, the Boreads intervene and successfully prevent the return. The narrator then describes their fate: because of their interference, Heracles will later kill the Boreads after the funeral games celebrated in honor of Pelias (*b*). Although the Argonauts are now back on course, the bad feelings of the νεῖκος have not dissipated. At this point, Glaucus appears; and, in a speech corresponding to the intervention of the Boreads, he informs them of Zeus's plan, telling them at the same time not to grieve for his loss. He also recounts to them the fates of all three of the Argonauts left behind (*b*). At the center of the ring lies the picturesque description of Glaucus's miraculous appearance (*c*). Apollonius gives special prominence to the event responsible for the abandonment of Heracles—Tiphys's call for a quick departure[6]—by placing it at the center of the whole episode as the transitional point from the portrait of Heracles to that of Jason (*B*).

Before the close of the episode, there is a brief epilogue (*C*) in which Apollonius repeats and expands upon the fates of Polyphemus, Heracles, and especially Hylas, regarding whom the poet cites the contemporary Cian practice of searching for Heracles' lost boyfriend (*a*). Following this digression there is a brief passage that serves as a bridge to the first episode of the next book (*b*), the sojourn among the Bebryces. Accordingly, the structure of the episode appears as follows:

---

6. One may well recall that Apollonius set Tiphys and Heracles in the thematic opposition of man of skill and man of strength in his description of the *Argo*'s departure from the Gulf of Pagasae; see Chapter 5, pp. 92–94.

HERACLES ABANDONED, 1153–1362

A. The Active Heroism of Heracles in
 Perspective (1153–1272)
  a. The Loss of Hylas (1153–1239)
   α. The Loss of Heracles' Oar;
    the Hungry Plowman
   β. The Acquisition of a New Oar
   α. The Loss of Hylas;
    the Hungry Heracles
  b. Reaction to the Loss of Hylas (1240–72)
   α. Polyphemus's Reaction: Animal Simile
   β. Polyphemus Informs Heracles of the Loss
   α. Heracles' Reaction: Animal Simile
B. Heracles Abandoned (1273–79)
A. The Passive Heroism of Jason
 in Perspective (1280–1344)
  a. Quarrel of Jason and Telamon
  b. Intervention of the Boreads; Their Fate
  c. Appearance of Glaucus
  b. Intervention of Glaucus;
   the Fates of Hylas, etc.
  a. Reconciliation of Jason and Telamon
C. Epilogue (1345–62)
  a. Final Words on the Abandoned Argonauts (1345–57)
  b. Bridge to Book 2 (1358–62)

A. The Active Heroism of Heracles in Perspective (1153–1272)

a. The Loss of Hylas (1153–1239)

Unable to use their sail because of the absence of wind as they leave Cyzicus, the Argonauts decide to have a rowing contest in which the winner will be the last crewman to give up. In the midst of the contest, the men succeed in driving the ship at such a speed that, in the words of the narrator, not even the horses of Poseidon would have overcome it (1157–58). Then, toward late afternoon, one by one they give up until Heracles rows alone and drives the *Argo* forward by himself, even causing the timbers of the ship to shake because of his massive strength. Thus Heracles can claim victory in the contest. But just as they are passing the Rhyndacus River and the tomb of Ægæon, the victor's oar breaks in two. With his oar now broken, the hero is reduced to a state of shock because, as the narrator tells us, his hands were unused to inactivity (1170–71).

Apollonius calls attention to the tomb of Ægæon not merely to parade his knowledge of local landmarks but because the tomb bears a thematic relevance to the loss of Heracles' oar and its consequences. The mythic figure Ægæon is not the Hesiodic Uranid here (cf. *Th.* 147–53, 617–20). According to Lucillus Tarrhæus (*apud* Σ *ad* 1.1165c, d [= fr. 11a Linnenkugel]), a first-century-A.D. commentator, Apollonius's Ægæon was the giant who fled from Eubœa and died near Phrygia. Tarrhæus draws his information from the *Heracleia* of Cinæthon (Davies p. 142 a),[7] who tells how Poseidon drowned Ægæon for competing against him.[8] Recognition that this is the Ægæon whose tomb the Argonauts pass is important for the understanding of events in this episode; for Ægæon and Heracles have something in common. Although it may not be immediately apparent, the contest that leads to Heracles' abandonment indirectly involves Poseidon. When the Argonauts get their vessel up to full speed, as mentioned just above, Apollonius states that not even the horses of Poseidon could have caught up with it (1157–58). Even after the rest of the men give up from exhaustion, Heracles continues to row the ship by himself. The authorial comment, in conjunction with the reference to Ægæon's tomb, suggests that the contest has gone too far: the Argonauts—and Heracles in particular—appear to be competing with Poseidon, a very risky challenge. The reader can find confirmation of the fact that the rowing contest has involved the god of the sea in that the Argonauts recognize the absence of Heracles just after they pass the Cape of Poseidon (cf. 1279), a notice that the poet has set at the center of the episode.

---

7. Cf. Vian 105 n. 2.
8. F. Vian, "Les ΓΗΓΕΝΕΙΣ de Cyzicus et la Grande Mère des Dieux," *RA* 72 (1970) 80–96, has discussed the importance of Poseidon and earthborn giants in this area.

There are other indications in the text that Heracles' behavior courts divine disfavor. In his amusing depiction of Heracles after he broke his oar, Apollonius alludes to an Odyssean episode in which Poseidon plays a central role. When Heracles holds on to one half of his oar as the other slips into the sea, he sits and stares in silent disbelief at what has happened to him:

> ἀτὰρ τρύφος ἄλλο μὲν αὐτὸς
> ἄμφω χερσὶν ἔχων πέσε δόχμιος, ἄλλο δὲ πόντος
> κλύζε παλιρροθίοισι φέρων. Ἀνὰ δ' ἕζετο σιγῇ
> παπταίνων· χεῖρες γὰρ ἀήθεσον ἠρεμέουσαι.
> (1168b-71)

> One piece he held in both his hands as he fell sideways; the sea, carrying away the other piece, swallowed it in its surf. He sat up, silently looking around; for his hands were unused to inaction.

The wording recalls the demise of the lesser Ajax in Book 4 of the *Odyssey*. After Poseidon had saved Ajax from the storm that wrecked so many ships of the Greek fleet, the arrogant boaster insisted that he had saved himself. The enraged god then split the rock on which he sat in two, one piece remaining fixed and the other falling into the sea:[9]

> φῆ ῥ' ἀέκητι θεῶν φυγέειν μέγα λαῖτμα θαλάσσης.
> τοῦ δὲ Ποσειδάων μεγάλ' ἔκλυεν αὐδήσαντος·
> αὐτίκ' ἔπειτα τρίαιναν ἑλὼν χερσὶ στιβαρῇσιν
> ἤλασε Γυραίην πέτρην, ἀπὸ δ' ἔσχισεν αὐτήν·
> καὶ τὸ μὲν αὐτόθι μεῖνε, τὸ δὲ τρύφος ἔμπεσε πόντῳ
> τῷ ῥ' Αἴας τὸ πρῶτον ἐφεζόμενος μέγ' ἀάσθη·
> τὸν δ' ἐφόρει κατὰ πόντον ἀπείρονα κυμαίνοντα.
> (*Od*.4.504-10)

> He [*sc*. Ajax] said that he had escaped the great depth of the sea
>   in spite of the gods.
> Poseidon heard him utter this hybristic boast
> and immediately upon taking his trident in his massive hands,
> he struck the Gyræan rock, splitting it in half.
> One part remained there, but the other slipped into the sea,

---

9. The parallel was noted by Mooney and Ardizzoni *ad* 1.1168 and Campbell *ad* 1.1168-69.

the part on which Ajax <u>was seated</u> when he made his deluded comment;
this carried him down within the swollen, boundless sea.

By inviting us to think of Ajax's hybristic defiance in Heracles' rowing of the *Argo* and in the breaking of his oar, Apollonius calls this remarkable feat into question. Comparison with the demise of Oilean Ajax encourages us to view Heracles' rowing as arrogant competition with the god of the sea.

Heracles broke his oar in the early evening (ὑπὸ δείελον, 1160). The Argonauts pull into the land of the Mysians around the dinner hour, as Apollonius makes clear in a simile:

<u>Ἦμος</u> δ' ἀγρόθεν εἶσι φυτοσκάφος ἤ τις <u>ἀροτρεὺς</u>
<u>ἀσπασίως</u> εἰς αὖλιν ἑήν, <u>δόρποιο χατίζων</u>
αὐτοῦ δ' ἐν προμολῇ τετρυμένα <u>γούνατ'</u> ἔκαμψεν
αὐσταλέος κονίῃσι, περιτριβέας δέ τε <u>χεῖρας</u>
εἰσορόων κακὰ πολλὰ ἑῇ ἠρήσατο γαστρί·
<u>τῆμος</u> ἄρ' οἵ γ' ἀφίκοντο Κιανίδος ἤθεα γαίης
ἀμφ' Ἀργανθώνειον ὄρος προχοάς τε Κίοιο.
(1172–78)

<u>At the time when</u> a gardener or <u>plowman</u> <u>eagerly</u> goes from the field toward his hut, <u>craving his dinner</u>,
and there at the entrance bends his worn <u>knees</u>,
caked with dust, and looking at his gnarled <u>hands</u>
utters many a curse against his stomach,
<u>at that time</u> the heroes reached the towns of the Cianian land around Mount Arganthoneion and the mouth of the Cius River.

The simile is a *contaminatio* of two Homeric similes: *Il.* 11.86–89 and *Od.* 13.31–35.[10] In the Iliadic simile, the Greek army breaks through the Trojan line at the time when a weary lumberjack has his lunch:

<u>ἦμος</u> δὲ δρυτόμος περ ἀνὴρ ὡπλίσσατο δεῖπνον
οὔρεος ἐν βήσσῃσιν, ἐπεί τ' ἐκορέσσατο <u>χεῖρας</u>
τάμνων δένδρεα μακρά, ἅδος τέ μιν ἵκετο θυμόν,

---

10. Cf. Mooney *ad* 1.1172–77, Vian 105 n. 4, and especially Campbell *ad* 1.1172ff.

σίτου τε γλυκεροῖο περὶ φρένας ἵμερος αἱρεῖ,
τῆμος σφῇ ἀρετῇ Δαναοὶ ῥήξαντο φάλαγγας.
(Il. 11.86-90)

At the time when a lumberjack prepared his dinner
in the mountain glens, after wearing out his hands
cutting tall trees and feeling within that he had had enough,
and desire for delicious food overcomes his thoughts,
at this time the Danaans courageously broke through the enemy
  lines.

In the Odyssean simile, the poet likens Odysseus, who longed for his last day on Phæacia to end, to a tired plowman who desires to go home for dinner:

ὡς δ' ὅτ' ἀνὴρ δόρποιο λιλαίεται, ᾧ τε πανῆμαρ
νειὸν ἀν' ἕλκητον βόε οἴνοπε πηκτὸν ἄροτρον·
ἀσπασίως δ' ἄρα τῷ κατέδυ φάος ἠελίοιο
δόρπον ἐποίχεσθαι, βλάβεται δέ τε γούνατ' ἰόντι·
ὣς 'Οδυσῆ' ἀσπαστὸν ἔδυ φάος ἠελίοιο.
(Od. 13.31-35)

As when a man craves his dinner, a man for whom all day long
a pair of dusky steers pulled his sturdy plow through the fallow
  land,
and the light of the sun set eagerly for him
so that he can go to prepare his dinner, his knees aching as he
  walked,
just so welcome was sunset for Odysseus.

In both Homeric similes, the occupation of the laborer and his sense of hunger, although poignant details, are of secondary importance to the issue of time. Apollonius, however, has heightened the importance of these details by making them equally relevant to the narrative, as will be seen below.[11]

Some have seen the gardener and plowman of the Apollonian simile as representing all the Argonauts, who likewise are weary and hungry from their rowing.[12] On the contrary, the one

---

11. Cf. A. W. James, "Some Examples of Imitation in the Similes of Later Greek Epic," *Antichthon* 3 (1969) 77-90, who argues that in general Apollonius improves on Homer's similes by producing more precise parallels between simile and narrative.

12. E.g., Blumberg 27 n. 31, Fränkel *ad* 1.1172-76b.

Argonaut whom the poet highlights in the contest is also the main focus of the simile. In his description of Heracles' rowing, Apollonius says that the hero creates furrows in the water (δὴ τότ' ἀνοχλίζων τετρηχότος οἴδματος ὁλκούς, 1167), and when his oar breaks, he sits and gazes silently. Although we are not told the object of his stare, the following comment gives us an idea: χεῖρες γὰρ ἀήθεσον ἠρεμέουσαι (1171b). Heracles, then, appears to stare at his hands.[13] In the simile that follows, the gardener or plowman, whose work entails the digging of furrows, like the Iliadic lumberjack stares at his hands (1175–76). Thus the Argonautic simile would appear to keep the reader's attention on Heracles. Besides occupation, weariness, and the time of day of their work, a more telling point of contact between Heracles and the laborers of all three similes is their hunger.[14] Heracles traditionally had an enormous appetite to match his great size, and this, as the reader will soon observe, is the source of his imminent troubles.

While the Argonauts prepare to eat their dinner, Heracles orders them to begin while he goes off to secure another oar. Fränkel has seen in his willingness to put off eating an indication of Heracles' Stoic commitment to duty.[15] Yet Heracles' frenzied response to the loss of Hylas belies such a philosophical stance. Although Apollonius does not make Heracles' feelings about his dinner explicit, the previous simile suggests that Heracles, like the agricultural laborers with whom he is compared, is not altogether pleased with having to work before his meal. In this case, the work will consist of finding and uprooting a small tree out of which to fashion his new oar. One can now better appreciate how thoroughly and successfully Apollonius "contaminated" the two Homeric similes. In the *Iliad* the hungry worker was a

---

13. *Pace* Collins 88–89, who believes that Heracles was staring at the other Argonauts to prevent their laughing at him.
14. Fränkel *ad* 1.1172–76b observes the importance of this feature of the simile; he compares Theocritus *Id.* 24.137–38, where, referring to Heracles' usual dinner fare, the poet says: δεῖπνον δὲ κρέα τ' ὀπτὰ καὶ ἐν κανέῳ μέγας ἄρτος / Δωρικός· ἀσφαλέως κε φυτοσκάφον [cf. *Argo.* 1.1172] ἄνδρα κορέσσαι.
15. H. Fränkel, "Das Argonautenepos des Apollonios," *MH* 14 (1957) 6–7 n. 5; cf. his suggestion in his commentary *ad* 1.1207–10 that Heracles was a water, as opposed to a wine, drinker because of his Stoic temperance.

lumberjack,[16] and in the *Odyssey* he was a plowman; in the *Argonautica*, Heracles digs furrows in the sea and then afterwards uproots a tree on land.

In describing the tree that Heracles plans to use for his oar, Apollonius imitates a line from an episode of the *Odyssey* in which another club-wielding figure of legend played a central role, the Cyclops Polyphemus. The Argonautic description runs as follows:

Εὗρεν ἔπειτ' ἐλάτην ἀλαλήμενος οὔτε τι πολλοῖς
ἀχθομένην ὄζοις οὐδὲ μέγα τηλεθόωσαν,
ἀλλ' οἷον ταναῆς ἔρνος πέλει αἰγείροιο·
<u>τόσση ὁμῶς μῆκός τε καὶ ἐς πάχος ἦεν ἰδέσθαι.</u>
                                                                (1190–93)

Then in his wanderings he [*sc.* Heracles] found a pine tree, neither laden
with too many branches nor excessively leafy,
but that was like the stock of a slender poplar;
<u>it appeared equal in length and thickness to the eye.</u>

When Odysseus and his men were inside Polyphemus's cave, they discovered his club, which Odysseus describes to his Phæacian audience in these words:[17]

Κύκλωπος γὰρ ἔκειτο μέγα ῥόπαλον παρὰ σηκῷ,
χλωρὸν ἐλαΐνεον· τὸ μὲν ἔκταμεν, ὄφρα φοροίη
αὐανθέν. τὸ μὲν ἄμμες ἐΐσκομεν εἰσορόωντες
ὅσσον θ' <u>ἱστὸν νηὸς</u> ἐεικοσόροιο μελαίνης,
φορτίδος εὐρείης, ἥ τ' ἐκπεράᾳ μέγα λαῖτμα·
<u>τόσσον ἔην μῆκος, τόσσον πάχος</u> εἰσοράασθαι.
                                                                (*Od.* 9.319–24)

For along the pen lay the Cyclops's great club,
made from the green branch of an olive tree that he had cut to carry
after it dried out. Upon seeing it we said it looked like

---

16. One might recall that in their battle with the Gegeneis, which featured Heracles and his style of heroics, Apollonius compared the felling of the giants to the work of lumberjacks.

17. Mooney, Ardizzoni, and Campbell *ad loc.* all note the imitation.

the <u>mast</u> of a black twenty-oared <u>ship</u>,
a wide freighter, which sails the deep sea;
<u>it was equal in length and thickness to look at.</u>

In addition to imitating *Od.* 9.324, a few lines later Apollonius also borrows the Odyssean ship simile; but instead of having it qualify the size of the tree (Homer has his simile qualify the size of Polyphemus's club), he applies it to Heracles' uprooting of the tree (Ὡς δ' ὅταν ἀπροφάτως <u>ἱστόν νεός</u>, 1201ff.), thereby equating the violence that Heracles uses to uproot the tree with the force of the sudden squall that tears out a ship's mast. Much like the allusion to Ajax, this Odyssean reference introduces a subtext that provides an inauspicious parallel for Heracles; for the huge and powerful Polyphemus was blinded by Odysseus, whom he describes insultingly as one lacking in stature (ἐὼν ὀλίγος τε καὶ οὐτιδανὸς καὶ ἄκικυς, *Od.* 9.515). In point of fact, the great hero was soon to experience intense pain at the loss of the young Hylas, whom one might well style ὀλίγος τε καὶ οὐτιδανὸς καὶ ἄκικυς. What is more, both Heracles and Polyphemus owe their suffering to their excessive appetites.

Reference to the Polyphemus episode continues in the third section of this first ring (α). When we first meet Hylas, he, like Heracles, also goes off to fetch something, in his case water for his master's dinner:

Τόφρα δ' Ὕλας χαλκέῃ σὺν κάλπιδι νόσφιν ὁμίλου
δίζητο κρήνης ἱερὸν ῥόον, ὥς κέ οἱ ὕδωρ
φθαίη ἀφυσσάμενος <u>ποτιδόρπιον</u>, ἄλλα τε πάντα
ὀτραλέως κατὰ κόσμον ἐπαρτίσσειεν ἰόντι.
                                              (1207–10)

In the meantime Hylas, taking a pitcher of bronze, set off apart from
the group in search of the holy stream of a fountain, so that he might
draw water <u>for dinner</u> and have all the other things
ready and in order before Heracles returned.

Before Apollonius, there are only three extant occurrences of the word ποτιδόρπιον: at *Od.* 9.234 and 249, and in a parody of these lines by Matron of Pitane, quoted by Athenæus (4.136f):[18]

φέρε δ' ὄβριμον ἄχθος
ὕλης ἀζαλέης, ἵνα οἱ <u>ποτιδόρπιον</u> εἴη.
ἔντοσθεν δ' ἄντροιο βαλὼν ὀρυμαγδὸν ἔθηκεν·
(*Od.* 9.233b–35)

He [*sc.* Polyphemus] carried a huge bundle
of dried wood so that it might be available to him <u>for his dinner</u>.
He brought it within his cave and threw it down with a crash.

ἥμισυ δ' αὖτ' ἔστησεν ἐν ἄγγεσιν, ὄφρα οἱ εἴη
πίνειν αἰνυμένῳ καὶ οἱ <u>ποτιδόρπιον</u> εἴη.
(*Od.* 9.248–49)

And [the other] half he poured into vessels, so that it might be
    at hand
to drink when he wanted and be available to him <u>for his dinner</u>.

ἦσθιε δ' ὥστε λέων, παλάμῃ δ' ἔχε τὸ σκέλος ἀμνοῦ,
ὄφρα οἱ οἴκαδ' ἰόντι πάλιν <u>ποτιδόρπιον</u> εἴη.
(Matron *apud* Athenæum, 4.136f)

He was as hungry as a lion and took in his hand the leg of a lamb,
so that it might be available to him <u>for his dinner</u> when he returned
    home.

Imitation of the Homeric δὶς λεγόμενον is particularly clever; for in the first instance, Polyphemus is bringing home wood for his dinner (≈ Heracles returning with the tree for his new oar), and in the second, he places milk in a vessel to drink with his dinner (≈ Hylas fetches a beverage for Heracles' dinner). I quote the parody by Matron not because I suppose that Apollonius necessarily had it in mind, but because the fourth-century-B.C. satirist uses the word when talking about the gluttonous parasite Chærephon. From its celebrated context in Homer, this word would appear to have become associated with men of voracious appetites.

---

18. Again, Mooney, Ardizzoni, and Campbell *ad loc.* cite the Homeric parallels; I found the reference to Matron in *TLG*.

To sum up what we have seen thus far: in the rowing contest Apollonius implicitly compared Heracles to Ægæon and Ajax, both of whom dared to rival Poseidon, and explicitly to a hungry farmer. In the securing of a new oar and in the preparation for Heracles' dinner, allusion to the cannibalistic Polyphemus, whose cave is filled with all sorts of foods, brings to mind a well-known Homeric figure who is characterized by his excessive hunger and irreverence toward the gods (cf. *Od.* 9.273–78). All three suffered as a result of their folly: both Ægæon and Ajax were killed at sea for daring to rival Poseidon, and Polyphemus, the son of Poseidon, was blinded by his own club because of his cruelty and appetite. These three figures provide the backdrop against which the story of how Heracles acquired Hylas should be read. They offer eloquent comment on why Heracles loses him.

Apollonius explains the speed and care of Hylas's preparations for Heracles' dinner in a brief digression. Heracles had trained the youth well in his duties ever since the time he had taken him from his father, Theiodamas, whom the hero killed over a draft ox.[19] The narrator informs us, however, that this was merely a pretext for initiating a war against the unjust Dryopians (1207–20). Apollonius's sketchy telling of the tale conflicts in several points with that of Callimachus, who many agree was Apollonius's model.[20] In the *Ætia* (fr. 22–25 Pf.), Callimachus combined two stories involving Heracles βουθοίνης: the sacrifice of Lindos and the tale of Theiodamas. In the former, Heracles took the draft ox (cf. *Ætia* fr. 22 Pf.) of an unnamed Lindian and consumed it *in toto*; while he did so, the innocent plowman hurled curses at him, a fact that explains why the people of Lindos continue the practice of sacrificing to Heracles with curses.[21] In the latter of the two

---

19. J. Cowell, "Hylas and Heracles," *Pegasus* 12 (1969) 44–48, argues that elements of Hylas's experience associate him with the ephebeia. Hunter (2) 448–52 makes a similar argument regarding Jason.
20. E.g., A. Ardizzoni, "Eracle e Teodamante in Callimaco e in Apollonio Rodio," *RFIC* 13 (1935) 452–67; C. Corbato, *Riprese callimachee in Apollonio Rodio* (Trieste 1955) 7–12; and more recently, A. Barigazzi, "Eracle e Tiodamante [*sic*] in Callimaco e Apollonio Rodio," *Prometheus* 2 (1976) 227–38.
21. This is also the version of Conon *Dieg.* 11 (*FGrHist* 26 F 1.11), Philostratus *Im.* 2.24, Lactantius *Div. Inst.* 1.21, among others; in Apollodorus 2.5.11, the ox pulls a cart, not a plow.

stories, the victim of Heracles' βουλιμία is not innocent. Heracles asks the Dryopian Theiodamas if he would give him some food from his lunch bag for his hungry son, Hyllus, which the cruel Theiodamas arrogantly refuses (cf. *Ætia* fr. 24.13 Pf.). As Vian observed, Apollonius's version is a *contaminatio* of the two Callimachean accounts: the wicked Theiodamas of the Dryopian tale in the *Argonautica* becomes the innocent plowman of the Lindian.²² The Apollonian Theiodamas is not a brute but a noble man (δίου, 1213), beset with troubles (ἀνίῃ βεβολημένος, 1216) and pitilessly killed by Heracles (νηλεῶς, 1214).²³ Heracles uses his encounter with the wretched Theiodamas—there is no mention of a hungry Hyllus—as a grim pretext (πρόφασιν ... λευγαλέην, 1218–19) for war against the unjust Dryopians. Even granting the low moral status of the Dryopians, Heracles' instigation of the war nonetheless evinces an equal disregard for justice; for he took it upon himself to begin a war by murdering an innocent plowman over a draft animal that, in fuller accounts of this story, he then ate. Apollonius stops short of mentioning this detail with a statement that he is digressing too far from his narrative (1220). Thus the simile comparing Heracles who plowed the sea and the hungry plowman of the simile who curses his hands, set in the section corresponding to this (Aa ≈ A*a*), assumes greater significance once one thinks of it in connection with Heracles' encounter with Theiodamas. The structural and thematic linkage invites us to see that in the rowing contest Heracles, the maritime plowman, has assumed the occupation of his victim, the wretched Theiodamas.²⁴ The simile of the plowman, then, is ironic and ominous, to say the least; for the rowing contest on which it comments will ultimately result in Heracles' loss of the plowman's son. Accordingly, all the indications in the narrative prior to the abduction of Hylas, textual and subtextual, show Heracles as an arrogant, violent, and gluttonous figure who will suffer some misfortune; for the great

---

22. Vian 46–48; in particular, Vian compares *Ætia* fr. 22 Pf. with *Argo.* 1214; cf. Feeney (supra n. 2) 56.

23. Fränkel (OCT) emends the first two to δήου and νηλεῦ and puts a dagger next to ἀνίῃ to suit his positive view of Heracles; cf. Fränkel *ad* 1.1187–89, 1210–20.

24. A comparable identification of victor and vanquished was observed in the previous chapter; cf. Chapter 7, pp. 173–74.

Heracles, this will be the painful loss of the son of the man he piteously killed.

In describing the rape of Heracles' young page, Apollonius focuses on the numinous setting and, within it, the reaction of the water nymph to Hylas's beauty. In doing so, he imitates certain features of the episode in the *Odyssey* in which Nausicaa fell in love with Odysseus.

When Hylas approaches the fountain into which he will eventually be drawn, the nymphs of the area are dancing in honor of Artemis:

> Οἱ δέ που ἄρτι
> <u>Νυμφάων</u> ἵσταντο χοροί· μέλε γάρ σφισι πάσαις
> ὅσσαι κεῖσ' ἐρατὸν Νύμφαι ῥίον ἀμφενέμοντο
> Ἄρτεμιν ἐννυχίῃσιν ἀεὶ μέλπεσθαι ἀοιδαῖς.
> <u>Αἱ μὲν ὅσαι σκοπιὰς ὀρέων λάχον ἢ καὶ ἐναύλους</u>,
> <u>αἵ γε μὲν ὑληωροὶ</u> ἀπόπροθεν ἐστιχόωντο·
> ἡ δὲ νέον κρήνης ἀνεδύετο καλλινάοιο
> Νύμφη ἐφυδατίη. Τὸν δὲ σχεδὸν εἰσενόησε
> <u>κάλλεῖ καὶ</u> γλυκερῇσιν ἐρευθόμενον <u>χαρίτεσσι</u>·

(1222b–30)

> Just then choruses
> <u>of nymphs</u> were beginning to form; for it was the duty of all
> the nymphs who lived thereabout on the lovely mountain
> to celebrate Artemis forever with nightly songs.
> <u>Those whose allotted homes were the peaks of mountains or
>   the streams</u>
> <u>and those living in the forest</u> were arranging themselves in lines
>   far away.
> But the nymph of the fair-flowing fountain just then rose up
> to the surface of the water and saw Hylas nearby,
> a flush of <u>beauty and sweet graces</u> ornamenting his face.

Apollonius has in mind the moment when Odysseus, after his exhausting swim to Phæacia, is roused from sleep by the voices of Nausicaa, who has just been compared to Artemis (*Od.* 6.102–9; cf. 149–52), and her servants:[25]

---

25. Mooney *ad* 1.1226 and Vian 108 n. 3 observed the imitation.

Ὤ μοι ἐγώ, τέων αὖτε βροτῶν ἐς γαῖαν ἱκάνω;
ἦ ῥ' οἵ γ' ὑβρισταί τε καὶ ἄγριοι οὐδὲ δίκαιοι,
ἦε φιλόξεινοι, καί σφιν νόος ἐστὶ θεουδής;
ὥς τέ με κουράων ἀμφήλυθε θῆλυς ἀϋτή,
<u>νυμφάων, αἳ ἔχουσ' ὀρέων αἰπεινὰ κάρηνα</u>
<u>καὶ πηγὰς ποταμῶν καὶ πίσεα ποιήεντα.</u>
(*Od.* 6.119–24)

Alas! Who are the people to whose land I have come?
Are they arrogant, savage, unjust?
Or do they welcome strangers and fear the gods?
The sound of girl's voices has reached me,
<u>like those of nymphs who inhabit the lofty peaks of mountains,</u>
<u>and the river springs, and the grassy dells.</u>

Apollonius has adapted the Odyssean division of nymphs into groups of three. He then describes the effect that Hylas has on the nymph in a way that recalls the effect that Odysseus had on Nausicaa after his bath:[26]

ἕζετ' ἔπειτ' ἀπάνευθε κιὼν ἐπὶ θῖνα θαλάσσης,
<u>κάλλεϊ καὶ χάρισι</u> στίλβων· θηεῖτο δὲ κούρη.
(*Od.* 6.236–37)

Then, going apart, he sat down upon the seashore
glistening with <u>beauty and sweet graces</u>. The young girl stared
   in amazement.

In his reference to this famous episode, the poet would seem to urge the reader to compare Hylas and the nymph to Odysseus and Nausicaa, and upon comparison we observe a significant inversion of the Homeric model: the young and effeminate[27] Hylas is cast in

---

26. Mooney and Ardizzoni *ad* 1.1230 noted this borrowing. κάλλεϊ occurs in this position only three other times in the Homeric corpus (*Il.* 3.392, 13.432; *Od.* 18.192), but only here does it accompany χάρισι; cf. *Argo.* 3.444.

27. Apollonius underscores Hylas's femininity by having him carry a κάλπις, for which Σ *ad* 1.1207b criticized the poet, pointing out that in Homer (he has *Od.* 7.20 in mind) παρθένοι normally carried such vessels. Although A. S. F. Gow, *Theocritus* (Cambridge 1952) *ad Id.* 13.46, and G. Serrao, "Problemi di poesia alesandrina," *Helikon* 5 (1965) 542–43 n. 8, are correct in pointing out that men are represented in classical art as carrying κάλπιδες, I believe that the sensitivity of the scholiast to what he perceives as a cultural, gender, or perhaps epochal infelicity should not be dismissed so easily.

Odysseus's role, and the aggressive nymph is placed in that of the demure Nausicaa.

Hylas is a passive young man who, when fetching water, causes a young nymph to fall desperately in love with him; he is also the antithesis both of the Homeric hero, with whom he is subtly compared, and his master, who has just rowed the *Argo* by himself and uprooted a tall tree. In the second half of this episode (A), Apollonius will turn his attention to Jason, another young man who, like Hylas, causes young women to fall desperately in love with him as he searches for the golden fleece. Like Hylas, Jason too stands in strong contrast with Heracles by virtue of his passive mode of action. But as will be seen in the second half of the episode, Jason's passivity and skills of leadership prove effective and, what is more, essential for an expedition without Heracles. One other point of comparison between Jason and Hylas emerges: like Hylas, the passive Jason will have a captivating effect on Medea, the key to the success of the expedition;[28] and like the nymph, Medea will not let go.

b. Reaction to the Loss of Hylas (1240–72)

As I pointed out in the previous chapter, Apollonius has a remarkable talent for forging elements from diverse and even contradictory traditions into a unified and convincing story line. Here too in his account of the loss of Hylas, the poet has successfully blended several divergent accounts,[29] aided, perhaps even influenced, by his predilection for the ring format. According to Autocharis (*FGrHist* 249 F 1), who provides us with the earliest extant tradition of the events in Mysia, Polyphemus the Argonaut founded the city of Cius,[30] and Hylas was a local divinity. Later

---

28. Apollonius will refer to the Odyssean episode just alluded to in the third book when Medea goes to meet Jason for the first time, imitating both the tripartite division of nymphs and the simile comparing Nausicaa to Artemis (*Argo.* 3.876–84). Before leaving this section of the episode, I would also add that just as Heracles reveals the enormous capacity of his physical strength by single-handedly plowing the sea (i.e., rowing the *Argo* by himself), Jason's great heroic feat in the poem similarly entails the single-handed plowing of the field of Ares with brazen, fire-breathing bulls (3.1326ff.); the ability to succeed in the latter task, however, comes not from Jason's own physical power, but from the drugs given him by the young woman whom he seduced.

29. For more details, see Delage 115, Händel 27–33, Vian 43–48.

30. A fact that Apollonius will mention; cf. 1321–33, 1345–47.

versions (e.g., Euphorion fr. 76 Powell, Socrates Πρὸς Εἰδοθέων *FGrHist* 310 F 15) combined these two elements of Mysian legend by making Polyphemus the lover of Hylas, and not Heracles as in the tradition followed by Apollonius and Theocritus.[31] Apollonius deals with this discrepancy by having Polyphemus hear the cry of Hylas as he is drawn into the nymph's pool and by having him report the disappearance of the youth to Heracles and share in the latter's hysterical response to the boy's unexplained disappearance. Apollonius articulates this doubling of Hylas's lovers neatly and economically through the ring structure. The reaction of each hero to Hylas's disappearance and an accompanying animal simile (bα, bα) frame the moment when Polyphemus meets Heracles and informs him of the situation (bβ).

In addition to incorporating a reference to the tradition in which Polyphemus was Hylas's lover, the ring format also invites a comparison between the reactions of the two heroes to the loss of Hylas; and just as he contrasted the different roles that Heracles and Jason played in the battles on Oros Arkton, here too Apollonius highlights the different reactions to Hylas's disappearance through animal similes. In this way, the poet uses Hylas's other lover as a foil for Heracles, who is clearly the main focal point of the first half of the episode.[32] While Polyphemus awaits Heracles' return,[33] he hears Hylas's shout and runs to the fountain like a wild and hungry animal (λιμῷ δ' αἰθόμενος, 1245) that searches for the sheep whose voices he heard from afar, bellowing as long as he can. Apollonius thus makes Polyphemus's association with Heracles in this episode all the closer by connecting him with the

---

31. Cf. *The Oxyrhynchus Papyri* 54 (1987) no. 3727 for the fragment of a second-century-B.C. poem that also makes Heracles the lover of Hylas; and G. L. Huxley, "Thracian Hylas," *JHS* 109 (1989) 185–86, for a brief discussion of this fragment. The relationship between Heracles and Hylas is not the equivalent of a father–son relationship (as D. N. Levin, "Apollonius' Heracles," *CJ* 67 [1971] 24–25, and M. Pulbrook, "The Hylas Myth in Apollonius of Rhodes and Theocritus," *Maynooth Review* 8 [1983] 25–31, cited by F. McGready, "Heracles' Love for Hylas," *CL* 3 [1983] 79–80). Heracles' reaction to Hylas's loss betrays clear signs that the hero was in love with the boy; see H. White, *Studies in Theocritus and Other Hellenistic Poets* (Amsterdam 1979) 63–73.

32. Cf. Levin (supra n. 31) 25, Palombi (supra n. 3) 84.

33. This is an especially nice touch; Polyphemus, as Blumberg 25 reminds us, is Heracles' brother-in-law, and so his concern is dramatically plausible.

hunger motif seen above; because of his "hunger" to find Hylas he, like Heracles, will be left behind.[34] The manner in which he responds to the emergency, however, differs significantly from Heracles'. In his frantic search for the boy, Polyphemus at least has a plan of action and gives some thought to what might have happened to Hylas. His constant shouts are meant to get a response from the boy; he believes that Hylas may be the prey of an animal or of some pirates, and for this reason draws his sword (bα, 1240-52). He is not, then, completely undone by the situation.

Heracles' response to the news is quite different. At the center of this ring, Polyphemus meets Heracles, informs him about Hylas, and offers his erroneous opinion about what has happened. In the following section, which corresponds to that giving the reaction of Polyphemus (bα, 1261-72),[35] Heracles does not act so logically. He begins to sweat and experience nausea, and then bolts off with no particular place in mind. Apollonius compares him to a bull stung by a gadfly who now runs and now stops to howl out of pain.[36] Like the bull, Heracles runs helter-skelter and every now and then stops to shout—not because he is calling out to locate Hylas, but because of the pain that the boy's loss has caused. Moreover, he describes the bull as κακῷ βεβολημένος οἴστρῳ (1269). Apollonius has just before stated that Hylas's father, Theiodamas, was ἀνίῃ βεβολημένος (1216) when Heracles encountered him. Much as the hungry-plowman simile in the context of Heracles' maritime plowing connected Heracles with Theiodamas, so too the significant recurrence of βεβολημένος in the bull simile drives home the fact that Heracles has suffered a loss comparable to that experienced by his victim, whose son Heracles too now loses. The striking repetition in the phrases that sum up the emotional experiences of Theiodamas (Hylas's father) and Heracles (Hylas's lover) heightens our awareness of the mutual bond of suffering between the

---

34. Cf. Fränkel ad 1.1245. The association of Polyphemus with Heracles' fate calls to mind the other Polyphemus, the Cyclops, whose hunger prompted his suffering, to which Odyssean episode Apollonius alluded in this section of the episode.

35. N.B. there is also a close numerical corresponsion between the parts of this subsection: 13 lines-8 lines-12 lines.

36. James (supra n. 11) 84 discusses the relationship of this simile to its Homeric model, Od. 22.299ff.

two and points to the ironic justice of Heracles' predicament. In short, Apollonius has Heracles reenact the occupation and suffering of the man he victimized. Comparison with Polyphemus the Argonaut underscores Heracles' complete inability to deal with the situation. Like Jason in the ensuing conflict arising over his abandonment, Heracles can well be described as ἀμηχανίηισιν ἀτυχθείς (1286).

B. Heracles Abandoned (1273-79)

Seven lines (1273-79) act as a bridge to the second half of the episode and contain an important detail that enhances our understanding of why Heracles is abandoned. While Polyphemus and Heracles search for Hylas, Tiphys gives the order to board the ship to take advantage of the winds. It is still dark, and for this reason the Argonauts do not notice that the three are missing. Since the men avail themselves of the winds, they would not have been at their oars, where the absence of the three would have been observed.[37] They remain unaware of the accidental abandonment of their comrades until they pass Cape Poseidon, after which dawn reveals the absence of the three men. Reference to the god's name, given the sequence of events, is significant. As I argued above, in the rowing contest Heracles is subtly associated with Ægæon and Ajax, both of whom vie with the god of the sea. By rowing the *Argo* at a speed said to be faster than the steeds of Poseidon, the Argonauts, and Heracles in particular, can be viewed as competing with the god. Thus, reference to Poseidon the moment the Argonauts come to see that they have left behind Heracles, Hylas, and Polyphemus admirably brings the first half of the episode to a close by hinting at the reason why Heracles is abandoned: like his mythological and literary analogues, Heracles is so confident in his strength that he can, and is willing to, act on his own. As Jason observed, the expedition to and from Colchis is a common concern. Heracles' godlike strength and self-sufficiency are completely inappropriate for a group of highly talented, but interdependent, heroes engaged in a

---

37. So Blumberg 28.

nautical ἄεθλος.[38] No wonder Poseidon finds Heracles' presence so offensive!

Heracles' hybris, moreover, is of a piece with his behavior toward Theiodamas and his people. Apollonius tells us that Heracles took it upon himself to concoct a grim pretext (πρόφασιν λευγαλέην, 1218-19) with which to initiate a war against the Dryopians, and thereby suggests that the murder of Theiodamas, regardless of its supposedly noble end, was a capricious act of aggression. For in order to provoke the unjust Dryopians into open hostilities, Heracles, we are explicitly told, killed the unfortunate Theiodamas for refusing the outrageous request that he give him the ox with which he was plowing. This murder in turn apparently precipitated the war between Heracles and the Dryopians.[39] As seen above, the manner of his punishment has been made in a most subtle way to fit his earlier crime: Heracles in the event leading up to, and in the very experience of, the loss of Hylas assumes the role of the wretched plowman whom he had killed.[40] In the second half of the episode, the narrator will provide further instances of Heracles' unforgiving and heavy-handed approach to justice,[41] which stands

---

38. Cf. G. Karl Galinsky, *The Herakles Theme* (Oxford 1972) 109, who states: "But before Herakles can row the boat out of contemporary reality, the oar snaps in the middle, and primitive heroic will and strength are defeated."

39. Apollonius also introduces into his literary collage a detail that makes reference to another story involving the Dryopians. Heracles was believed to have fought with the Dryopians while staying at the home of Ceyx, king of Trachis (cf. Apollodorus 2.7). According to Hesiod's *Ceykos Gamos* (fr. 263 M&W), this event would have occurred just after Heracles was abandoned at Aphetae. By having Heracles require the Cians to send hostages to Trachis, thus ensuring their continuation of the search (1354-57), and by telling the story of the Dryopians in the context of Heracles' abandonment, Apollonius would seem to have the Hesiodic poem in mind. Although this poem is too fragmentary to afford us any clear insight into what Apollonius might have had in mind, if anything, through such a subtle reference, nonetheless I find it significant that in the Hesiodic poem Heracles had an eating contest with a certain Lepreus, whom he went on to kill *ob indignationem æmulæ virtutis* (cf. fr. 265 M&W).

40. I wonder if it might also be significant that Heracles is compared to a bull, given the fact that he ate Theiodamas's steer.

41. Many have viewed Heracles' behavior here and elsewhere in the poem in a favorable light, arguing that he was a Stoic saint, human benefactor, or the great hero of grand epic (cf. Chapter 6, pp. 139-40): e.g., A. Ardizzoni, *L'Eracle "semnós" nel poema di Apollonio* (Catania 1937); Fränkel *ad* 1.855ff., 1187-89, 1207-10; Palombi (supra n. 3) 83; and Barigazzi (supra n. 20) 232

in sharp contrast to Jason's more conciliatory mode of behavior. The latter is the focus of the second half of the episode.

A. The Passive Heroism of Jason in Perspective (1280-1344)

Scholarly interest in the Argonautic sojourn in Mysia has focused, by and large, on the story of Heracles and Hylas, and especially on how it compares with the Theocritean version of the tale. Few critics have observed how Apollonius successfully integrated this etiological story within its larger context, appreciation of which does not depend on knowledge of the relative dating of the two third-century versions.[42] As becomes readily apparent once one perceives the balanced structure of the episode, Heracles' reaction to the loss of Hylas stands in sharp contrast to Jason's response to the loss of Heracles. In this way, Apollonius has brought the story of Hylas fully within the larger framework of his thematic contrast between the man of strength and the man of skill, and in particular between Heracles and Jason.

When the Argonauts notice that their three comrades are missing, a νεῖκος (1284) ensues. This νεῖκος, like that on the beach at Pagasae, threatens to undermine the unity of the group, an extremely dangerous situation, since unified action is even more important now that the Argonauts cannot count on the assistance of Heracles. The crisis is real, and the way in which Apollonius describes their dispute is significant:

> Ἐν δέ σφιν κρατερὸν νεῖκος πέσεν, ἐν δὲ κολῳὸς
> ἄσπετος, εἰ τὸν ἄριστον ἀποπρολιπόντες ἔβησαν
> σφωιτέρον ἑτάρων.
>
> (1284-86a)

---

and 236-37. Others have questioned the seriousness of this character in their analysis of the text (e.g., Lawall 2 argues that Heracles is too large for reality and is without any sensitivity; and Collins 86ff., that Heracles lacks dignity and wisdom; cf. Levin [supra n. 31] 25, who tries to steer a middle course between the august and the brutish Heracles); but where a subtext exists, it should be taken into consideration, especially with regard to interpretations of the central characters of the poem. In this episode, the Homeric models used in his portrayal of Heracles are blasphemous brutes.

42. I have not myself been able to decide whether Theocritus or Apollonius is the imitator in this case, and so leave this issue aside in the present discussion. In any event, even if Apollonius were imitating Theocritus, as Köhnken argues (supra n. 4; cf. Vian 48), my interpretation of this episode would not change substantially.

Among them a violent disagreement ensued, an unspeakable argument as to whether they left behind the best of their comrades when they set off.

The question behind the dispute is worded ambiguously. Although the νεῖκος appears to arise over the reason for Heracles' abandonment—whether or not it was deliberate[43]—a second glance at the wording reveals another side to the issue at hand: Have they left behind the best of the Argonauts? This now becomes the central question of the episode, and its answer becomes the climactic finish of the book as a whole.

There is no doubt that Heracles is the strongest of the Argonauts. Apollonius has just given us a vivid portrayal of his enormous strength in the rowing contest. Elsewhere in the poem there are not only clear indications of what his contemporaries thought of him,[44] but also unambiguous indications that he could have performed the expedition by himself.[45] Strength, however, is not the sole factor to be considered in determining the nature or identity of the best of the Argonauts. At Pagasae, Jason described the best man as the one who concerns himself with all the details, especially those involving treaties (συνθεσίαι) and the settlement of conflicts (νείκεα). As it happens, Jason was describing his own approach to leadership. Besides taking care of all the details prior to their departure, Jason also intervened successfully in the argument (νεῖκος, 492) between Idas and Idmon at Pagasae (cf. 494). He will likewise succeed in managing the present argument (νεῖκος, 1284), one that questions whether in leaving behind Heracles they have abandoned the best of the Argonauts.

When the Argonauts realize that Heracles is no longer among them, Jason at first finds himself at a complete loss and neither does nor says anything:[46]

---

43. Cf. Giangrande 14–15.
44. Besides the election, where the Argonauts immediately judge him the best among them (1.341–43), cf. 2.145–50, 774–95; the narrator makes it clear that Heracles is the strongest among the group twice, at 1.197 and 3.1232–34.
45. See above, pp. 176–77.
46. Hurst 66 has aptly observed that his silent aporia corresponds to that of Heracles at the beginning of the episode, when he too sat in silent disbelief at the breaking of his oar.

> Ὁ δ' ἀμηχανίῃσιν ἀτυχθεὶς
> οὐδέ τι τοῖον ἔπος μετεφώνεεν οὐδέ τι τοῖον
> Αἰσονίδης, ἀλλ' ἧστο βαρείῃ νειόθεν ἄτῃ
> θυμὸν ἔδων.
>
> (1286b-89a)

> Stunned and helpless,
> the son of Æson spoke not a word either this way
> or that, but sat, eating his heart out
> because of this grievous misfortune.

Telamon reacts to the loss of his friend just as Heracles reacted to the loss of Hylas: immediately and without any reflection. Like Idas at Pagasae, he misinterprets Jason's silence and, as a result, becomes furious, believing that Jason had schemed to abandon Heracles (1290–93). The suspicion that Telamon entertains—that Jason wanted to get rid of the one whose glorious achievements would far outshine his own—is erroneous. But it is not implausible, especially given the issue of κῦδος, which was at stake in the election (cf. 1.351). First of all, Telamon's strong feelings toward Heracles are understandable given his close association with Heracles on several expeditions, chiefly those against the Amazons and the Trojans, as Σ *ad* 1.1289–91 observed.[47] Second, the men had originally chosen Heracles as their leader, and on Lemnos Heracles had even taken Jason to task for the excessive amount of time he spent with Hypsipyle, thereby delaying their expedition. For these reasons, Jason might well have harbored bad feelings against Heracles. Moreover, Jason's inability to respond could appear to signify acceptance of Telamon's charges.[48]

At the conclusion of his brief speech, Telamon states that he will return to Mysia to find Heracles. His words recall a climactic moment in the *Iliad,* when Achilles realizes that although he

---

47. Cf. J. Schmidt, "Telamon," Roscher 5.219–23; N.B. at *Idyll* 13.38 Theocritus has Hylas fetch water for Heracles and Telamon who share the same table; and Valerius Flaccus *Argo.* 1.353–54 has them share the same bench. U. von Wilamowitz-Moellendorf, *Die Textgeschichte der griechischen Bukoliker* (Berlin 1906) 178, argues for Theocritean imitation on this point; cf. Serrao (supra n. 27) 560–61.

48. Cf. Blumberg 28.

has everything that Zeus promised, he has lost his dear comrade Patroclus:[49]

Ἀλλὰ τί μύθων ἦδος; Ἐπεὶ καὶ νόσφιν ἑταίρων
εἶμι τεῶν οἳ τόνδε δόλον συνετεκτήναντο.
                                                    (1294–95)

But what profit is there in words? For I shall go even despite your comrades who have fabricated this plot together with you.

μῆτερ ἐμή, τὰ μὲν ἄρ' μοι Ὀλύμπιος ἐξετέλεσσεν·
ἀλλὰ τί μοι τῶν ἦδος, ἐπεὶ φίλος ὤλεθ' ἑταῖρος,
Πάτροκλος, τὸν ἐγὼ περὶ πάντων τῖον ἑταίρων,
ἶσον ἐμῇ κεφαλῇ·
                                                (Il. 18.79–82a)

Mother of mine, the Olympian god has fulfilled my wishes.
But what profit is there in this, since my dear comrade has died,
Patroclus, whom I honored above all comrades,
even as I do myself.

The contrast between the Argonautic passage and its model is striking. In the Homeric context, Achilles, enraged by the death of Patroclus, which took away any enjoyment he might have had of the fulfillment of Zeus's promises, chose to rejoin his compatriots and do battle with Hector, which he knew would lead to his own death. On the other hand, Telamon is about to abandon the expedition after jumping to a mistaken conclusion about the abandonment of his companion, who, at the time the Argonauts disembarked, was engaged in the futile and frantic search for his boyfriend. The imitation invests Telamon's angry reaction with epic coloration; but as we already know and the poet will have Glaucus reveal, the reasons for his anger are unsubstantiated; his Achillean wrath is empty.[50]

---

49. Mooney, Ardizzoni, and Campbell ad 1.1294 all note the imitation. The clever change from μοι τῶν to μύθων is particularly noteworthy.

50. Hunter (2) 444 suggests that this first stage of the argument between Jason and Telamon has as its model the quarrel between Achilles and Agamemnon in *Iliad* 1. There are, however, no discernible textual points of contact, although it is true, as he and others have pointed out, that the resolution of the Argonautic argument looks to that of the Iliadic; see immediately below.

After blaming Jason for the abandonment of Heracles, Telamon turns against Tiphys, who ordered the sailing, and would have succeeded in having the ship return to Mysia, despite the opposition of the wind and the current, had the Boreads not prevented this through their harsh words (1300–1301). The narrator then digresses and informs us of their fate: years later they will pay for their intervention when Heracles kills them after the funeral games in honor of Pelias, and, as a memorial of this, one of their funeral markers will sway to the blasts of their father, Boreas. Although the Argonauts are now proceeding ahead as they should, nonetheless a problem remains: they still harbor the bad feelings and suspicions that the abandonment of Heracles evoked. What is needed is a remedy for the mistrust elicited by the νεῖκος, something comparable to Orpheus's song at Pagasae. The appearance of Glaucus, whose report clears Jason of all suspicion, makes this possible.

To return briefly to the structure of this section of the episode, the outbreak of the νεῖκος containing Telamon's speech (a) corresponds to the reconciliation in which Telamon apologizes for his unwarranted accusation (a). In between these two subsections lie two corresponding interventions: that of the Boreads, who successfully contravene Telamon's plans (b), and that of Glaucus, who explains Heracles' abandonment (b), each containing references to the future of the missing Argonauts. For Glaucus, like the Boreads, instructs the Argonauts not to return to search for Heracles; and, like the narrator, he mentions the fates of the abandoned Argonauts: Heracles must complete his labors, Polyphemus will found the city of Cius, and Hylas will become the husband of the water nymph who abducted him. These subsections in turn frame the colorful portrait of Glaucus's sudden appearance, which is situated at the center of this ring (c). This symmetrical arrangement thus focuses on the picture of Glaucus rising out of the sea with his hand on the stern post (ὁλκαῖον) of the ship.

Apollonius did not invent the involvement of this minor sea divinity in the Argonautic legend. According to Philostratus (*Imag.* 2.15) and Diodorus (4.48), there was a tradition that Glaucus appeared to the Argonauts in the Black Sea, where he gave them prophecies. Diodorus even has him predict for Heracles the completion of his labors and his future immortality. According to Possis of Magnesia (*FGrHist* 480 F 2), Glaucus built the

Argo and was its helmsman in a battle against the Tyrrhenians. Afterwards, in accordance with Zeus's wishes, he disappeared into the depths of the sea (κατὰ δὲ Διὸς βούλησιν ἐν τῷ τῆς θαλάσσης βυθῷ ἀφανισθῆναι) and was transformed into a sea divinity. If Possis, who may have come after Apollonius (Jacoby *ad loc.* reluctantly dates him to around 200 B.C.), did not invent the metamorphosis of Glaucus,[51] but instead passes on an older tradition, Apollonius may well have this in mind in his portrayal of Glaucus as he emerges from the depths of the sea (Τοῖσιν δὲ Γλαῦκος βρυχίης ἁλὸς ἐξεφαάνθη, 1310) and reports to the Argonauts that they should not proceed contrary to the will of Zeus (Τίπτε παρὲx μεγάλοιο Διὸς μενεαίνετε βουλήν; 1315).[52] The fact that Apollonius's Glaucus holds on to the stern post to control the ship, as Apollonius recounts the story, may allude to his having been the helmsman in one version of the expedition. The central position of this image might suggest that a literary reference underlies the epiphany here. Be that as it may, a tradition that Glaucus was originally a mortal who became immortal goes back to Æschylus (*Glaucus* fr. 28–29 Radt). Apollonius's contemporary Alexander Ætolus also mentions this in his *Halieus* (121-22 Powell). In this respect, it is appropriate that Glaucus, a man become god, should intervene and announce the future apotheosis of Heracles, especially since the thrust of Glaucus's message is that Heracles does not belong among the Argonauts precisely because he is on his way to becoming a god. Gods, however, are not interdependent, and Jason stated on the beach at Pagasae that their expedition required a joint effort (336–37). Heracles, who can drive the *Argo* by himself, and take the golden apples of the Hesperides from a tree guarded by Ladon by himself, is out of place in such a group. His independence stands in opposition to the unity of the group; but Jason's dependence on the group and his skill in settling νείκεα, which Apollonius evinces in this concluding episode of Book 1, draw the men closer together. In this lies the strength of Jason's weakness. The appearance of Glaucus

---

51. As U. von Wilamowitz-Moellendorff, *Hellenistische Dichtung in der Zeit des Kallimachos* (reprint: Dublin 1973) 2.222 n. 1, avers.
52. Cf. Sophocles *Ph.* 1413–16, where Heracles appears to announce to Philoctetes τὰ Διός ... βουλεύματα in order to turn him to a different course.

thus allows both heroes to pursue their goals in the ways that best suit their personalities and abilities.

After Heracles' abandonment is discovered, Jason is stricken with ἀμηχανίη (1286). He has no idea what to do, and does nothing. In contrast, Telamon, Heracles' good friend and his counterpart in this half of the episode, as Hylas was Jason's counterpart in the first half, takes immediate action. Like Heracles on Lemnos, he usurps command momentarily, ordering a return to Mysia until the Boreads intervene. Jason has again temporarily yielded his command, and the result is chaos. Glaucus clears the air of suspicion. But the harmony that Telamon had destroyed through his most uncomplimentary accusation against Jason must be restored for the expedition to continue. It is in this context that we can perceive a crucial difference between Heracles and Jason. On the one hand, Heracles, who ultimately attains immortality by virtue of his extraordinary feats, will respond to the Boreads' intervention with unforgiving violence in a manner similar to his harsh treatment of Theiodamas and the Dryopians. In this way, Heracles stands apart from the others by virtue of his ruthless savagery and superhuman power, and acts as the foil against which we are to measure Jason, with whom he is overtly contrasted in this episode. Jason, on the other hand, is easily—and often—reduced to ἀμηχανίη; but, like the optimal leader he described at Pagasae (339-40), he knows how to ponder details, settle conflicts, and make compacts. Without Heracles, the only means of success lies in unified action and in skillful manipulation of those who can provide assistance. It happens that Jason is fully capable of preserving harmony and attracting others to his side. As the reader will see in the course of the poem, this brand of heroism is ultimately just as effective as that shown by the great Heracles. Through the assistance of Medea, Jason will come to complete the ἄεθλος that Æëtes assigns and secure the golden fleece guarded by the dragon, just as Heracles will complete the ἄεθλοι that Eurystheus set upon him. Apollonius includes an account of the acquisition of the golden apples of the Hesperides near the end of the poem to make the comparison with Jason's ἄεθλος perfectly clear.[53] Since Heracles'

---

53. Cf. M. G. Palombi, "Apollonio e il dodecathlon," *Prometheus* 11 (1985) 131-33.

power is so massive, one never doubts his ability to succeed. That a young man of the people (δημόθεν, 7) who is not especially powerful but rather prone to ἀμηχανίη—yet very adept at dealing with people—should manage to perform a feat comparable to the greatest of the Greek heroes is truly astonishing.

The cosmopolitan and sophisticated audience of Apollonius's day, like the heroes of the *Argonautica*, must also have left behind their belief in the great Heraclean hero. The figure of a Heracles was doubtless as unreal to them as Lynceus's sighting of Heracles in the Libyan desert (4.1477-80). In an age so absorbed with realism,[54] the real-life hero does not single-handedly row ships, but rather must know how to navigate seas of conflicting interests, foreign and internal squabbles, and the many obstacles—foreign customs, places, and peoples—that beset his quest for success. It is no longer the age of the old hero who could throw a huge boulder by himself. The epic magnitude of the challenge has not changed. But when the performer of a great ἄεθλος is only one of however many men it takes to lift up the huge stone that was once thrown with ease by a hero of the lost past, success entails finding the others who will assist.[55]

Who, then, is the best of the Argonauts? Apollonius colors the reader's response to this question, which is implicit in the νεῖκος, by having us see the reconciliation between Telamon and Jason against a Homeric backdrop. And the story of the reconciliation provides at least a partial answer.

In his apology to Jason, Telamon excuses his importunate words and asks Jason to cast his atrocious behavior to the winds:

---

54. G. Zanker, *Realism in Alexandrian Poetry: A Literature and Its Audience* (London 1987), provides an excellent study of this feature of Hellenistic thought; on realism in Apollonius in particular, cf. M. Lombardi, "Aspetti del realismo nelle *Argonautiche* di Apollonio Rodio," *Orpheus* 6 (1985) 250-69. Realism was a hallmark of Hellenistic art in general; cf. T. B. L. Webster, *Hellenistic Poetry and Art* (London 1964); J. J. Pollitt, *Art in the Hellenistic Age* (Cambridge 1986); and even more recently B. H. Fowler, *The Hellenistic Æsthetic* (Madison 1989).

55. Cf. 3.1365-67, where Apollonius uses this Homeric trope when Jason throws the stone that causes the earth-born men sprung from the dragon's teeth to fight among themselves (see Hunter *ad loc.*).

Αἰσονίδη, μή μοί τι χολώσεαι, ἀφραδίῃσιν
εἴ τί περ <u>ἀασάμην</u>· πέρι γὰρ μ' ἄχος ἧκεν ἐνισπεῖν
μῦθον ὑπερφίαλόν τε καὶ ἄσχετον. Ἀλλ' ἀνέμοισι
<u>δώομεν ἀμπλακίην</u>, ὡς καὶ πάρος εὐμενέοντες.

(1332–35)

Son of Æson, do not be angry with me if in my ignorance
<u>I acted foolishly</u>. Excessive grief led me to make
so arrogant and intolerable a speech. <u>But let us cast
this mistake to the winds</u> and be friendly toward each other as
before.

In the Homeric corpus, the form ἀασάμην is used only three times, always by the same man and with regard to the same event. Twice within the same speech Agamemnon uses it to describe his insulting behavior toward Achilles (*Il.* 9.116, 119), and once again when he apologizes directly to Achilles (*Il.* 19.137).[56] In a completely different context Agamemnon also asks another hero whom he has insulted to overlook his ill-spoken remarks.[57] In the so-called Ἀγαμέμνονος Ἐπιπώλησις, Agamemnon rebukes Mnestheus and Odysseus for holding back, saying that they are not so hesitant to be the first in line when the king gives a banquet (*Il.* 4.338–48). To Odysseus's furious retort (350–55), Agamemnon says:

διογενὲς Λαερτιάδη, πολυμήχαν' Ὀδυσσεῦ,
οὔτε σε νεικείω περιώσιον οὔτε κελεύω·
οἶδα γὰρ ὥς τοι θυμὸς ἐνὶ στήθεσσι φίλοισιν
ἤπια δήνεα οἶδε· τὰ γὰρ φρονέεις ἅ τ' ἐγώ περ.
ἀλλ' ἴθι, ταῦτα δ' ὄπισθεν ἀρεσσόμεθ', <u>εἴ τι κακὸν νῦν
εἴρηται</u>,[58] <u>τὰ δὲ πάντα θεοὶ μεταμώνια θεῖεν</u>.

(*Il.* 4.358–63)

Zeus-born son of Laërtes, clever Odysseus,
I have no intention of rebuking you excessively or ordering you about,
for I know that the feelings you hold within
are well-meaning, since you think along the same lines as I.

---

56. Cf. Ardizzoni *ad* 1333; N.B. in the last two instances the word is in the same metrical *sedes* as in the Argonautic passage.
57. Mooney *ad* 1.1330 noted the parallel.
58. Cf. εἴ τί περ ἀασάμην (1333).

But, come now, let's settle these things later if anything untoward has just now been said, and may the gods annul all unpleasantries between us.

Like Agamemnon, Telamon has incorrectly interpreted his comrade's inactivity and has spoken out of line; and like Agamemnon, he asks that his impertinent statement be rendered null and void.

Campbell has pointed out another parallel to Telamon's apology that merits close attention.[59] During Odysseus's brief stay on Phæacia, Euryalus insulted his anonymous guest for refusing to take part in the athletic contests:

οὐ γάρ σ' οὐδέ, ξεῖνε, δαήμονι φωτὶ ἐίσκω
ἄθλων, οἷά τε πολλὰ μετ' ἀνθρώποισι πέλονται,
ἀλλὰ τῷ ὅς θ' ἅμα νηὶ πολυκληῖδι θαμίζων,
ἀρχὸς ναυτάων οἵ τε πρηκτῆρες ἔασι,
φόρτου τε μνήμων καὶ ἐπίσκοπος ᾗσιν ὁδαίων
κερδέων θ' ἁρπαλέων· οὐδ' ἀθλητῆρι ἔοικας.
(Od. 8.159-64)

Stranger, I do not make you out to be a man skilled in the many
athletic contests that there are in the world,
but one who travels about in a many-oared ship,
a captain of sailors who are in the business of trading merchandise;
a man who thinks only of his freight and watches out for his cargo
and eagerly sought gain. But you do not look like one who cares
   for ἄεθλοι.

As in the Iliadic passage discussed immediately above, Odysseus's hesitation to act—in the Odyssean context, to compete—is misinterpreted. After he defeated all the athletes in the discus contest, it became clear to all the Phæacians that Odysseus did not hesitate out of inability or cowardice; and Euryalus apologizes for his foolish remark:

Χαῖρε, πάτερ ὦ ξεῖνε· ἔπος δ' εἴ πέρ τι βέβαχται
δεινόν, ἄφαρ τὸ φέροιεν ἀναρπάξασαι ἄελλαι.
σοὶ δὲ θεοὶ ἄλοχον ἰδέειν καὶ πατρίδ' ἱκέσθαι
δοῖεν, ἐπεὶ δὴ δηθὰ φίλων ἄπο πήματα πάσχεις.
(Od. 8.408-11)

---

59. Campbell ad 1.1332ff.

> Hail, honored stranger. If some terrible word has been
> uttered, may the breezes snatch it up and carry it away.
> May the gods grant that you see your wife and arrive in your
> fatherland, since you have suffered for a long time far away from
> your loved ones.

It would seem that Apollonius also had the phrasing of Euryalus's apology in mind in his articulation of Telamon's. In addition to the similar phraseology, this Odyssean dispute in general parallels the Argonautic argument: Euryalus makes the mistaken judgment that Odysseus does not know how to succeed in ἄεθλοι, and Odysseus proves him wrong. To Telamon and the others, Jason did not seem to be the best of the Argonauts. In their estimation, as we have seen in the the election, Heracles, the man of strength, was the best. In the argument following Heracles' abandonment, Telamon's position reflects this opinion. Yet Apollonius underscores the empty bluster of the latter's accusation and apology by having the reader compare his words with those of three Homeric characters. His Achillean wrath is thoroughly misdirected and divisive, and his apology smacks at once of the shallowness of Agamemnon and the foolishness of Euryalus. When seen in the light of their Homeric models, Heracles and Telamon both come off badly. On the other hand, in this νεῖκος Jason resembles the Odysseus of the Homeric subtext in that he too at first remains aloof and thereby encounters Telamon's rebuff. But in his masterful handling of the situation he shows that he is the best leader for the Argonautic mission, a mission characterized as ξυνός, and one capable after all of competing in ἄεθλοι.

Faced with the possible abandonment of the expedition, Jason, as we have seen, is at first incapable of action, and his temporary paralysis leads immediately to chaos and disorder. Yet, as I stated above, even after the Boreads get the Argonauts on the proper course and Glaucus clears Jason of Telamon's charge, the crisis is not yet completely resolved. Jason must find some way to restore unity and resume command of his expedition. Telamon offers that opportunity in his apology, which Jason accepts graciously, even putting Telamon in his debt:

> Ἀλλ' οὐ θήν τοι ἀδευκέα μῆνιν ἀέξω,
> πρίν περ ἀνιηθείς, ἐπεὶ οὐ περὶ πώεσι μήλων

οὐδὲ περὶ κτεάτεσσι χαλεψάμενος μενέηνας,
ἀλλ' ἑτάρου περὶ φωτός. Ἔολπα δέ τοι σὲ καὶ ἄλλῳ
ἀμφ' ἐμεῦ, εἰ τοιόνδε πέλοι ποτέ, δηρίσασθαι.
(1339b-43)

But I shall not harbor bitter wrath against you,
despite my earlier distress, since not about flocks of sheep
or about possessions did you experience such anger and rage,
but about a man who was your comrade. I hope that you might
even fight
another on my behalf, should such a situation ever arise.

The heart of Jason's acceptance is modeled on a comment that the Homeric narrator made as Achilles pursued Hector around the walls of Troy:[60]

τῇ ῥα παραδραμέτην, φεύγων, ὁ δ' ὄπισθε διώκων·
πρόσθε μὲν ἐσθλὸς ἔφευγε, δίωκε δέ μιν μέγ' ἀμείνων
καρπαλίμως, ἐπεὶ οὐχ ἱερήιον οὐδὲ βοείην
ἀρνύσθην, ἅ τε ποσσὶν ἀέθλια γίγνεται ἀνδρῶν,
ἀλλὰ περὶ ψυχῆς θέον Ἕκτορος ἱπποδάμοιο.
(Il. 22.157-61)

The two ran along, the one fleeing and the one behind in pursuit.
A noble man fled in front, but a much better man held him in hot
pursuit, since they were not vying for a sacrificial animal
or a leather hide, which are prizes for footraces,
but they were running for the life of horse-taming Hector.

Like the narrator of the *Iliad*, Jason stands apart as an observer of the action, and in this he differs markedly from the other Argonauts. This aloofness from action comes across at first as unheroic passivity; yet it enables him to achieve a better perspective on the relative importance of this and other events. As wrong as Telamon was, Jason acknowledges that his concerns were at least not ignoble. In a masterful stroke of diplomacy he dismisses Telamon's insulting accusation and suggests that one day Telamon might even fight as valiantly on his behalf; these are the kinds of pacts

---

60. Observed by Mooney *ad* 1.1330, Campbell *ad* 1.1339-42, Vian 113 n. 4; cf. R. W. Garson, "Homeric Echoes in Apollonius Rhodius' *Argonautica*," *CP* 67 (1972) 6.

the Jasonian hero makes best, as his dealings with Medea will demonstrate.

The crisis following the abandonment of Heracles is also enlightening on another related issue. Jason may be skilled in taking care of the details of the expedition and in settling arguments, but, as is quite evident here, he does not create the opportunities for his diplomatic successes. Rather, his passive style requires that he depend on forces and occurrences outside his making; he waits for opportunities that he can turn to the benefit of the group.[61] This approach differs from the active style of a Heracles and a Telamon, which locks them into a perversely egotistic and divisive course of action. Rather, for Jason the goal of the whole group takes precedence over the personal pique of the one: ξυνὸς γὰρ νόστος, ξυναὶ δὲ κέλευθοι. When Jason finishes speaking, Apollonius confirms the success of his approach: he spoke, and, united as before, they took their seats (Ἦ ῥα καί, ἀρθμηθέντες ὅπῃ πάρος, ἑδριόωντο, 1344). The group has regained its lost unity, and the expedition can continue.[62]

THROUGHOUT the rest of the poem Jason will maintain this passive style. He does not make things happen but waits for the dust to settle before taking advantage of the opportunities that others—mortal and divine—have provided. Jason's talents include the ability to attract women, to take care of the quotidian details of running an expedition, and to make the best of bad situations through skillful crisis management. These are not the qualities one normally associates with the best of the Greek heroes. In the Iliadic Catalogue of Ships, which Apollonius's Catalogue pointedly calls to mind, Homer asked who the best of the Achæans was, and gave as his answer Telamonian Ajax—that is, as long as Achilles was absent. Likewise, on several occasions in Book 1 Apollonius poses the question, Who is the best of the Argonauts? At the conclusion of this book the reader has an answer. In the

---

61. Cf. F. Vian, "ΙΗΣΩΝ ΑΜΗΧΑΝΕΩΝ," *Studi in honore di Anthos Ardizzoni*, ed. E. Livrea and G. A. Privitera (Rome 1978), 1025–41, who views Jason's ἀμηχανίη as beneficial in that it allows the gods to intervene.

62. On the importance of unity as a theme in the poem, cf. Vian 48–49, Hunter (2) 445, and "Apollo and the Argonauts: Two Notes on Ap. Rhod. 2.669–719," *MH* 43 (1986) 50–54.

absence of Heracles—or in the absence of some one like Heracles; that is, in the absence of a totally self-sufficient man of godlike strength—Jason, a totally dependent man of limited skills, proves to be the best of the Argonauts.

At the conclusion of Book 1, we have seen the old Homeric hero redefined. Jason has emerged as a new, Alexandrian epic hero, the best among his peers at completing heroic ἄεθλοι. How we are to read the following three books depends very much on our understanding of this redefined hero. In calling the traditional hero into question and creating a more realistic hero, Apollonius significantly advanced the writing of epic poetry.[63] As the reader prepares to follow the Argonauts on their journey through the Symplegades and beyond, he or she can observe how this new kind of hero engages in a mission best suited for a traditional hero like Heracles. Jason will single-mindedly pursue his quest: νόστος with the fleece in hand. And he will succeed. Yet, we are left at the end of the book with a trenchant irony. At the climax of Book 1, Jason confirms his leadership and his status as the best of the Argonauts through his diplomatic skills, in particular his ability to solve νείκεα. Just as Heracles' great strength both brings about and is of no avail in the loss of Hylas, so too Jason will ultimately suffer a devastating loss in the death of his sons when his "heroic" skill of making pacts and settling arguments, in particular with foreigners, fails him in his final ἄεθλος with Medea.

---

63. Fraser's generally negative view of the *Argonautica* (*Ptolemaic Alexandria* [Oxford 1972] 1.626, 640), with its focus on geography, etiology, and Alexandrian vocabulary, is symptomatic of an older school of thought. I would add that his styling of Apollonius's imitations and allusions as "plagiarism" (751) is equally dated.

The age demanded an image
Of its accelerated grimace,
Something for the modern stage,
Not, at any rate, an Attic grace.

EZRA POUND, HUGH SELWYN MAUBERLY II.21–24

SELECT BIBLIOGRAPHY

Allen, T. W., W. R. Halliday, and E. E. Sikes, eds. *The Homeric Hymns*. Oxford 1963.
Anderson, W. D. "Notes on the Simile in Homer and His Successors, I." *CJ* 53 (1957) 81–87.
Ardizzoni, A. "Apollonio Rodio I.177." *Helikon* 5 (1965) 532–33.
———. "Cleite, ovvero la Fonte delle Lacrime." In *Mythos: Scripta in Honorem M. Untersteiner*, 37–42. Genoa 1970.
———. "Echi pitagorici in Apollonio Rodio e Callimaco." *RFIC* 93 (1965) 257–67.
———. "Eracle e Teodamante in Callimaco e in Apollonio Rodio." *RFIC* 63 (1935) 452–67.
———. *L'Eracle "semnós" nel poema di Apollonio*. Catania 1937.
———. "Note apolloniane." *Maia* 20 (1968) 11–14.
———. "Il pianto di Medea e la similitudine della giovane vedova (Apollonio Rodio 3.656-657)." *GIF* 28 (1976) 233–40.
———. "Riflessioni sul testo di Apollonio Rodio." *GIF* 31 (1979) 261–67.
———. "'Trappole' e infortuni apolloniani." *GIF* 30 (1978) 275–87.
———. "Una presa di posizione di Apollonio Rodio riguardo a un particolare mitico in Pindaro." *BIFG* 1 (1974) 164–72.
———. "Vergine vedova o solo giovane vedova? Intorno ad una similitudine di Apollonio Rodio." In *Studi in onore di A. Colonna*, 7–9. Perugia 1982.
Bacon, J. R. *The Voyage of the Argonauts*. London 1925.
Bahrenfuss, W. "Das Abenteuer der Argonauten auf Lemnos bei Apollonios Rhodios (*Argo.* 1.601 bis 909), Valerius Flaccus (*Argo.* 2.72 bis 430), Papinius Statius (*Theb.* 4.746 bis 5.498)." Diss. Kiel 1951.
Barrigazzi, A. "Eracle e Teodamante in Callimaco e Apollonio Rodio." *Prometheus* 2 (1976) 227–38.

Belloni, L. "A proposito di alcuni omerismi in Apollonio Rodio." *Aevum* 53 (1979) 66–71.
Beye, C. R. "Jason as Love-Hero in Apollonius' *Argonautica*." *GRBS* 10 (1969) 31–55.
Bremer, J. M. "Full Moon and Marriage in Apollonius' *Argonautica*." *CQ* 37 (1987) 423–26.
Brunel, J. "Jason μονοκρήπις." *RA* 4 (1934) 34–43.
Bulloch, A. W. "Apollonius Rhodius *Argonautica* 1.177: A Case Study in Hellenistic Poetic Style." *Hermes* 101 (1973) 496–98.
———. *Callimachus: The Fifth Hymn*. Cambridge 1985.
———. "Hellenistic Poetry." In *The Cambridge History of Classical Literature* 1, 541–621. Cambridge 1985.
Bundy, E. "The Quarrel between Kallimachos and Apollonios, Part I: The Epilogue of Kallimachos' Hymn to Apollo." *CSCA* 5 (1972) 39–94.
Burkert, W. *Greek Religion*. Trans. J. Raffan. Cambridge, Mass., 1985.
———. *Homo Necans*. Trans. P. Bing. Berkeley and Los Angeles 1983.
———. *Structure and History in Greek Mythology and Ritual*. Berkeley and Los Angeles 1979.
Caggia, G. "Un caso di bivalenza semantica in Apollonio Rodio." *GIF* 26 (1974) 33–40.
———. "Due parole omeriche in Apollonio Rodio (ἐψιάομαι in 1.459 e ἀΐδηλος in 3.1132)." *RFIC* 100 (1972) 23–31.
Cahen, E. *Callimaque et son œuvre poétique*. Paris 1929.
Campbell, M. "Ap. Rhod. 1.26:ff. Again." *GIF* 30 (1978) 288–89.
———. "Ap. Rhod. 1.74–76." *GIF* 33 (1981) 207–8.
———. "Ap. Rhod. 1.1187." *RhM* 125 (1982) 192.
———. "Apollonian and Homeric Book Division." *Mnemosyne* 36 (1983) 154–55.
———. "βώσεσθε Again." *CQ* 27 (1977) 467.
———. "ΔΟΔΕΚΑ ΑΠΟΛΛΟΝΙΟΥ." In *Studi in honore di Anthos Ardizzoni*, ed. E. Livrea and G. A. Privitera, 119–25. Rome 1978.
———. "Some Methodological Problems in Alexandrian Poetry: A Reply to Dr. Giangrande." *CQ* 22 (1972) 110–12.
———. "Some Unnoticed Apollonian Testimonia." *RhM* 131 (1988) 98.
———. *Studies in the Third Book of Apollonius Rhodius' Argonautica*. Hildesheim 1983.
———. "Three Notes on Alexandrine Poetry." *Hermes* 102 (1974) 38–46.

Carspecken, J. F. "Apollonius Rhodius and the Homeric Epic." *YClS* 13 (1952) 33–143.
Cataudella, Q. "Note critiche al testo delle Argonautiche di Apollonio Rodio." In *Miscellanea di studi alessandrini in memoria di A. Rostagni*, 356–62. Turin 1963.
Ciani, M. G. "Apollonio Rodio: Gli studi moderni e le prospettive attuali." *A&R* 15 (1970) 80–88.
———. "Poesia come enigma (Considerazioni sulla poesia di Apollonio Rodio)." *Scritti in onore di C. Diano*, 77–111. Bologna 1975.
———. "Scelti e usi lessicali in Apollonio Rodio." In *Studi in honore di Anthos Ardizzoni*, ed. E. Livrea and G. A. Privitera, 199–216. Rome 1978.
Clack, J. "The Medea Similes of Apollonius Rhodius." *CJ* 68 (1973) 310–15.
Clauss, J. J. "Hellenistic Imitations of Hesiod, *Catalogue of Women* fr. 1.6–7 M&W." *QUCC*, n.s., 36 (1990) 129–40.
———. "Lies and Allusions: The Addressee and Date of Callimachus' *Hymn to Zeus*." *ClAnt* 5 (1986) 155–70.
———. "A Mythological Thaumatrope in Apollonius Rhodius." *Hermes* 119 (1991) 484–88.
———. "Two Curious Reflections in the Argonautic Looking-glass (*Argo.* 1.577 and 603)." *GIF* 41 (1989) 195–207.
———. Review of R. L. Hunter, ed., *Apollonius of Rhodes: Argonautica Book III* (Cambridge 1989). *EMC*, n.s., 11 (1992) 63–76.
———. Review of E.-R. Schwinge, *Künstlichkeit von Kunst* (Munich 1986). *AJP* 109 (1988) 447–49.
Cole, S. G. *Theoi Megaloi: The Cult of the Great Gods at Samothrace*. Leiden 1984.
Colonna, A. "Apoll. Rhod. 1.1237." *Maia* 18 (1966) 281.
Corbato, C. *Riprese callimachee in Apollonio Rodio*. Trieste 1955.
Cowell, J. "Hylas and Heracles." *Pegasus* 12 (1969) 44–48.
DeForest, M. M. *Heroes in a Toy Boat*. Forthcoming.
Delage, E. *Biographie d'Apollonios de Rhodes*. Paris 1930.
De Marco, V. "Osservazioni su Apolloniio Rodio, I. 1–22." In *Miscellanea di studi alessandrini in memoria di A. Rostagni*, 350–55. Turin 1963.
Dufner, C. M. "The *Odyssey* in the *Argonautica*: Reminiscence, Revision, Reconstruction." Diss. Princeton 1988.
Dyck, A. R. "On the Way from Colchis to Corinth: Medea in Book 4 of the *Argonautica*." *Hermes* 117 (1989) 445–70.
Edwards, A. T. *Achilles in the Odyssey: Ideologues of Heroism in the Homeric Epic*. Königstein 1985.

Eichgrün, E. "Kallimachos und Apollonios Rhodios." Diss. Freie U. Berlin 1961.
Elderkin, G. W. "Repetitions in the *Argonautica* of Apollonius." *AJP* 34 (1913) 198–201.
Erbse, H. "Homerscholien und hellenistische Glossare bei Apollonios Rhodios." *Hermes* 81 (1953) 163–96.
——— . "Versumstellungen in den *Argonautika* des Apollonios Rhodios." *RhM* 106 (1963) 229–51.
Faerber, H. "Zur dichterischen Kunst in Apollonios Rhodios' *Argonautika* (Die Gleichnisse)." Diss. Berlin 1932.
Fantuzzi, M. "Omero 'autore' di Apollonio Rodio: Le formule introduttive al discorso diretto." *MD* 13 (1986) 7–105.
——— . "Varianti d' autore nelle *Argonautiche* d'Apollonio Rodio." *A&A* 29 (1983) 146–61.
Farrell, J. *Vergil's Georgics and the Traditions of Ancient Epic*. Oxford 1991.
Feeney, D. C. *The Gods in Epic: Poets and Critics of the Classical Tradition*. Oxford 1991.
——— . "Epic Hero and Epic Fable." *CompLit* 38 (1986) 137–58.
——— . "Following after Hercules in Virgil and Apollonius." *PVS* 18 (1986) 47–85.
Fitch, E. "Apollonius Rhodius and Cyzicus." *AJP* 33 (1912) 43–56.
Fowler, B. H. *The Hellenistic Æsthetic*. Madison 1989.
Fränkel, H. "Apollonius Rhodius as a Narrator in Argonautica II.1–40." *TAPhA* 83 (1952) 144–55.
——— . "Das Argonautenepos des Apollonios." *MH* 14 (1957) 1–19.
——— . "Ein Don Quijote unter den Argonauten des Apollonios." *MH* 17 (1960) 1–20.
Fraser, P. M. *Ptolemaic Alexandria*. 3 vols. Oxford 1972.
Frazer, J. G. *Apollodorus: The Library*. 2 vols. London 1921.
Fusillo, M. "Descrizione e racconto: Sulla retorica dell'oggeto in Apollonio Rodio." *MD* 10–11 (1983) 65–103.
——— . *Il tempo delle Argonautiche: Un'analisi del racconto in Apollonio Rodio*. Rome 1985.
Gaisser, J. H. "A Structural Analysis of the Digressions in the *Iliad* and *Odyssey*." *HSCPh* 73 (1969) 1–43.
Galinsky, G. Karl. *The Herakles Theme*. Oxford 1972.
Garson, R. W. "Homeric Echoes in Apollonius Rhodius' *Argonautica*." *CP* 67 (1972) 1–9.
Gaunt, D. M. "*Argo* and the Gods in Apollonius Rhodius." *G&R* 19 (1972) 117–26.

———. "The Creation-Theme in Epic Poetry," *CompLit* 29 (1977) 213-20.
Gentili, B., and C. Prato, eds. *Poetae Elegiaci Pars II*. Leipzig 1985.
George, E. V. "Poet and Characters in Apollonius Rhodius' Lemnian Episode." *Hermes* 100 (1972) 47-62.
Gerke, A. "Alexandrinische Studien (Der Streit mit Apollonios)." *RhM* 44 (1884) 127-50, 240-57.
Giangrande, G. "'Arte allusiva' and Alexandrian Epic Poetry." *CQ* 17 (1967) 85-97.
———. "Aspects of Apollonius Rhodius' Language." In *Papers of the Liverpool Latin Seminar, 1976*, ed. F. Cairns, 271-91. Liverpool 1977.
———. "Hellenistic Poetry and Homer." *AC* 39 (1970) 46-77.
———. "A Passage in Apollonius." *CQ* 21 (1971) 146-48.
———. "Polisemia del linguaggio nella poesia alessandrina." *QUCC* 24 (1977) 97-106.
———. "Der stilistische Gebrauch der Dorismen im Epos." *Hermes* 98 (1970) 257-77.
———. "The Utilization of Homeric Variants by Apollonius Rhodius: A Methodological Canon of Research." *QUCC* 15 (1973) 73-81.
———. *Zu Sprachgebrauch, Technik und Text des Apollonios Rhodios*. Amsterdam 1973.
Gillies, M. M. *The Argonautica of Apollonius Rhodius: Book III*. Cambridge 1928.
Goldberg, S. *Understanding Terence*. Princeton 1986.
Goldhill, S. *The Poet's Voice: Essays on Poetics and Greek Literature*. Cambridge 1991.
Gow, A. S. F. *Theocritus*. Cambridge 1952.
———. "The Thirteenth Idyll of Theocritus." *CQ* 32 (1938) 10-17.
Grajew, G. "Untersuchungen über die Bedeutung der Gebärden in der griechischen Epik." Diss. Königsberg 1934.
Grillo, A. *Tra filologia e narratologia*. Rome 1988.
Griffiths, A. H. "Six Passages in Callimachus and the Anthology." *BICS* 17 (1970) 32-43.
van Groningen, B. A. *La composition littéraire archaïque grecque*. Amsterdam 1958.
———. "Un passage difficile d'Apollonios de Rhodes (*Argonautiques* 1.1071-1077)." *Mnemosyne* 15 (1962) 268-70.
Hadas, M. "Apollonius Called the Rhodian." *CW* 26 (1932) 41-46, 49-54.
———. "The Tradition of a Feeble Jason." *CP* 31 (1936) 166-69.

Händel, P. "Die Götter des Apollonios als Personen." In *Miscellanea di Studi alessandrini in memoria di A. Rostagni*, 363–81. Turin 1963.
Hainsworth, J. B. *The Idea of Epic*. Berkeley and Los Angeles 1991.
Haslam, M. W. "Apollonius Rhodius and the Papyri." *ICS* 3 (1978) 47–73.
Hasluck, F. *Cyzicus*. Cambridge 1910.
Henrichs, A. "Apollonios Rhodios I.317–331 (P. Colon. inv. 929)." *ZPE* 1 (1967) 113–16.
———. "Apollonios Rhodios I.699–719 (P. Mil. 6 und P. Colon. inv. 522)." *ZPE* 5 (1970) 49–56.
———. "Callimachus *Epigram* 28: A Fastidious Priamel." *HSCPh* 83 (1979) 207–12.
Herter, H. "Apollonius, der Epiker." *RE* Suppl. 13 (1973) 15–56.
———. "Bericht über die Literatur zur hellenistischen Dichtung seit dem Jahre 1921, II: Apollonios von Rhodos." *JAW* 285 (1944–55) 213–410.
———. "Hera spricht mit Thetis: Eine Szene des Apollonios Rhodios." *SO* 35 (1959) 40–54.
———. "Zum Lebensgeschichte des Apollonios von Rhodos." *RhM* 91 (1942) 310–26.
Heubeck, A., S. West, and A. J. Hainsworth. *A Commentary on Homer's Odyssey*. Vol. 1. Oxford 1988.
Hopkinson, N. *Callimachus: Hymn to Demeter*. Cambridge 1984.
———. *A Hellenistic Anthology*. Cambridge 1988.
Huebscher, P. A. "Die Charakteristik der Personen in Apollonios' Argonautika." Diss. Freiberg 1936 [1940].
Hunter, R. L. "Apollo and the Argonauts: Two Notes on Ap. Rhod. 2.669–719." *MH* 43 (1986) 50–60.
———. "Medea's Flight: The Fourth Book of the *Argonautica*." *CQ* 37 (1987) 129–39.
Hurst, A. "Le retour nocturne des Argonautes." *MH* 21 (1964) 232–37.
Hutchinson, G. O. *Hellenistic Poetry*. Oxford 1988.
Huxley, G. L. "Thracian Hylas." *JHS* 109 (1989) 185–86.
———. "Kallimachos, the Assyrian River and the Bees of Demeter." *GRBS* 12 (1971) 211–15.
Ibscher, R. "Gestalt der Szene und Form der Rede in den *Argonautika* des Apollonios Rhodios." Diss. Munich 1939.
James, A. W. "Some Examples of Imitation in the Similes of Later Greek Epic." *Antichthon* 3 (1969) 77–90.
———. "Apollonius Rhodius and His Sources: Interpretative Notes on the *Argonautica*." *CL* 1 (1981) 59–86.
Janko, R. "βώσεσθε Revisited." *CQ* 39 (1979) 215–16.

Kirk, G. S., ed. *The Iliad: A Commentary*. Cambridge 1985- .
Klein, T. M. "Apollonius Rhodius, *Vates Ludens*: Eros' Golden Ball (*Arg.* 3.113-50)." *CW* 74 (1980-81) 225-27.
―――――. "Apollonius' Jason: Hero and Scoundrel." *QUCC*, n.s., 13 (1983) 115-26.
―――――. "Callimachus' Two Ætia Prologues." *ZAnt* 26 (1976) 357-61.
―――――. "Callimachus, Apollonius Rhodius, and the Concept of the Big Book." *Eranos* (1975) 16-25.
―――――. "The Role of Callimachus in the Development of the Concept of Counter-Genre." *Latomus* 33 (1974) 217-31.
Knight, V. "Apollonius Rhodius, *Argonautica* 4.167-70 and Euripides' *Medea*." *CQ* 41 (1991) 248-50.
Köhnken, A. *Apollonios Rhodios und Theokrit: Die Hylas- und die Amykosgeschichten beider Dichter und die Frage der Priorität*. Hypomnemata 12. Gottingen 1965.
―――――. "Der Schrei des Hylas." *RhM* 113 (1970) 69-79.
van Krevelen, D. A. "Die Bedeutung von αὐτίκα in den *Argonautika* des Apollonios, 2.946; 3.521; 4.1547." *RhM* 117 (1974) 359-60.
―――――. "Bemerkungen zur Characteristik der in den *Argonautika* des Apollonius auftretenden Personen." *RhM* 99 (1956) 3-8.
―――――. "Kritische und exegetische Bemerkungen zu Apollonios Rhodios." *SIFC* 25 (1951) 95-103.
―――――. "Der Kybelekult in den *Argonautika* des Apollonios von Rhodos I.1078-1153." *RhM* 97 (1954) 75-82.
―――――. "Zu Apollonios Rhodios' *Argonautika*." *Hermes* 99 (1971) 242-43.
―――――. "Zu Apollonios von Rhodos." *Mnemosyne* 4 (1953) 46-55.
Kumpf, M. M. *Four Indices of the Homeric Hapax Legomena*. Hildesheim 1984.
Lefkowitz, M. R. "The Quarrel between Callimachus and Apollonius." *ZPE* 40 (1980) 1-19.
Lennox, P. G. "Apollonius, *Argonautica* 3.1ff. and Homer." *Hermes* 108 (1980) 45-73.
Lesky, A. *Thalatta: Der Weg der Griechen zum Meer*. Vienna 1947.
Levin, D. N. "Apollonius' Heracles." *CJ* 67 (1971) 22-28.
―――――. "Δίπλαξ πορφυρέη." *RFIC* 98 (1970) 12-36.
Livrea, E. "Apoll. Rh. I.262." *GIF* 29 (1977) 29-33.
―――――. "Da Pagasai a Lemnos." *SIFC* 51 (1979) 146-54.
―――――. "Un' eco saffica in Apollonio Rodio." *Helikon* 8 (1968) 447.
―――――. "L'épos philologique: Apollonios de Rhodes et quelques homérismes méconnus." *AC* 49 (1980) 146-60.

———. "Una 'tecnica allusiva' apolloniana alla luce dell'esegesi omerica alessandrina." *SIFC* 44 (1972) 231-43.
Lombardi, M. "Aspetti del realismo nelle *Argonautiche* di Apollonio Rodio." *Orpheus* 6 (1985) 250-69.
———. "Note al libro I delle *Argonautiche* di Apollonio Rodio." *Helikon* 20-12 (1980-81) [1983] 335-49.
Martin, J. *Arati Phænomena*. Florence 1956.
Marxer, G. "Die Sprache des Apollonius Rhodius." Diss. Zurich 1935.
Mawet, F. "Evolution d'une structure sémantique: Le vocabulaire de la douleur. Apollonius de Rhodes et Homère." *AC* 50 (1981) 499-516.
McGready, F. "Heracles' Love for Hylas." *CL* 3 (1983) 79-80.
McLennan, G. R. *Callimachus: Hymn to Zeus*. Rome 1977.
Merkel, R. *Apollonii Argonautica*. Leipzig 1854.
Nagy, G. *The Best of the Achæans*. Baltimore 1979.
———. *Greek Mythology and Poetics*. Ithaca 1990.
Nelis, D. P. "Iphias: Apollonius Rhodius, *Argonautica* 1.311-16." *CQ* 41 (1991) 96-105.
Newman, J. K. *The Classical Epic Tradition*. Madison 1986.
Paduano, G. *Apollonio Rodio: Le Argonautiche*. Milan 1986.
———. "Struttura e significato del monologo in Apollonio Rodio." *QUCC* 9 (1970) 24-66.
———. *Studi su Apollonio Rodio*. Rome 1972.
Paduano Faedo, L. "L'inversione del rapporto poeta-musa nella cultura ellenistica." *ASNP* 39 (1970) 377-86.
Palombi, M. G. "Apollonio e il dodecathlon." *Prometheus* 11 (1985) 126-36.
———. "Eracle e Ila nelle *Argonautiche* di Apollonio Rodio." *SCO* 35 (1985) 71-92.
Paskiewicz, T. M. "Aitia in the Second Book of Apollonius' *Argonautica*." *ICS* 13 (1988) 57-61.
Pavlock, B. *Eros, Imitation, and the Epic Tradition*. Ithaca 1990.
Pearson, L. "Apollonius of Rhodes and the Old Geographers." *AJP* 59 (1938) 443-59.
Petrusevski, M. D. "Perewote-Doroqo Sowote." *ZAnt* 15 (1965-66) 201.
Phinney, E. "Hellenistic Painting and the Poetic Style of Apollonius." *CJ* 62 (1967) 145-49.
———. "Narrative Unity in the *Argonautica*: The Medea-Jason Romance." *TAPhA* 98 (1967) 327-41.
Pike, D. L. "The Comic Aspects of the Strongman-Hero in Greek Myth." *AClass* 23 (1980) 37-44.
Platt, A. "Apollonius Again." *Journal of Philology* 34 (1918) 129-41.
———. "Apollonius III." *Journal of Philology* 35 (1919) 72-85.

Pollitt, J. J. *Art in the Hellenistic Age*. Cambridge 1986.
Preininger. J. *Der Aufbau der Argonautica des Apollonios Rhodios*. Vienna 1976.
Pulbrook, M. "The Hylas Myth in Apollonius of Rhodes and Theocritus." *Maynooth Review* 8 (1983) 25-31.
Race, W. H. *The Classical Priamel from Homer to Boethius*. Mnemosyne Supplement 74. Leiden 1982.
Richardson, N. J. *The Homeric Hymn to Demeter*. Oxford 1974.
Robert, L. "Géographie et philologie, ou la terre et le papier." In *Association G. Budé, Actes du VIIIe Congrès*, 67-86. Paris 1969.
Rose, A. R. "Clothing Imagery in Apollonius' *Argonautica*." *QUCC*, n.s., 21 (1985) 29-44.
———. "Three Narrative Themes in Apollonios' Bebrykian Episode (*Argonautica* 2.1-163)." *WS* 18 (1984) 115-35.
Rossi, L. E. "La fine allesandrina dell'*Odissea* e lo ζῆλος ὁμηρικός di Apollonio Rodio." *RFIC* 96 (1968) 151-63.
Roux, G. "Commentaires sur Theocrite, Apollonios et quelques epigrammes de l'*Anthologie*." *RPh* 37 (1963) 76-92.
Roux, R. *Le problème des Argonautes: Recherches sur les aspects religieux de la légende*. Paris 1949.
Rusten, J. S. *Dionysius Scytobrachion*. Opladen 1982.
Saussez, M. "La caractère de Jason dans les *Argonautiques* d'Apollonius de Rhodes." Diss. Louvain 1941.
Schwinge, E.-R. *Künstlichkeit von Kunst: Zur Geschichtlichkeit der alexandrinischen Poesie*. Munich 1986.
Seaton, R. C. "Notes on Ap. Rhod. with Reference to Liddell and Scott." *CR* 2 (1888) 83-84.
Segal, C. P. *Orpheus: The Myth of the Poet*. Baltimore 1989.
Serrao, G. "Problemi di poesia alessandrina." *Helikon* 5 (1965) 541-65.
Shapiro, H. A. "Jason's Cloak." *TAPhA* 110 (1980) 263-86.
Sisti, F. "Apollonio I.177." *Helikon* 11-12 (1971-72) 491-93.
Skutsch, O. "βώσεσθε." *CQ* 23 (1973) 60.
Slatkin, L. M. "The Wrath of Thetis." *TAPhA* 116 (1986) 1-24.
Smid, T. C. "Tsunamis in Greek Literature." *G&R* 17 (1970) 100-104.
Smiley, M. T. "The Quarrel between Callimachus and Apollonius." *Hermathena* 39 (1913) 280-94.
Steffen, W. "Avant l'expédition des Argonautes à la recherche de la toison d'or: Apollonios de Rhodes I 228-360." *Meander* 35 (1980) 59-62.
———. "De Veteribus et Novis Elementis Poeticis in Apollonii Rhodii Argonautis Obviis." *Meander* 19 (1964) 77-87.

Stössl, F. *Apollonios Rhodios: Interpretationen zur Erzählungskunst und Quellenverwertung.* Bern 1941.

Thierstein, P. *Bau der Szenen in den Argonautika des Apollonios Rhodios.* Bern 1971.

Thomas, R. F. "Vergil's *Georgics* and the Art of Reference." *HSCPh* 90 (1986) 171–98.

Vian, F. "Apollonios de Rhodes et le renouveau de la poésie épique." *IL* 15 (1963) 25–30.

———. "Apollonios de Rhodes, *Argonautiques* I.105, 1012: Deux notes critiques." *REG* 80 (1967) 256–57.

———. "Les ΓΗΓΕΝΕΙΣ de Cyzique et la Grande Mère des Dieux." *RA* 37 (1951) 14–25.

———. "L'isthme de Cyzique d'après Apollonios de Rhodes (I.936–941)." *REG* 91 (1978) 96–106.

———. "ΙΗΣΩΝ ΑΜΗΧΑΝΕΩΝ." In *Studi in honore di Anthos Ardizzoni,* ed. E. Livrea. and G. A. Privitera, 1025–41. Rome 1978.

———. "Notes critiques au chant I des 'Argonautiques' d'Apollonios de Rhodes." *REA* 72 (1970) 80–96.

———. Review of D. N. Levin, *Apollonius' Argonautica Re-examined, I: The Neglected First and Second Books,* Mnemosyne Supplement 13 (Leiden 1971). *Gnomon* 46 (1974) 346–53.

Walther, R. "De Apollonii Rhodii Argonauticorum Rebus Geographicis." Diss. Halle 1894.

Webster, T. B. L. "Chronological Problems in Early Alexandrian Poetry." *WS* 76 (1963) 68–78.

———. *Hellenistic Poetry and Art.* London 1964.

Wehrli, F. "Apollonios von Rhodos und Kallimachos." *Hermes* 74 (1941) 14–21.

Weigel, G. "Kritische Bemerkungen zu Apollonios Rhodios." *Hermes* 86 (1958) 255–56.

West, D., and T. Woodman. *Creative Imitation and Latin Literature.* London 1979.

West, M. L. "Critical Notes on Apollonius Rhodius." *CR* 13 (1963) 9–12.

———. *Hesiod: Theogony.* Oxford 1966.

White, H. *Studies in Theocritus and Other Hellenistic Poets.* Amsterdam 1979.

von Wilamowitz-Moellendorf, U. *Hellenistische Dichtung in der Zeit des Kallimachos.* 2 vols. Berlin 1924.

———. *Die Textgeschichte der griechischen Bukoliker.* Berlin 1906.

Wilkins, E. G. "A Classification of the Similes in the *Argonautica* of Apollonius Rhodius." *CW* 14 (1921) 162–68.

Wyss, R. "Die Komposition von Apollonios' *Argonautika*." Diss. Zurich 1931.

Zanker, G. "The Love Theme in Apollonius Rhodius' *Argonautica*." *WS* 13 (1979) 52–75.

——— . *Realism in Alexandrian Poetry: A Literature and Its Audience*. London 1987.

GENERAL INDEX

Abas, 32n24
Acarnania, 126
Acastus, 28–34 *passim*, 57, 59–60, 67, 81, 86
Achilles, 1, 3n5, 35, 43n13, 174n50; as slayer of Hector, 46, 49, 52, 55; and Agamemnon as models for Jason and Heracles, 64–65; and Odysseus as models for Idas and Idmon, 68–87 *passim*; as infant, 88, 90, 97–98, 101; as model for Jason on Lemnos, 121–23; as model for Telamon, 200–201, 208–11 *passim*
Acrisius, 112
Actius, 74
Admetus, 35n28
Adonis, 165n35
Adrasteia, 170
Adrastus, 155
Agamemnon, 139; and Achilles as models for Jason and Heracles, 64–65; and the sacrifice of Iphigeneia, 105; as model for Hypsipyle, 116–17; as model for Jason, 120; and Odysseus as models for Jason and Telamon, 206–8
Ajax, son of Œleus: his argument with Idomeneus, 82, 86; as model for Heracles, 182–87
Ajax, son of Telamon, 1n5, 35, 47n18, 210
Alcestis, 30n23
Alcimede, her reaction to the departure of Jason, 35, 38–54 *passim*, 62, 95

Alcinous: as model for Jason, 66–69, 70n24, 80; as model for Hypsipyle, 133, 144; as model for Cyzicus, 159
Allusion: general discussion of, 4–13; some specific examples of, 48, 74, 79, 92–93, 97n18, 119, 129, 133n40, 135, 141n47, 144, 161, 187–88
Aloadae, 80
Amaltheia, 169
Amazons, 200
Amphiaraus, 80
Amphion, 27n9, 109, 124, 126
Amphius, 155
Amycus, 34
Amymone, 28n11
Anaphe, 77, 79, 86
Anaurus, 24
Andromache, as model for Alcimede, 8, 41n8, 42–55 *passim*
Andromeda, 125
Anticleia, 145
Antimachus, 10, 93n11
Antiphates, 159–60
Antiphus, 118
Aphetae Argous, 88–105 *passim*, 176n1, 197n39
Aphrodite, 77n34; restores male population of Lemnos, 103–4, 135, 142; on Jason's cloak, 109, 125, 125n29; punishes Lemnian women, 111, 111n6
Apollo, 10, 11n27, 14–25 *passim*, 32n24, 39, 52–53, 57–87 *passim*, 92–97 *passim*, 105n33, 126, 133; Actian and

227

Apollo (*continued*)
  Embasian Apollo, 74; Altar of Jasonian Apollo, 149
Apollonius: literary strategies of, 1-13; his relationship with the Muses, 14-20; his originality in dealing with sources and models (e.g.), 148-50; his attitude toward the "Best of the Argonauts," 205
Apsyrtus, 126, 172n48
Aratus, 18-22
Arcadia, 30, 72, 169-71
Areius, 29, 31, 35n28
Ares, 109, 125, 125n29; Field of Ares, 193n28
Arganthoneion, 183
Argo: driven by Heracles, 5, 183, 193, 196; voyage of, 9, 67, 88-105 *passim*, 111, 178n6; crew of, 28n13, 29, 146; building of, 20-21, 28, 69n21, 202-3; as sacrificial victim, 70; talking, 88, 127; at Oros Arkton, 149, 172; dedication of its anchor, 151, 158-59
Argonautica of Apollonius of Rhodes: as a Callimachean and Hellenistic epic, 1-3, 10, 205; as an example of the "presque homérique," 5-7; influence of Greek tragedy on, 9, 45n15; structural composition of, 11-13, *et passim*; the literary program of, 14-25; influence of the *Hecale* on, 8n20; Homeric etiquette in, 160n28; its temporal relationship with Callimachus's *Hymn to Zeus*, 170
Ariadne, 9, 98n21
Artemis: contrasted with Apollo, 16n8, 39, 53; her association with Medea, 55n30, 191, 193n28; her association with Thetis and Medea, 89-105 *passim*
Asteris, 156
Asterius, 27n9
Astyanax, 42, 43-55 *passim*
Atalanta, 129
Athena, 49, 75-79, 85-86, 109, 111, 133; helped build the Argo, 20; provides for Jason, 51, 120; shrine of Jasonian Athena, 151-52, 158-59
Athos, Mount, 91, 102, 103
Attire, significance of, 32-34, 59-61, 122n26, 124
Atys, 165n35
Audience, expectations of, 6, 10, 46, 50, 51, 60, 65, 84, 105, 205
Augeas, 26n9, 32n24
Aulis, 104-6, 146n52

Bebryces, 179
Bias, 29, 31
Boreads, Zetes and Calas, 27-31 *passim*, 179, 202-9 *passim*
Briareus, 165

Cabiri, 151
Callimachus, his influence on the *Argonautica*, 1-2, 8-10, 14-22, 8n20, 29n15, 30n19, 77-79, 169, 169-72, 189
Calliope, 32n24
Calypso, as model for Hypsipyle, 106, 129, 131, 132, 134, 145
Catalogue of Argonauts, 4, 18, 22, 26-36, 39, 58, 60, 67, 72n30, 97-98, 124-26, 210
Ceyx, 197n39
Chariclo, 90, 97
Chios, 112
Chiron, 84n49, 88-100 *passim*
Chytus Harbor, 152, 161, 172
Circe, as model for Hypsipyle, 106, 130-37, 144-45
Cius, 183, 193, 202
Cleite, 149-55 *passim*, 165
Clymene, 35
Cnossus, 169, 170
Colchis: journey to and from, 5, 18, 57, 66, 72, 77, 92, 94, 98, 101, 106, 108, 126-28, 148, 172, 196; Idas at, 82n44; arrival of Heracles at, 176, 176n3
Cottus, 165
Crete, 169-70
Cronus, 84, 169
Curetes, 169
Cybele, 168n40
Cyllenus, 169-70
Cyzicus, 4, 93n12, 107, 148-79 *passim*, 180

Dardanus, 168, 171

GENERAL INDEX 229

Delphi, 75, 81
Demeter, 99n24
Demetrius, 156
Demodocus, 47, 125n29; as model for Orpheus, 67–68, 80, 82n44, 83
Dindymon, 10, 149–74 passim
Diomedes, 3n5, 82, 117
Dionysus, 32n24
Dioscuri, 114n12; Castor, 32n24; Polydeuces, 34; Tyndaridae, 79
Divorce, of Peleus and Thetis compared with that of Jason and Medea, 98–101, 125n29
Doliones, 4, 148–74 passim
Dolops, 90, 100, 104
Dryopians, 178, 189, 197, 204

Echion, 32n24
Ecphrasis of Jason's Cloak, 109, 120–29
Electryon, 109, 125
Eleius, 32n24
Empedocles, 84
Epiphany: of Apollo, 77; of Athena, 85–86; of Glaucus, 202–3
Erato, 17
Erginus, 32n24
Eros, 77n34, 125, 126
Erymanthian Boar, 30, 72n30, 124
Erytus, 32n24
Eumelus, steeds of, 35
Euneus, son of Jason and Hypsipyle, 98n20
Euphemus, 32n24, 35n28
Euryalus, 207–8
Eurydice, 31n23
Eurylochus, as model for Heracles, 136, 138
Eurynome, 84
Eurynomus, 118
Eurystheus, 204

Gaia, 165
Gegeneis, 4, 148–74 passim, 186n16
Gigantomachy, 33n25
Glaucus, 5, 94, 173, 179, 201–8 passim
Greek tragedy, influence of, 9, 45n15

Hecate, 96
Hecatonchires, 164
Hector, 3n5, 80, 117; as model for Jason departing from home, 8, 40–55 passim, 146; in battle against Achilles, 122–23, 174n50, 201, 209
Hecuba, as model for Alcimede, 51
Helius, 32n24
Hera: her love for Jason and hatred of Pelias, 22–24, 173; assists Jason, 77n34, 94, 150; her hatred of Heracles, 161
Heracles: as old fashioned hero, 2, 13; abandonment of, 4, 72n28, 83, 100–101, 196–210 passim; his victory over Nemean Lion, 15; the dodecathlon of, 26n11, 204n53; as man of strength, 29–36 passim, 92–99 passim; election of, 57, 61–66; his seating on the Argo, 72; participates in the sacrifice to Apollo, 74–79; rowing of the Argo by, 92–99 passim; and the Apples of the Hesperides, 124–25, 176–77; his reaction to women of Lemnos, 135–46; his battle with the Gegeneis, 149–50, 157, 161, 172; contrasts with Jason in battle, 172–74; his arrival in Colchis, 176, 176n1, 176n3; loses his oar, 180–82; his hunger, 184–89; his relationship with Hylas, 187–96; his brutal treatment of the Boreads, 202; contrasts with Jason in general, 205, 210–11
Hermes, 32n24; his first sacrifice and the launch of the Argo, 70–87 passim; his assistance to Odysseus, 132, 135
Hesperides, 124, 174, 177, 202, 204
Hippodamia, 109, 126
Hippolyte, the Amazon, 94n13
Hippolyte, sister of Jason, 41n8
Homer, as major model for Apollonius, 5–9
Hylas, 29n15, 31, 94, 140, 176–212 passim
Hyllus, 190
Hypsipyle, 9, 43n12, 55–56, 157n22; as compared with Medea, 89, 95–96, 98; in the roles of Calypso, Nausicaa, and Circe, 106–47 passim; Jason's dalliance in bed with, 177, 200

Idas: his argument with Idmon, 57–86 *passim*, 199; his rejection of Medea's help, 176

Idmon, 29, 32n24, 41n10; his argument with Idas, 57–86 *passim*, 199

Idomeneus, as model for Idmon, 82, 86

Ilissus, 31

Ino, 72, 127

Inversion of the model, 43n13, 53, 65, 111, 113, 117, 157n22, 192

Iolcus, 35, 37–56 *passim*, 90n6, 94, 126

Iphianassa, 95n14

Iphias, 39, 44, 52–55 *passim*, 95

Iphiclus, 29, 31, 35n28, 72n30

Iphigeneia, 104

Ithaca, 1n5, 3n7, 70n24, 111n6, 118, 119, 132, 156

Jason: as real-life hero, 2, 7, 24–25, 205; handles the loss of Heracles, 4, 198–210 *passim*; his future dealings with Medea, 9, 96–97, 211; loses his sandal, 22–25; enlists the Argonauts, 26; his quest, 32; as diplomatic hero, 33, 209–10, 198–210 *passim*; his departure from home, 37–56; his speech to Alcimede, 48–52; his comparison to Apollo, 52–55, 92–95; definition of and election as leader, 61–66; his handling of quarrels, 66–86 *passim*, 198–210 *passim*; his sacrifice to Apollo, 74–79; his cloak, 120–29; his encounter with Hypsipyle (parallel with Odysseus's), 129–46; as love hero, 138; his experience at Oros Arkton parallels Odysseus's with Ægeus, 160–67; his celebration of Samothracian and Cyzicene mysteries as prelude to heroic action, 167–74; his argument with Telamon, 198–210 *passim*

Ladon, 174, 177, 203

Lemnos, 4, 9, 43n12, 88–147 *passim*, 173, 176, 177, 200, 204

Leodocus, 29, 31, 35n28

Lepreus, 197n39

Lindos, 189

Lynceus, 205

Lysanias, 14

Macries, 149, 157

Magnesia, 88–102 *passim*

Mariandyni, 94

Medea: invaluable assistance of, 3, 82n44, 84, 124–26, 173–74, 176, 204; her future dealings with Jason, 4, 9, 89, 98; her love for Jason, 10; her departure from Colchis, 17, 126; her future abandonment by Jason, 54, 97, 212; her association with Artemis, 55n30; birth of son, Medeius, to, 98–100; frightening nature of, 104n30; her comparison with Hypsipyle, 128, 146; murder of Apsyrtus by, 172n48; comparison of with Hylas, 193

Medeius, 98–101

Medes/Persians, 99–100

Melampus, 31–32, 72n30

Meleager, 29, 129n34

Menelaus, 76

Mentor, 76

Merops, 148, 154, 155

Meter, 150, 151, 167–69

Minyadae, 26–35 *passim*

Mnestheus, 207

Molorchus, 15, 29n15

Mopsus, 29, 164–67, 171

Muses, 17–25 *passim*

Myrine, 103, 108–45 *passim*, 144

Myrtilus, 126

Mysia, 5, 94, 107, 146, 151, 176–202 *passim*

Mytilene, 176n1

Nauplius, 28n11, 32n24

Nausicaa: as model for Hypsipyle, 106–47 *passim*; her welcome of Odysseus, 159–60; as model for the nymph who abducts Hylas, 191–93

Neda, 169–70

Neleus, 31

Nestor: as model for Iphias, 53–54; his sacrifice at Pylos as model for the sacrifice at Pagasae, 75–77, 79, 86

Odysseus, 1, 3n5, 8, 43n13, 47, 89n3; and Achilles as models for Idas and Idmon, 66–74 *passim*, 80, 82–87; as model for Jason on Lemnos, 106

118–19, 123n27, 129–46, 174n50; as model for Jason on Oros Arkton, 159–64, 171; and Polyphemus as models for Heracles and Hylas, 184–88; and Nausicaa as models for Hylas and the nymph, 191–93; and Euryalus as models for Jason and Telamon, 207–9
Œdipus, 175n51
Olympus, Mount, 103, 104n30, 124
Omphale, 176n1
Ophion, 84
Oracle: for Pelias, 18–25, 60; for Jason, 51, 68–79; for Cyzicus, 148–74; establishing the sanctuary of Jasonian Athena, 158
Oreithyia, 31
Oros Arkton, 4, 148–74 passim, 177, 194
Orpheus, 4; as symbol for the man of brain, 26–32 passim; in role of Demodocus, 66–87; his cosmogonical song, 83–85, 123–24, 202; as coxswain, 89–95, 105; his song on Oros Arkton, 169
Ortygia, 78–79

Pagasae, 4, 10, 29, 33, 37, 57–87 passim, 88–105 passim, 198–202
Pallene, 91, 102
Panormus, 158n24
Patroclus, 43n13; death of, 64, 82, 174n50, 200–201
Peisistratus, 76
Pelasgi, 149, 157, 168 (see also Macries)
Peleus, 4, 41n8, 50, 97–105 passim
Pelias: as fearsome, 4, 7, 38, 45, 54n27, 128, 132n39; his fears about the man with one sandal, 19, 22–24, 60; death of, 99n24, 173, 202
Pelion, Mount, 88, 90, 97
Pellene, 26n9
Pelopia, 33, 59
Pelops, 109, 126
Penelope, 3n5, 21, 51n21, 119
Percote, 154
Pergamon, Altar of Zeus, 33n25
Perseus, 112, 125
Persians/Medes, 99–100
Phasis, 158n24

Phemius, 20n21, 21
Phineus, 125, 160n30
Phleias, 32n24
Phorbas, 32n24
Phrixus, 45, 72, 109, 127
Phrygia, 156, 168, 170, 181
Phylace, 31
Phylacus, 31
Pieria, 30, 70, 72, 124
Pimpleia, 27n8
Piraeus, 89n5
Polyphemus, the Argonaut, 32n24, 177–80, 193–96, 202
Polyphemus, the Cyclops, 118; as model for Heracles, 186–88; his association with Polyphemus the Argonaut, 195n34
Polyxo, 108–41 passim
Poseidon, 22, 32n24, 86, 159; his implicit anger with Heracles, 180–96 passim
Posidippus, 93n11
Priam, as model for Æëtes, 40–55 passim
Priolaus, 94n13
Proecdosis, 46n15, 89n5, 131n36
Proemium, 4, 11, 13, 14–25 passim, 27, 28, 37, 56, 60
Propontis, 156, 160, 160n30, 162
Ptolemies, 168n40
Pylos, 30, 75
Pytho, 52, 68, 77–79

Realism, contemporary taste for, 69, 205, 205n54
Reconciliation: of Agamemnon and Achilles, 65; of Hermes and Apollo, 72–74; cosmic, 87; between Argonauts and Doliones, 166; between Jason and Telamon, 205
Rhea, 10, 84; anger of on Oros Arkton, 150–72 passim

Samothrace, 108n4, 151–54, 167–68, 174
Sciathus, 100
Selene, 15n8
Sepias Acte, 91, 99–101
Seriphos, 112
Sicily, 89n5

Sicinus, 111–13
Sintian men and women, 102–4
Subtext, influence of, 10, 39, 44, 50–51, 57, 68–69, 74, 89, 129, 171, 187, 197–98n41
Symplegades, 13, 211

Talaus, 29, 31, 35n28
Talos, 97n18, 125
Taphian Pirates/Teleboans, 125
Telamon, 5, 35, 176–211 *passim*
Telchines, 92n11
Teleboans/Taphian Pirates, 125
Telemachus, 51n21, 157; as model for Jason, 76–86 *passim*; as model for Hypsipyle, 118–19
Thebes, 124
Theiodamas, 177–204 *passim*
Thermopylae, 91, 100
Thersites, as model for Heracles, 138–46 *passim*
Theseus, 98n21
Thetis, 4, 77n34, 120, 123; her anger with Peleus as subtext, 88–105 *passim*; parallels Medea, 125n29, 146n52

Thoas, 107–16, *passim*, 132
Thrace, 27, 30
Thrasymedes, 76
Tiphys, 28n13, 29, 41n10, 158; contrasts with Heracles, 89, 92–94; his order to leave Mysia, 179, 196, 202
Tiresias, 114n12
Tithonus, 15
Titias, 94n13, 169–70
Tityus, 109, 126
Trachis, 197n39
Troy, 50, 64, 81–83, 119, 122
Typheus, 80

Uranus, 165

Xanthus, 52

Zenodotus, 64n15
Zethus, 109, 124, 126
Zeus, 32n24; in the prologue of Aratus's *Phænomena*, 18; his punishment of Idas, 82n44; and the thunderbolt as his weapon, 84, 121–27 *passim*; his birth, 169–72; his plan for Heracles, 179, 201–3

INDEX LOCORUM

PASSAGES ALLUDED TO IN *ARGONAUTICA 1*

Aratus
 Phænomena
  1–18: 18, 19, 19n19

Callimachus
 Ætia
  fr. 18.1–13 Pf.: 78–79
 Hymn to Zeus
  1–9, *et passim*: 169–71
 SH
  250–51: 79n36

Herodotus
 7.183ff.: 91, 100
 7.193: 99, 100–1

Hesiod
 Catalogue of Women
  1.6–7 M&W: 62n8, 97n18
 Theogony
  147–53: 164–65, 164n34
  671–73: 164n34
  1000–1002: 99, 101

Homer
 Iliad
  1.592–94: 103
  1.594: 102n29
  2.87–93a: 141
  2.229–33a: 139
  2.235: 144
  2.335–38: 139
  2.484ff.: 26
  2.484–93: 27
  2.494–759: 30
  2.761–79: 35
  2.816–77: 30
  2.830–34: 155
  3.125–28: 122
  4.338–48: 206
  4.358–63: 206–7
  6.410b–11a: 46
  6.411b–30: 46
  6.429–30: 55n29
  6.447–65: 46
  6.450–81: 55
  6.486: 49n20
  6.486–93: 51
  11.86–89: 183–84
  14.39–40: 53–54
  14.107–8: 117
  18.79–82a: 201
  18.372–79: 121
  19.40–46: 64
  19.56–73: 64
  19.74–77: 64
  19.78–144: 64
  19.145–53: 64–65
  22.25–32: 122
  22.157–61: 209
  22.440–41: 122
  22.481: 46
  22.496–500a: 43
  23.450–72: 82
  23.488–91: 82
  23.499–500: 82
  24.160–68: 40–41, 52n23
  24.218–19: 52
  24.525–26: 49
  24.534–42: 50
  24.549–51: 49
  24.725–45: 46
  24.742: 46
 Odyssey
  1.55–57a: 131–32
  1.337–42: 21
  2.14–22: 118
  3.329–36: 85–86
  3.375–76: 76
  3.444b–46: 75–76
  3.447–54: 76
  4.504–10: 182–83
  4.844–47: 156
  6.119–24: 192
  6.236–37: 192
  6.238–45: 133, 133n40
  6.255–315: 159
  6.263b–67: 158–59
  7.309–16: 133–34, 133n40
  8.34–45: 66–69
  8.50–55: 69

233

Odyssey (continued)
8.72–82: 67–69, 81
8.78: 82
8.81–82: 83
8.159–64: 207
8.408–11: 207–8
8.461–69: 143–44
8.462: 142n49
8.521–31: 47
8.523: 8
9.233b–35: 188
9.248–49: 188
9.273–78: 189
9.319–24: 186–87
9.515: 187
10.48–49: 89n6, 163
10.72–75: 164
10.103–8: 159–60
10.124: 160
10.212–19: 130
10.233: 131n36
10.281–301: 135
10.301: 144
10.312–15: 131
10.314: 131n36
10.366: 131n36
10.401–5: 134
10.443–48: 136
10.447: 136n43
10.469–74: 137
10.490–95: 114n12
11.142–43: 145
11.302–4: 114n12
13.31–35: 183–84
14.434–38: 71–72
22.299ff.: 195n36
Homeric Hymns
  h. Merc
    112–29: 70
    128a: 69
    313: 70n23
    416a–35: 73
    423b–34: 73–74
  h. Hom. 32
    18–19: 16

OTHER PASSAGES DISCUSSED OR MENTIONED IN THE PRESENT WORK

Æschylus
  Cabiri
    fr. 95–97a Radt: 153
  Dictyulci
    fr. 464 Radt: 112
  Glaucus
    fr. 28–29 Radt: 203
  Supplices
    892: 164n33
Alexander Ætolus
  Halieus
    fr. 121–22 Powell: 203
Anaximenes of Lampsacus
  (*apud* Strabonem)
    14.635: 157
Antimachus
  Lyde
    fr. 58 Wyss: 93n11
Apollodorus
  1.3.5: 104n30
  1.9.19: 72n28, 93n11
  1.9.27: 54n27
  2.5.11: 189n21
  2.7: 197n39
  3.6.4: 112

Apollonius of Rhodes
  Argonautica
    1.1: 18
    1.1–2: 15
    1.1–4: 18, 22, 26
    1.1–22: 14–25
    1.5–17: 22
    1.18–19: 26, 77n34
    1.18–22: 18, 20, 22
    1.22: 17, 27
    1.23: 29
    1.23–223: 30–32
    1.23–233: 26–36
    1.28–31: 30
    1.69–70: 98
    1.97–100: 98
    1.109–10: 77n34
    1.115–17: 98
    1.118–32: 72n30
    1.120–21: 31
    1.123: 29
    1.124–29: 30
    1.131–32: 31
    1.146–50: 98
    1.164–71: 98
    1.177: 27n9
    1.190–96: 98
    1.211–18: 31
    1.224–27: 28, 32–34
    1.228–33: 34–36
    1.229–33: 34–35
    1.234–316: 37–56
    1.246: 38n4
    1.251–52: 54
    1.261–64: 40–41, 52n23
    1.261–77: 40–44
    1.262: 46n17
    1.266–77a: 42
    1.270: 46–48
    1.273: 43
    1.278–91: 44–46
    1.278–94: 44–48
    1.286b–87: 54
    1.295–305: 48–52
    1.306–16: 52–55, 95
    1.315–16: 44, 95
    1.317: 58n2
    1.317–30: 59–61
    1.317–518: 57–87
    1.321–26: 33, 67
    1.322: 60
    1.324–26: 59–61
    1.331–62: 61–66
    1.332–50: 33, 36
    1.336–37: 3, 132n39
    1.336–40: 62–66
    1.339b: 80

INDEX LOCORUM

1.341–44: 64–65, 199n44
1.351: 80
1.351–52: 64
1.354b–58: 67
1.363–401: 69–74
1.363–518: 66–86
1.364b–66: 69–70
1.394: 58n2, 70–71
1.395: 71
1.396b–40: 72
1.402–47: 74–79
1.408b–10: 75–76
1.411–16a: 76–77
1.412–14: 81
1.416b–19: 78–79
1.439: 77n34
1.448–95: 79–83
1.450: 58n2
1.460: 83
1.479–80a: 80
1.492: 68
1.492–95: 81–83
1.494: 80
1.496–511: 73, 80, 83–86, 124
1.512–18: 85–86
1.516–18: 85–86
1.519–79: 92–99
1.519–608: 88–105
1.525–27: 127n32
1.531–33: 92–93
1.534–35: 89n6
1.542–43: 93
1.554: 99
1.559–62: 93
1.568: 94
1.577: 105
1.580–608: 99–104
1.601–10: 102–3
1.609–720: 111–19
1.609–909: 106–46
1.620–23a: 112
1.623b–26: 113
1.633: 111n5
1.644–45: 114n12
1.647–48: 114n12
1.648–49: 114, 154
1.665–66: 116
1.666: 116n15

1.672: 117n17
1.667–74: 118
1.702–3: 133n41
1.702–7: 115
1.710–16: 154
1.712–16: 115–16
1.721–24: 77n34
1.721–73: 33, 120–29
1.722: 60, 121–22
1.725–26: 124
1.725–28a: 128
1.730–34: 120–21, 123–24
1.735–41: 124–25
1.742–46: 125
1.747–51: 125–26
1.752–58: 126
1.759–62: 126
1.763–67: 127
1.774–909: 129–46
1.786b–90: 130–131
1.791–92: 131
1.809–17: 43n12
1.827–31: 132
1.832–33: 134
1.840–41: 135
1.849–52: 104
1.854b–56: 135–6
1.861–64: 95
1.861–68: 136–37
1.866–67: 139
1.869–74: 138
1.875–76: 145
1.879–85: 140
1.886–97a: 96
1.894b–97: 143
1.896: 142n49
1.900–903: 143
1.900–909: 55, 142
1.904–9: 98
1.910: 96, 143
1.910–12a: 108n4
1.910–60: 153–60
1.910–1152: 148–75
1.936–40: 155–56
1.944–46: 164
1.954b–60: 158
1.961–1117: 160–67
1.970: 160
1.974–76a: 154

1.979: 71
1.980–84: 162
1.991: 160
1.1015–18a: 162–63
1.1071b–72a: 166n37
1.1088: 150
1.1094: 164
1.1116: 170n45
1.1117–52: 167–74
1.1128–50: 170
1.1153–1239: 180–93
1.1153–1272: 180–96
1.1153–1362: 176–211
1.1161b–64: 62–63
1.1168b–71: 182
1.1172–78: 183
1.1179–80: 171n46
1.1190–93: 186
1.1195: 60
1.1207–10: 187–88
1.1221–39: 94n13
1.1222b–30: 191
1.1240–72: 193–96
1.1273ff.: 94
1.1273–79: 193–98
1.1280–1309: 94
1.1280–1344: 36, 198–210
1.1284–86a: 198–99
1.1286: 83n45
1.1286b–89a: 200
1.1294–95: 201
1.1310–25: 94
1.1332–35: 206
1.1339b–43: 208–9
1.1345–57: 94n13
2.30–34: 34
2.67–97: 34
2.145–50: 176, 199n44
2.145–53: 63
2.410: 83n45
2.423–25: 77n34
2.495: 71
2.537–614: 77n34
2.623: 83n45
2.674–84a: 77n34
2.774–95: 199n44
2.775–85: 94n13

Argonautica (continued)
2.815: 32n24
2.830b–31: 82n44
2.851–57: 94
2.859–63: 94
2.864–66a: 94
2.864–68: 77n34
2.885: 83n45
2.1123–24: 171n46
3.1–5: 18
3.7–112: 77n34
3.25–111: 77n34
3.61–73: 24
3.210–14: 77n34
3.250: 77n34
3.275–98: 77n34, 126
3.336: 83n45
3.423: 83n45
3.432: 83n45
3.444: 192n26
3.504: 83n45
3.540–54: 77n34
3.556–63: 176
3.558–68: 82n44
3.818: 77n34
3.876–84: 96, 193n28
3.919–23: 77n34
3.997–1007: 98n21
3.1066b–70a: 96
3.1074–76: 98n21
3.1096–1108: 98n21
3.1105: 71n26
3.1109–11: 96
3.1131–36: 77n34
3.1198: 71n26
3.1226ff.: 193n28
3.1232b–34: 63, 177
3.1252–54: 82n44
3.1265–67: 84–85
3.1365–67: 205n55
4.1–5: 18
4.66–97: 55
4.338–54: 147
4.338–410: 55, 96
4.424–34: 98n21
4.507–10: 77n34
4.529–32a: 77n34
4.552–65: 18
4.576b–80a: 77n34
4.640–48: 77n34
4.659–752: 172n48
4.753–865: 77n34
4.758ff.: 77n34
4.760ff.: 77n34
4.865–79: 97, 99n24
4.956–67: 77n34
4.1131–67: 55
4.1151b–52: 77n34
4.1161–69: 55
4.1183b–85a: 77n34
4.1199–1200: 77n34
4.1203: 71n26
4.1318: 83n45
4.1393–1405: 177
4.1477–80: 205
4.1547–49: 77n34
4.1641–44: 97n18
4.1694–1730: 77
4.1701b–30: 77n34
4.1704–5: 79

Aratus
  Phænomena
    993: 69n22
Aristotle
  De Generatione Animalium
    3.10: 141n48
  Historia Animalium
    2.51: 141n48
Arrian
  Periplus
    9.2: 158n24
Athenæus
  Deipnosophistæ
    1.16b: 85n51
    4.136f: 188
    10.428f: 153
Autocharis
  FGrHist 249 F 1: 193

Callimachus
  Ætia
    fr. 1 Pf.: 15
    fr. 1.21–28 Pf.: 21
    fr. 3–7 Pf.: 15
    fr. 7–21 Pf.: 15, 29n15
    fr. 22–25 Pf.: 189–90
    fr. 108–9 Pf.: 29n15, 158n24
    fr. 110 Pf.: 15
  Schol. Flor. ad Ætia
    1–12 Pf.: 93n11
  Hecala
    fr. 299 Pf. (Hollis fr. 116): 170n45
  Iambi
    13, fr. 203 Pf.: 16
  Epigr. 28 Pf.: 14
  SH
    250–51: 15
    254–69: 15
    260A5: 31
Cinæthon
  Heracleia
    Davies p. 142 a: 181
Columella
  De Re Rustica
    9.2.4: 141n48
Conon
  FGrHist 26 F 1: 149n6, 189n21
Crinagoras
  A. P. 7.645.5: 71n27

Deiochus
  FGrHist 471 F 4–10: 148n3
  FGrHist 471 F 7–8: 149n4
Demetrius of Scepsis (*apud* Strabonem)
  1.59: 156
  10.456: 156
Diodorus
  4.43.1–2: 153
  4.48: 202
  4.50.1: 54n27
  5.49: 168
Dionysius of Byzantium
  De Bospori Navigatione
    87: 158n24
Dionysius of Mytilene (Scytobrachion)
  FGrHist 42 F 2b: 176n1

INDEX LOCORUM 237

Ephorus
  FGrHist 70 F 61:
    149n6
  FGrHist 70 F 104: 168
Euphorion
  fr. 76 Powell: 194
Euripides
  Hecuba
    716: 71n27
    1977: 71n27
  Hippolytus
    324: 46n16
    1376: 71n27
  Hypsipyle
    fr. 1.3.8–14 Bond:
      28n13
    fr. 64.93 Bond: 106
  Medea
    1032–37: 54n27
  Orestes
    1041, 1085: 46n16
Eusebius
  Præparatio Evangelica
    5.8.7: 17n13

Herodorus
  FGrHist 31 F 7, 41:
    150n9, 10
  FGrHist 31 F 41:
    176n1
Herodotus
  4.76: 150n11
  4.145: 112
  7.193: 176n1
Hesiod
  Catalogue of Women
    40 M&W: 84n49
  Ceycos Gamos
    fr. 263 M&W:
      176n1, 197n39
    fr. 265 M&W:
      197n39
  Theogony
    147–53: 181
    617–20: 181
Homer
  Iliad
    1.503–10: 65
    1.594: 102n29
    2.573–74: 27n9

  2.619: 27n9
  2.811: 156
  2.872: 43n13
  3.392: 192n26
  5.4–6: 122
  5.103, 414: 3n5
  7.289: 3n5
  7.467–69: 98n20
  9.116, 119: 206
  10.256: 136n43
  11.62–64: 122
  11.711, 722: 156
  13.32: 156
  13.313–14: 3n5
  13.432: 192n26
  16.7: 43n13
  18.394–405: 104n30
  19.137: 206
  23.745–47: 98n20
  Odyssey
    1.374: 71
    2.139: 71
    3.293: 156
    5.97–115: 132
    5.160–70: 132
    6.130–36: 123n27
    8.38: 71
    8.294: 102n29
    11.186: 71
    13.23: 71
    17.234: 43n13
    18.192: 192n26
  Ilias Parva
    fr. 1 Davies: 17
  Nostoi
    fr. 6 Davies: 99n24
Homeric Hymns
  h. Ap.
    317–21: 104n30
  h. Cer.
    237–41: 99n24
  h. Merc.
    361: 71
    476: 71
  h. Ven.
    11: 71
    228: 117n17
Hyginus
  Fabulæ
    Præf. 14: 100n26

  120: 112

Ibycus
  fr. 301 PMG: 41n8

Lactantius
  Divinæ Institutiones
    1.21: 189n21
Lucillus Tarrhæus
  fr. 11a Linnenkugel:
    181

Matron
  (apud Athenæum)
    4.136f: 188
Metrodorus
  A.P. 14.116.2, 119.1,
    120.7: 71n27

Neanthes
  FGrHist 84 F 11–12:
    150n11
Nicander
  fr. 48 Schneider: 63n12
Nonnus
  Dionysiaca
    3.61–78: 168
  Paraphrasis Sancti
    Evvangelii Joannei
    5.157: 17n13
Nymphis
  FGrHist 432 F 5b:
    94n13

Oppian
  Haleutica
    1.121: 69n22
    5.650: 69n22
Orphic Argonautica
  464: 100n26

Pherecydes
  FGrHist 3 F 4: 28n11
  FGrHist 3 F 111:
    93n11, 176n1
Philostratus
  Imagines
    2.15: 202
    2.24: 189n21

INDEX LOCORUM

Pindar
  Pæan
    fr. 62 (Snell): 150,
      167
  Pythian
    4.70–171: 24
    4.102–3: 84n49
    4.252ff.: 106
  Hypothesis *ad Epi.*
    Nem.
    p. 424 Boeckh: 112
Possis of Magnesia
  FGrHist 480 F 2: 202

Quintus Smyrnæus
  Posthomerica
    5.529–30: 42n10
    5.444: 47n18

Scylax
  Periplus
    94 *GGM*: 157
Servius
  ad Æn. 3.167: 168
Simonides
  fr. 543.1–2 PMG: 112
Socrates of Argos
  FGrHist 310 F 15: 194
Sophocles
  Œdipus Tyrannos
    1504: 46n16
  Philoctetes
    391: 164n33
    1413–16: 203n52
Statius
  Thebaid
    5.284–91: 112
Strabo
  1.59: 156
  10.456: 156
  14.635: 157
  9.436: 99

Theocritus
  Idylls
    13.38: 200n47
    13.73–75: 176n1
    24.137–38: 185n14
Thucydides
  6.30–32: 89n5

Valerius Flaccus
  Argonautica
    1.353–54: 200n47
    1.777ff.: 54n27
    2.242–310: 112
    2.439–42: 168

Xenagoras
  FGrHist 240 F 31: 112

Compositor:	Theodora S. MacKay
Formatting:	NEP Format by P. A. MacKay based on D. E. Knuth's TeX
Text Font:	Computer Modern
Greek Font:	by Silvio Levy adapted by P. A. MacKay

www.ingramcontent.com/pod-product-compliance
Lightning Source LLC
Chambersburg PA
CBHW021700230426
43668CB00008B/686